The Employment Revolution

The Employment Revolution:
Young American Women in the 1970s

Edited by Frank L. Mott

with contributions by

R. Jean Haurin

Nan L. Maxwell

Sylvia F. Moore

Frank L. Mott

David Shapiro

Lois B. Shaw

Anne Statham

The MIT Press
Cambridge, Massachusetts
London, England

This report was prepared under a contract with the Employment and
Training Administration, U.S. Department of Labor, under the authority
of the Comprehensive Employment and Training Act. Researchers
undertaking such projects under government sponsorship are encouraged to express their own judgments. Interpretations or viewpoints
stated in this document do not necessarily represent the official position or policy of the Department of Labor.

This book was set in VIP Univers by Achorn Graphic Services,
Inc., and printed and bound by The Murray Printing Company in
the United States of America.

Library of Congress Cataloging in Publication Data
Main entry under title:

The Employment revolution.

  Bibliography: p.
  Includes index.
  1. Women—Employment—United States.
I. Mott, Frank. II. Haurin, R. Jean.
HD6095.E46 1982   331.4'0973   82-10011
ISBN 0-262-13186-2   AACR2

Contents

List of Figures

Preface

In 1968 the Center for Human Resource Research of The Ohio State University and the U.S. Bureau of the Census, under separate contracts with the Employment and Training Administration of the U.S. Department of Labor, initiated the National Longitudinal Survey of Work Experience of Young Women. In this survey a nationally representative sample of 5,159 (3,638 white and 1,459 black) women 14 to 24 years of age were initially interviewed during the first few months of 1968, were reinterviewed with lengthy personal interviews each year until 1973, with shorter telephone interviews in 1975 and 1977 and longer personal interviews in 1978. The research presented in this book covers this 1968 to 1978 period, years when many of these young women completed their schooling, formed families of their own, and began a life-long attachment to the work force. Interviews with these women are planned at least until 1983, at which time the cohort will be between the ages of 29 and 39.

In the tenth interview year in 1978, the Census Bureau completed interviews with 3,902 (2,794 white and 1,064 black) women or over 75 percent of the original sample. Although the sample loss was not completely random, there were no apparent major biases due to attrition, so that the substantive conclusions drawn here for the most part can be generalized to the population of American women passing through late adolescence and early adulthood during the late 1960s and early 1970s. The breadth and depth of the available data have permitted careful analyses of the dynamics of change as they relate to education, the family, and the labor force. With most cross-sectional surveys it is possible only to examine the status of individuals at one point in time, as a snapshot permits a careful look at a person at a certain point. Longitudinal data in effect permit one to construct a series of snapshots of the same person over time so that the advantage of longitudinal over cross-sectional data is somewhat akin to the advantage that a filmstrip has over a photograph. The principal objective of the National Longitudinal Survey of Work Experience of Young Women is to permit the examination in great detail of the processes whereby women reach adulthood and make career and family choices. The overriding objective of this book has been to examine how and why women make labor force attachments.

Paralleling the interviews with the young women over the

past decade have been interviews with nationally representative samples of young men 14 to 24 in 1966, men 45 to 59 years of age in 1966, and women 30 to 44 years of age in 1967. These surveys have also been carried out by the Census Bureau, under the direction of the Center for Human Resource Research and funded by the Employment and Training Administration of the U.S. Department of Labor. From the inception of the surveys until 1979, the surveys were administered by Herbert Parnes. Since Professor Parnes's retirement, Michael Borus has taken over the administration of the project and in addition has administered the new youth cohort of the National Longitudinal Survey of Work Experience. This survey includes interviews with over 12,000 young Americans 14 to 21 years of age in 1979 with subsequent annual interviews through 1984. This survey has been primarily sponsored by the U.S. Department of Labor with the interviews being conducted by the National Opinion Research Center at the University of Chicago.

While retaining ultimate responsibility for all limitations of this research, we wish to acknowledge our debt to many people who have made this research possible. In particular, we wish to thank Kezia Sproat, whose overall editorial supervision for the book immeasurably improved its quality and readability, and Sherry McNamara, whose scrupulous attention to the details of the production process was invaluable. In this regard she was frequently assisted by Kathy Niehaus. We also wish to thank Jean Haurin who maintained quality checks over all the tables and figures in this book.

Over the years the professional staff at the Center for Human Resource Research have maintained a close liaison with their counterparts in the Department of Labor. In particular we wish to thank Howard Rosen, who was responsible for initiating these surveys and having the foresight and perseverance to maintain their funding and professional integrity over the years. Since Dr. Rosen's retirement, Burt Barnow has continued to play this important role. We also thank Ellen Sehgal, the current Labor Department liaison for the surveys, not only for her professional assistance but also as the key person who has helped smooth the governmental administrative procedures with regard to expediting funding, clearance procedures, and other areas essential to a project of this magnitude. Also we wish to thank the many Census Bureau personnel who over the years have ridden herd on the interview schedules and have maintained a remarkably high sample retention rate without jeopardizing the high quality of the data collected.

Within the center we wish to thank Helene Churchill, Mary Ann Harmon, Mary Janson, Rufus Milstead, Michael Motto, Joel Rath, Pat Shannon, Carol Sheets, Pam Sparrow, and Steve Strohl for their outstanding programming and other technical assistance in a process that extended over more than a year and included thousands of hours of help. Finally we are indebted to Michael Borus, Jody Crowley, Ron D'Amico, Tom Daymont, Steve Hills, Choongsoo Kim, Gil Nestel, Tom Pollard, Pat Rhoton, and Richard Santos for their review of earlier versions of these chapters and their gracious technical assistance.

The Employment Revolution

Chapter 1

Women: The Employment Revolution

Frank L. Mott

While American society still differentiates the roles of men and women, their behaviors and attitudes are certainly much less differentiated than was true only one or two decades ago. Men and women are becoming more equal contributors and beneficiaries in the educational process, the family, and the marketplace. More men are taking an active role in child raising, and many more women are gainfully employed, even at the life-cycle stage where they have traditionally avoided paid activities outside the home. In 1960 only 15 percent of married women with children under the age of 3 were in the work force, but by 1970 this percentage had grown to about 26 percent, and by 1980 fully 41 percent of women with preschool children were either on the job or looking for work (Bureau of Labor Statistics 1980; Waldman and Young 1971; Schiffman, 1961).

Despite the recent large increase in descriptive information about the changing roles of women in society, we still have only limited understanding of why these changes have been happening, how the process of change works, and, perhaps most important, whether and how far these transitions are happening unevenly within the society. This last question is important because behavioral disparities, particularly when they can be linked to other familial and nonfamilial attitudes and behaviors, can help explain why observed overall changes are taking place. This book uses some unique data to help explain the process of change, particularly in regard to the labor market, for a group of women who are demographically at the cutting edge of the women's movement—young women who were passing through their adolescent years in the 1960s and reaching adulthood in the turbulent years of the 1960s and 1970s. Many of this generation are currently in the forefront of the women's movement.

In early 1968 the U.S. Bureau of the Census interviewed for the first time a group of about 5,000 young women who were then 14 to 24 years of age. In a far-ranging interview, the Census Bureau collected from this nationally representative sample of 1,500 black and 3,500 white women information about their family and educational experiences, their thoughts about their current and future home, educational, and work activities, and a detailed profile of their employment. This survey, known as the National Longitudinal Survey (NLS) of Work Experience of Young Women, has continued, under the sponsorship of the

U.S. Department of Labor.[1] The vast majority of these young women have been reinterviewed eight times since 1968. The Census Bureau carried out personal interviews each year between 1968 and 1973, shorter telephone interviews in 1975 and 1977, and in 1978 a lengthy personal interview with the 4,200 young women of the original 5,159 who could still be located and who agreed to be interviewed.[2] Thus in contrast to most other data-collection efforts, which gather information about the behaviors or attitudes of individuals at one point in time, this unique longitudinal survey has interviewed the same young women repeatedly over a decade. The NLS has followed them through schooling into an adulthood of family and work responsibilities, repeatedly gathering information about their life-styles and life circumstances. The early interviews focused on educational experiences, family background, and attitudes about the future. As the cohort aged, the focus shifted to family and work considerations and the transition from youth to adulthood. With a variety of attitudinal questions, the interviews probed how effectively youth-to-adult transitions were being made, how earlier priorities and values were being replaced by new concerns, and the extent to which the social climate of the 1970s contributed to a transition away from sex role stereotypes toward more egalitarian ideas about appropriate activities for men and women.

The longitudinal nature of the data set makes it possible to follow these young women through various life-cycle stages— from their parental homes, through the completion of their education, and into their own family units. In addition the unique manner in which the NLS samples were selected permits more comprehensive family and cross-generational research than is usually possible. How are demographic, social, and economic forces juxtaposing to reorient American women toward the economic mainstream? Using this unique longitudinal data set, we can examine in some detail various aspects of this fundamental process of social change in American society. This book inquires into the intensity and extensiveness of the relationship between woman's work activity and her behavior and attitudes about childbearing. It also considers how the employment revolution relates to changes in marriage, fertility, divorce, and remarriage patterns. Making use of data from other NLS cohorts, it examines some of the mechanisms whereby young women learn roles from their mothers and how brothers and sisters are differentially socialized. These analyses concentrate not only on the mechanisms through which transitions occur but also on the educational and employment-related results of different role-learning processes.[3]

The research is cross-disciplinary. The disciplines of economics and sociology frequently offer theoretical orientations that complement each other, thus offering fuller explanations of behavior. In particular traditional neoclassical labor supply theory focuses on how competing family- and market-related factors influence a woman's labor force decisions. On the other hand, sociological orientations have been more concerned with what might be termed precipitating or inhibiting factors, which condition or predispose a woman either toward or away from gainful employment. The research in this book continually supports the notion that both perspectives are fundamental to a more complete understanding of how and why women work in the marketplace. Essentially women will react in the marketplace in ways similar to men subject to significant constraints, reflecting forces from their own and their husband's earlier adult and childhood environment. The decisions women make about family and work reflect not only a balancing act between contemporary market and home forces but, perhaps as important, a life-long socialization process. This process is intimately linked not only with earlier adult experiences but also with a vast array of earlier peer, sibling, parental, and other institutional forces. These forces, commonly subsumed under the rubric of what economists call "tastes," are not necessarily independent of an adult woman's economic behavior. Not considering these factors can, in some instances at least, distort traditional attempts at economic explanation and interpretation.

Societal Transitions and the Stereotyping of "Atypical" Behavior

The work activity of young adult women is conditioned by earlier experiences but constrained by the tempo of life-cycle events such as school leaving, marriage, and children. Early school leaving not only implies less educational and skill development but is also frequently associated with early marriage and childbearing. Although an early start on parenthood does not necessarily imply a lifetime at home, career progression is less viable. An earlier start on family building has traditionally been associated with larger families, lower incomes, and fewer career opportunities. Data from the mature and young

3

women's NLS cohorts suggest how demographic change over the past three decades has partly paralleled and partly flown in the face of social change, particularly with respect to the relationship of school leaving, marriage, and family formation. Focusing on women aged 20 to 24 at various points in time, table 1.1 shows that for both white and black women, the median age at school leaving has moved progressively upward. In the immediate post–World War II period, the average woman left school before age 18. This statistic showed only modest change until the decade of the 1960s. But by the early 1970s, reflecting partly the increasing proportions of women attending college, the average white woman remained in school until almost age 20 and her black counterpart until 19.5 years of age.

Whereas the educational transition has been inexorably toward more and more attendance, other demographic changes

Table 1.1
Median age for occurrence of selected life-cycle events and average length of time between events for women age 20 to 24 years at selected points in time, by race

Race/ year	Median age			Gap between median dates (years)		
	At school leaving	At marriage	At first birth	Between school and marriage	Between school and first child	Between marriage and first child
Total						
1948	17.8	20.9	22.7	3.1	4.9	1.8
1953	18.0	20.5	22.1	2.5	4.1	1.6
1958	18.2	20.2	21.3	2.0	3.2	1.2
1968	19.5	20.8	22.8	1.3	3.3	2.0
1973	19.8	21.1	24.1	1.3	4.3	3.0
Whites						
1948	17.9	20.9	22.8	3.0	4.9	1.9
1953	18.0	20.5	22.3	2.5	4.3	1.8
1958	18.2	20.2	21.5	2.0	3.3	1.3
1968	19.5	20.7	23.2	1.2	3.7	2.5
1973	19.8	21.0	24.7	1.2	5.0	3.8
Blacks						
1948	17.6	20.5	21.7	2.9	4.1	1.2
1953	17.3	19.7	19.4	2.4	2.2	−0.2
1958	17.9	19.7	19.2	1.8	1.4	−0.4
1968	19.0	21.4	20.2	2.5	1.2	−1.3
1973	19.5	23.1	20.5	3.5	0.9	−2.6

Note: Information for women who were 20 to 24 in 1948, 1953, and 1958 was derived from the retrospective records of women who were 30 to 44 in 1967. Information for women who were 20 to 24 in 1968 and 1973 was derived from the retrospective records of women who were 24 to 34 in 1978, that is, the mature and young women's cohorts of the NLS.

have been more erratic. Paralleling the baby boom dynamics, the median age at marriage for white and black women declined during the 1950s and then gradually rose, reaching 21 for white women in 1973 and a dramatic 23 years for their black counterparts.[4] However, while first births have followed a pattern generally similar to the marriage curve, the magnitudes suggest a radically different story. From a low of 21.5 for white women age 20 to 24 in 1958, the median age at first birth climbed to almost 25 years of age for white women who were age 20 to 24 in 1973. Unfortunately from a career perspective, the trend of first births among blacks showed only modest increases to a median of 20.5 in 1973. Thus the average young black woman has fewer years than her white counterpart between school leaving and family formation in which to gain a solid foothold on the employment ladder. Indeed the radical dissimilarity between the white and black marriage-birth relationship in 1973 has important and contrasting socioeconomic implications for women of both races.

The impact of these dramatic demographic transitions over the past three decades cannot be underestimated. While many women can and do begin lifetime work attachments both contiguous with and following their early family formation, career development is definitely smoother for women who gain a foothold in the marketplace during the early postschool years. The contraceptive revolution and changing norms regarding optimum family size have had a major impact on the family-career relationship (table 1.1). Between the 1940s and 1970s rapid increases in the age of schooling but only modest increases in the age at marriage led to a phenomenal decline for white women in the average gap between school leaving and marriage. However, the direct impact of this narrowing on female employment has been only modest, reflecting the general acceptability of work for young married women in our society. From social perspectives other than employment, the long-term implications of closing the school-marriage gap remain uncertain. Indeed to the extent that the school years are ones of rapid social and psychological development for many young men and women and years when ideas about the future are in flux, the increase in the proportions of the population marrying while in school (albeit college) may be one major force behind the current high divorce rates for young adults.

Although the gap between school and marriage has narrowed, for white women the period between school leaving and childbearing has increased considerably in recent years. The group age 20 to 24 in 1973 showed an average of five years between school leaving and the birth of a first child, reflecting a lengthy gap of about 3.8 years between first marriage and first birth. This average five-year gap permits many women to gain a substantial foothold on the career employment ladder before beginning a family.

The situation for black women is far less satisfactory. Although the young black woman waits substantially longer to marry, she begins a family rapidly. The net result is that the average young black woman has 3.5 years between school leaving and marriage but only about a year between school leaving and childbirth; she is then less likely to find and maintain meaningful employment and also less likely to have the economic support of a husband if she does not have a job. These demographic events in the early adult years have all-pervading implications that are difficult, though not impossible, to alter.

Most discussions of demographic phenomena focus on what might be termed "normal" transitions, as in fact, the above trend analysis has done. For most people there has historically been a neat, logical sequence in the way they matured and lived. Usually marriage has not occurred until school has been completed, and children have not been conceived and born until after marriage. Employment for women has always been fairly common in the years between school leaving and marriage but far less common following marriage, particularly when young children are present in the home. This typically neat ordering of life-cycle events made social science research into the activities of women quite easy and also quite uninteresting.

But witness what has been happening in recent years. Whereas only about 18 percent of white women age 20 to 24 in 1948 married before completing school, about 40 percent of contemporary women marry while they are still students (table 1.2). Thus a substantial proportion of American women are following what might be termed a nonnormative behavior path. The increase in student marriages may be a major contributor to the social revolution in marriage and divorce. Whether it has a significant impact on long-term employment trends is somewhat less clear.

On the other hand, whereas more than one of five white

Table 1.2
Prevalence of "nontraditional" behavior for women age 20 to 24 years at selected points in time, by race

Race/ year	Percent marrying before completing school	Percent having a first birth before leaving school	Percent having a first birth before marrying[a]
Total			
1948	18.8	14.3	18.2
1953	21.9	15.1	18.7
1958	25.3	19.4	22.7
1968	42.1	23.9	16.1
1973	37.3	17.1	15.5
Whites			
1948	18.1	13.3	15.9
1953	21.3	13.6	16.1
1958	25.2	18.4	19.9
1968	43.1	22.2	12.1
1973	38.2	13.7	10.5
Blacks			
1948	27.1	23.3	37.4
1953	26.1	26.9	40.6
1958	26.8	28.3	47.2
1968	35.4	37.9	46.6
1973	30.7	40.4	50.7

a. Includes women who never married. See table 1.1 for definition of sample. To the extent that school leaving, marriage or first birth events occur after age 30 to 44 for the women who were 30 to 44 in 1967 (the 1948, 1953, and 1958 age cohorts) or after age 24 to 34 for women who were 14 to 24 in 1968 (the 1968 and 1973 cohorts), the estimates in this table may be subject to some minor truncation biases.

women were having their first child while still in school during the late 1960s and early 1970s, this trend has dramatically reversed. Also changing familial values in conjunction with the contraceptive revolution have significantly lessened the magnitude of the early pregnancy problem for white women and have permitted more and more women not only to begin a career but, just as important, to complete their education. By the mid-1970s the prevalence of in-school fertility among white women was no higher than it had been in the immediate postwar years.

As might be anticipated on the basis of the results of table 1.1, young black women are less likely to marry while still in school but more likely to have a child. Although their average

age at school leaving is now only modestly below that for white women, fully 40 percent of black women who were age 20 to 24 in 1973 had had a child before leaving school. Thus in many instances their potential for gaining necessary vocational skills, adequately searching the job market, and maintaining ties with a job was effectively curtailed. While normal demographic progression in life-cycle events is not a necessary prerequisite to career and life success, its importance for most people should not be underestimated. The links joining these demographic transitions, earlier activities, and later work and nonwork events form the core of this book. Any understanding of the attitudes and behaviors of adult women—how they see their role in American society and what they view as constraints or facilitating factors—is heavily contingent on understanding their early adult demographics.

Figure 1.1 suggests how young American women are at least partially coming to grips with their changing outlook on life. Focusing on the status of 20- to 24-year-old women, we see that substantial proportions are continuing their education well into their twenties and frequently returning to school following lengthy interruptions. In fact about one of every eight women in our sample have already returned to school by their mid-twenties. Those who return had an average interruption of over 3 years before returning if they were white and 6.7 years if black (table 1.3). The majority of those who returned did not leave school the second time until after age 27.

Demographic sequences are not predetermined or positioned. Although the early breaks in education cannot be easily remedied and returning to school is not a complete solution, our social system demonstrates increasing flexibility in meeting the requirements of a population highly diverse in capabilities and needs. It offers considerable potential for overcoming early demographic "mistakes," if you will.

The Decade of the 1970s: Maturation and Change for Young American Women

In a quarter-century of demographic history an enormous transition has made possible for most women a greater consonance between their diversified life-styles and their demographic behavior—that is, their education, marriage, and childbearing patterns. This change does not mean that the progression to adulthood is now easy, but very large proportions of women are now reaching adulthood in a position to follow more diverse life-styles than was true for their mothers' generation.

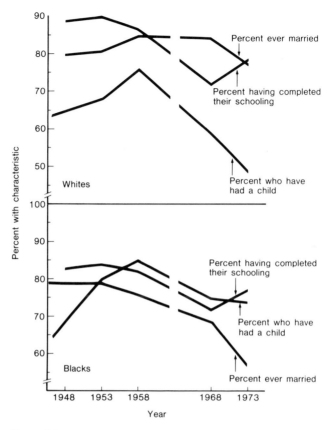

Figure 1.1
Life-cycle characteristics at age 24, by race, 1948–1973

For the most part these secular trends are also more likely to leave an adult woman in a better position to maintain a close continuing tie with the labor force.

We now focus on the group who are central to this study: young women age 14 to 24 in 1968, the generation reaching adulthood in the 1970s. We will examine the extent to which transitions for these young women reflected their own maturation, as well as continuing secular change within American society. Table 1.4 shows how women who were age 20 to 24 in 1968 and 1973 altered their behaviors by the time they reached age 25 to 29, in 1973 and 1978, respectively. A comparison of the socioeconomic characteristics and economic well-being of those who were age 20 to 24 in 1968 and 1973 and age 25 to 29 in 1973 and 1978 indicates how the situation of adult women has been changing within the past decade.

9

Table 1.3
School-leaving patterns for women age 24 to 34 years in 1978, by age in 1968 and 1973 and race

Characteristic and age	Median age at first school leaving	Median age returned	Median age at second school leaving
Whites			
20–24 in 1968			
Total	19.3		
Nonreturnees	18.5		
Returnees	21.4	24.7	27.2
Percent returnees	12.1		
20–24 in 1973			
Total	19.3		
Nonreturnees	19.0		
Returnees	21.1	24.9	a
Percent returnees	12.8		
Blacks			
20–24 in 1968			
Total	18.7		
Nonreturnees	18.4		
Returnees	19.2	25.9	27.5
Percent returnees	8.2		
20–24 in 1973			
Total	18.9		
Nonreturnees	18.8		
Returnees	19.5	24.6	
Percent returnees	15.6		

a. Because the majority are still enrolled, a median value could not be constructed.

The demographic trends emphasized previously were accelerating as the 1970s progressed. For white women the pace of marriage and childbearing continued to slow, as can be seen by comparing the five-year transition of young women age 20 to 24 in 1968 with that of their 1973 counterparts. For example, the average white woman age 20 to 24 in 1968 had 0.67 children and 1.42 children five years later at age 25 to 29. The comparable figures for the cohort age 20 to 24 in 1973 were 0.52 and 1.09.

Enrollments showed a modest increase for white women over the decade. The 1973 group was relatively more likely than the 1968 group to be enrolled and to have attended college by the time they had attained age 25 to 29.

Through the 1970s young black women showed no significant decline in the probability of having had a child, while their likelihood of having a husband declined sharply; however, although their likelihood of having a child showed no change, their average number of children declined sharply, suggesting that as the decade progressed, young black mothers were significantly slowing down their pace of childbearing. This decline in the probability of having a second child will enhance the ability of many black women to overcome the premature school leaving and employment termination associated with their characteristically earlier first births. This decline is also consistent with the substantial increase in school enrollment and college attendance among young black women over the 1970s (table 1.4).

Table 1.4 presents a synthesis of several important indicators of work and economic success. The attachment of young white women to the work force, shown in the employment and labor force participation rates, increased substantially between the 1968 and 1973 cohorts. Although the employment and labor force rates, as well as the average weeks worked in the year, for the 1968 cohort declined by the time they attained the ages of 25 to 29 in 1973, the trend for the 1973 cohort was in the opposite direction. Thus there is evidence that the historical pattern of declines in the overall level of female labor force participation associated with movement into the peak childbearing years may have reversed. As the research in this book suggests, this fundamental change reflects the overall decline in American fertility and the greater work propensities of women who do have children.

While there is a clear secular increase in female employment over the decade, parallel improvements in remuneration and status are less in evidence. Mean increases in real annual earnings for women who worked at some time during the year showed insignificant change, real hourly wages declined, and the average occupational status of white workers also was unchanged. Real family income for white women also declined substantially, but reflecting demographic forces, per-capita income increased. Because the average family in the later years of the decade included fewer children, the difference between family income and the poverty line increased considerably. In sum the work involvement of white women continued to rise over the period despite the fact that those white women who

Table 1.4
Maturation and secular change between 1968 and 1978: personal, demographic, and employment characteristics, by age and race in 1968, 1973, and 1978

Characteristic and age	Total			White			Black		
	1968	1973	1978	1968	1973	1978	1968	1973	1978
Percent married, with husband present									
20–24	58.0	54.3		59.6	56.9		45.3	36.1	
25–29		79.4	69.2		82.5	72.8		53.9	43.6
Percent with a child									
20–24	44.4	39.9		42.0	36.5		63.7	63.8	
25–29		72.4	63.2		71.0	60.6		81.0	81.9
Mean number of children									
20–24	0.73	0.58		0.67	0.52		1.23	1.03	
25–29		1.49	1.16		1.42	1.09		2.12	1.68
Percent enrolled in school									
20–24	16.2	17.8		17.3	18.2		7.5	15.2	
25–29		5.6	7.9		5.6	7.9		5.3	8.2
Percent having attended college									
20–24	35.1	35.9		37.1	38.0		18.1	21.4	
25–29		36.6	40.8		38.5	42.5		20.8	29.4
Percent employed survey week									
20–24	51.7	59.1		52.2	60.1		48.0	51.8	
25–29		51.2	62.7		50.0	62.7		52.7	62.8
Labor force participation rate									
20–24	57.9	64.3		57.9	64.4		57.5	63.0	
25–29		54.2	67.4		53.8	66.8		57.5	71.9
Mean weeks worked in year (total population)									
20–24	28.4	29.2		28.6	29.6		26.8	25.7	
25–29		25.4	32.9		25.3	33.0		25.9	32.1
Mean annual earnings (total population)									
20–24	3,204	3,509		3,301	3,586		2,407	2,954	
25–29		3,813	4,937		3,862	4,953		3,416	4,826

Table 1.4 (continued)

Characteristic and age	Total			White			Black		
	1968	1973	1978	1968	1973	1978	1968	1973	1978
Mean annual earnings (workers only)[a]									
20–24	4,273	4,408		4,409	4,476		3,188	3,883	
25–29		5,992	6,571		6,112	6,588		5,060	6,446
Mean hourly wage (workers only)									
20–24	3.82	3.65		3.88	3.68		3.28	3.40	
25–29		4.37	4.59		4.50	4.64		3.47	4.30
Mean occupational (Bose) status (workers only)[b]									
20–24	49.8	49.4		50.9	50.1		39.5	43.2	
25–29		51.5	51.7		52.7	52.3		42.1	47.3
Family income[a]									
20–24	15,162	14,061		15,745	14,622		10,363	9,864	
25–29		16,022	15,014		16,707	15,605		10,556	10,801
Ratio of family income to poverty level									
20–24	2.88	2.93		2.72	3.09		1.61	1.80	
25–29		3.24	3.31		2.72	3.45		1.86	2.27
Percent expect- ing to work at age 35									
20–24	31.5	52.1		29.9	50.6		44.6	63.4	
25–29		57.4	77.0		56.5	75.7		63.0	86.0
Mean atypicality score of occu- pation expected at age 35[c]									
20–24	29.0	28.0		27.2	27.3		39.1	32.4	
25–29		28.0	21.8		27.2	21.7		34.1	22.2

Note: The measures included in this table are for women in the young women's cohort who were 15 to 24 years of age in 1968. Thus, there are no data available for women who were 25 to 29 in 1968 or 20 to 24 in 1978. These two groups were outside the scope of the original cohort.
a. Constant 1978 dollars.
b. The Bose Index is an ordinal measure of occupational prestige based upon the prestige rankings of 110 occupations. The average rank within each occupation was transformed into a metric ranging from 0 to 100.
c. An atypicality score is the difference between the percentage of women found in the occupational category desired by the respondent (measured as of the 1970 Census) and the percentage of women represented in the experienced civilian labor force in 1970. For example, in 1970 women were 38.1 percent of the experienced civilian labor force. Women were also 4.6 percent of all architects. Therefore the atypicality score for a woman who desires to be an architect is 4.6 − 38.1 = −33.5. The larger the positive value of the atypicality score, the more typical is the occupation for women. The larger the negative value of the atypicality score, the more atypical the occupation is for women.

did work showed no substantial income or status gains. The families of these women improved their real well-being primarily by having fewer children as the absolute level of their real family income declined.

Among black women increasing participation in the work force reflected both the aging process and a secular trend toward greater attachment to the work force. In contrast to the modest pattern of real increase in earnings for white women, black workers showed major increases in hourly wage rates, occupational status, and annual earnings. The wage and status gap between white and black women narrowed considerably over the decade. Particularly striking has been the sharp increase in well-being for black women who were 20 to 24 in 1973. Over the 1973–1978 period black women who were employed at some time during the year increased their real annual earnings (in 1978 dollars) from about $3,900 to $6,500. While this increase partly reflected an increase in mean weeks worked, a major part of it resulted from real hourly wage increases from $3.40 to $4.30 an hour. Overall the trends indicated by these data suggest continuing increases in work attachment for women of both races, with black women gaining on their white counterparts in their ability to attain income and status equality in the labor market.

Transitions in Role Attitudes

The depth of the transition toward greater female attachment to the work force and movement away from traditional ideas about women's behavior can be seen most clearly and directly by noting the responses of the young women to questions on their ideas about appropriate roles for women in general and their own long-term work intentions. The speed with which women's perceptions have been changing is startling. It is considered virtually universally acceptable for a married young mother to work if it is economically necessary to do so, just as it was when the NLS surveys were initiated in the late 1960s (table 1.5). However, positive attitudes regarding more generalized ideas about the appropriateness of young mothers' work behavior are more recent. A question about the appropriateness of woman's work "if she prefers to work and her husband agrees" even if "trusted relatives are available for child care" drew a 32 percent negative response from a cross-section of women age 20 to 24 in 1968. By 1972 a comparable cohort gave only an 18 percent negative response rate, and by

Table 1.5

Percentage agreeing with specified attitudes toward employment for selected survey years, by age and race

Attitude and age	Total			White			Black		
	1968	1972	1978	1968	1972	1978	1968	1972	1978
All right to work if necessary									
20–24	92.0	95.0		92.1	94.9		91.2	95.9	
25–29		96.0	97.8		96.0	97.9		95.6	97.1
All right to work if husband agrees									
20–24	67.8	82.2		65.8	80.6		84.7	93.4	
25–29		86.0	94.2		85.2	94.0		93.3	95.5
All right to work if husband disagrees									
20–24	13.6	23.7		13.1	23.3		17.4	26.8	
25–29		26.9	53.2		26.4	53.6		31.1	50.1

Note: See table 1.4. The full attitude question is: "Now I'd like you to think about a family where there is a mother, a father who works full time, and several children under school age. A trusted relative who can care for the children lives nearby. In this family situation, how do you feel about the mother taking a full-time job outside the home (a) if it is absolutely necessary to make ends meet? (b) if she prefers to work and her husband agrees? and (c) if she prefers to work, but her husband doesn't particularly like it?" The possible responses were "definitely all right," "probably all right," "probably not all right," "definitely not all right," and "no opinion, undecided."

the time this same group had aged to 25 to 29, agreement with this item was almost universal. Thus in one decade it has become virtually totally acceptable among young women to work for noneconomic reasons, as long as there is intrafamily consensus. Societal norms have changed from the immediate post–World War II years when most married women who worked did so only because of economic compulsion (Milkman 1976; Smuts 1971; Cain 1966).

Perhaps the most striking statistics, however, are related to positive responses from women to a question that potentially implies a considerable level of intrafamily conflict. More directly than almost any other measure I have seen, it is symptomatic of the recent radical transitions in perceptions of the roles of men and women. In 1968 only about 14 percent of women age 20 to 24 felt that it was all right for a woman to work "if she prefers to work, but her husband doesn't particularly like it." By 1972 this percentage had almost doubled to about 24 percent for a later cohort of 20 to 24 year olds, and by the time this group had reached age 25 to 29, over half indi-

Table 1.6
Percentage expecting to work at age 35: stability of responses over five-year period, by age

Age	Changed from expect to don't expect to work	Changed from don't expect to expect to work	Expect to work both points	Do not expect to work both points
20–24 in 1968	8.3	34.0	23.4	34.3
20–24 in 1973	7.0	31.2	45.8	16.1

cated that work by a wife with young children was acceptable, even if her husband disagreed.

Paralleling these responses about the appropriateness of work, by 1978 about 77 percent of women age 25 to 29 said that they planned to be working at age 35, substantially above the anticipated work rate of just a few years earlier (table 1.4). While young women are more likely to respond positively regarding future work intentions than had been true a few years earlier, many of these positive work values tend to be acquired as women approach adulthood, reflecting a greater awareness of the economic need for and psychic desirability of work outside the home. This level of awareness has undoubtedly increased in recent years as young women become aware of the increasing social acceptability of women's work and the greater range of occupational opportunities now open to them. Table 1.6 documents the magnitude of this transition in intentions. When one compares the future work intentions of women age 20 to 24 in 1968 with their intentions five years later, we see that only 23 percent had indicated in both 1968 and 1973 that they expected to be working at age 35, 34 percent indicated no intentions toward future work at both dates, and a substantial 34 percent changed their ideas from a home toward a work orientation. Following a group age 20 to 24 in 1973 to 1978, one finds that only 16 percent said at both points that they did not plan future work, and fully 45 percent stated at both points that they planned to be working at age 35. The net effect was that between 1973 and 1978, the percentage of women age 25 to 29 at these dates who expected to be working only five to ten years later increased from 57 to 77 percent.

Whether this trend toward increasing work intentions will continue in the years immediately ahead is uncertain, but several facts are already clear. From a somewhat mundane academic perspective, the increasing desire of women for the freedom to seek employment and the increasing intensity with which they are doing so—for all sorts of reasons—suggests that traditional theoretical orientations for explaining male work behavior will predict with increasing effectiveness women's work participation. Just as men have worked and continue to work for a wide variety of reasons, regardless of family or personal considerations, women will also work for all reasons and in all situations. Most of the research in this book supports this thesis.

We have obviously not yet reached a stage of psychological equality regarding role behavior between the sexes. This book will show how women are still constrained overtly and perhaps also less consciously by a host of factors. Chapter 2 demonstrates how influences from one's family of origin differentially affect the ability of boys and girls to progress educationally, by virtue of the effect that parents have on both educational goals and actual educational attainment. Chapter 4 shows how the ideas mothers have about appropriate role behaviors for women have a lasting influence on daughters' work behavior patterns.

On the other hand, linkages can be broken. Although evidence suggests that fertility intentions are indeed conditioned by contemporary life-style attitudes (in chapter 6), they also are directly influenced by earlier work experiences (in chapter 3). Finally although several of the chapters demonstrate that for most women the short-term effect of having a birth is to depress the level of work activity, strong evidence in chapters 5 and 7 supports the notion that substantial proportions of women with children, both in and outside of marriage, plan life-long commitments to their jobs, every bit as strong as the work commitments shown by men. These women are demonstrably at center stage in the employment revolution.

Notes

I thank Jean Haurin and Nan Maxwell for their outstanding research assistance.

1. See appendix to chapter 1 for a detailed discussion of the survey.

2. See appendix to chapter 1 for a more detailed statement about the sample loss and potential attrition biases.

3. There are four separate age cohorts in the original National Longitudinal Survey of Work Experience. They include about 5,000 men 14 to 24 and 45 to 59 first interviewed in 1966, 5,000 women 30 to 44 in 1967, and 5,000 women 14 to 24 in 1968, the group who are the principal focus of this research. In drawing the original cohort samples, the

Census Bureau permitted multiple respondents from the same household. Thus, for example, a 30- to 44-year-old woman in the mature women's cohort and a 14- to 24-year-old woman in the young women's cohort might both have been selected for interview. There are many such cross-cohort matches possible, detailed in the relevant chapters in Center for Human Resource Research (1981).

4. The analysis in this section focuses on age cohorts who were 20 to 24 years of age in the years noted. The reference years for the medians were 1967 and 1978 (see table 1.1).

References

Bureau of Labor Statistics. 1980. *Marital and Family Characteristics of Workers, March 1980*. USDOL 80-767. Washington, D.C.: U.S. Government Printing Office.

Cain, G. 1966. *Married Women in the Labor Force, An Economic Analysis*. Chicago: University of Chicago Press.

Center for Human Resource Research. 1981. *The National Longitudinal Surveys Handbook 1981*. Columbus, Ohio: The Ohio State University.

Milkman, R. 1976. Women's work and economic crisis: some lessons of the great depression. *Review of Radical Political Economics* 8:73–97.

Schiffman, J. 1961. Marital and family characteristics of workers, March 1960. *Monthly Labor Review* 84:1–10.

Smuts, R. W. 1971. *Women and Work in America*. New York: New York University Press.

Waldman, E., and Young, A. M. 1971. Marital and family characteristics of workers, March 1970. *Monthly Labor Review* 94:46–50.

Chapter 2

Variations
in the
Educational
Progress
and Career
Orientations of
Brothers and
Sisters

Frank L. Mott
and
R. Jean Haurin

In American society the principal mechanism by which people have improved their socioeconomic status across generations has been education. Higher levels of education are prerequisites for most higher-status and better-paying occupations. Although women have historically had difficulty entering many occupational areas, to a considerable degree these structural barriers are being eroded. As women gain access to an increasingly broad array of occupational opportunities, adequate educational preparation becomes even more important.

As a prelude to the research on the determinants and consequences of female employment encompassed in most of this book, in this chapter we examine some of the reasons why young women may already be a step behind young men in their career development process before they have even gained a foothold on the employment ladder. Some unique data permit an examination of the extent to which young women are handicapped in their educational progress compared with young men—how their differential socialization varies across socioeconomic levels, is affected by household structure and sibling placement within the family, and is conditioned by a youth's ability and how he or she perceives encouragement from parents. Here we also examine how these same background factors affect a young women's career choices.

The Data Set

The NLS young women's cohort was originally interviewed in 1968. Beginning in 1966 a nationally representative sample of about 5,000 young men age 14 to 24 were interviewed, and like the young women, they were repeatedly interviewed over the following decade about their family, education, and employment experiences and attitudes. By the tenth survey year (1976 for men and 1978 for women), the 3,700 young men and 4,200 young women still being interviewed were age 24 to 34, and the vast majority had completed their formal education. Thus we are able to examine their educational progress without introducing any serious truncation biases.

In the initial sample selection process, if a household included a young man who was 14 to 24 in 1966 and a young woman who was 14 to 24 in 1968, the U.S. Bureau of the Census included them both in the samples selected. Although these young men and women could be related to each other in many different ways, they were typically brother and sister.

We constrained the sample to brother and sister pairs where both siblings were still being interviewed after ten years. This and other constraints left a total of 749 matched pairs of brothers and sisters: 522 white, 214 black, and 13 of other races.[1] Because of the relatively small number of black and other race pairs, the analyses here are limited to white youth.

The principal rationale for using matched brother-sister pairs is to control more properly for commonality of background. To gain the assurance that our matched pairs are generally comparable in demographic and socioeconomic characteristics to a nationally representative population group of similar age, we compared them with the full nationally representative NLS samples of young men and women with respect to a number of socioeconomic characteristics. In virtually all cases our sample and the overall nationally representative samples matched up well.[2] Further details regarding the sample selection procedure and the nature of the sample may be found in appendix 2A. This data set offers distinct advantages over some used in previous status attainment research by allowing greater generalizability and more contemporary information.[3] Furthermore we can control for common background factors better than has been possible in other research.[4]

The General Research Plan

Our general aim in this chapter is to examine the educational patterns of brothers and sisters to see if they vary according to major determinants of educational progress. The unique sibling match permits us to examine differences in the educational attainment of brothers and sisters as a function of a variety of factors commonly assumed to affect them. Our basic assumption, consistent with previous findings, is that on average the sister in the sibling pair will be handicapped in her educational development (as measured by high school completion, college attendance, college completion, and ultimate educational attainment) compared with her brother. This handicap is due to a variety of factors, all of which cannot be treated extensively in this chapter (Adams and Meidam 1968; Sewell and Shah 1968; Alexander and Eckland 1974; Hout and Morgan 1975; Marini 1978; Marini and Greenberger 1978). We also hypothesize parallel sex differences in educational goals as measured by anticipation of college attendance or completion and anticipated educational attainment.[5] The broad categories of independent variables included in our multivariate analysis may be subsumed under sibling effects, socioeco-nomic effects, environmental effects, and other background factors.

The available literature is ambiguous about how important sibling influences are as predictors of actual educational prog-ress or goals. Although a number of studies have shown that the effect of family size is inversely related to educational achievement and educational expectations (Hout and Morgan 1975; Blau and Duncan 1967; Olneck and Bills 1979), other studies suggest that family size may affect one sex to a greater extent than the other (McClendon 1976; Rosen and Aneshensel 1978), perhaps reflecting a differential distribution of family resources by sex of child, particularly when available resources are severely constrained.

Some studies also report that sibling placement is a use-ful predictor of actual and prospective educational success. Whereas some studies find no sibling placement effects, par-ticularly when family size is controlled (Adams and Meidam 1968; Olneck and Bills 1979), others find that birth order makes a difference. The most general finding is that being the first born is associated with higher educational attainment (Adams 1972).

More important some researchers have pointed out that birth order alone is not always an important factor in the so-cialization process or in educational outcomes but that the sex of one's siblings matters. Sutton-Smith and Rosenberg (1970) extensively discuss the effects of different sibling relationships upon personality development and role modeling throughout childhood into the adolescent and adult years. Lin and Oliver (1979) note that girls have higher educational aspirations when they have older sisters, and Adams and Meidam (1968) show that male siblings can handicap a girl's educational progress, particularly in blue-collar families. In general, however, the available literature on cross-sex sibling effects is sparse, a fur-ther reason for an examination of these types of effects.

This study measures the independent effects of family size, sibling placement, and sex of siblings on educational prog-ress. Our multivariate analyses will include the number of sib-lings outside the brother-sister pair (a measure of family size), whether the boy in the pair is older than the girl (a measure of sibling placement), and a variable that captures the sex mix of siblings who are older than the pair. Youth are assumed to be most affected by the sex of older rather than younger siblings in terms of their being potential role models.

The literature on socioeconomic and other background effects is somewhat more substantial than that on sibling influences, but it is also far from conclusive. Both socioeconomic background and ability generally have been found to exert positive and independent effects on educational goals and attainment. Background status tends to have greater impact on the educational progress of females, and ability shows substantial influence upon males (Sewell and Shah 1967; Alexander and Eckland 1974).

Although most studies have used a composite measure of socioeconomic status, usually incorporating both mother's and father's education, father's occupation, and/or family income, few have examined the separate effects of these measures. Sewell and Hauser (1972) found each component to have approximately equal effect upon educational attainment. On the other hand Treiman and Terrell (1975) found parental education to be the strongest predictor of educational attainment, with a slight tendency toward a like-sexed parent effect. McClendon (1976) found mother's education to be a stronger predictor than father's education regardless of the sex of the child. This study contributes to the dialogue by including in its models an interactive variable that separately identifies the father's and the mother's educational attainment.[6]

Independent of a status measure based upon parental education, we also include a measure of the ability of the brother and sister, an IQ score obtained, for the most part, during the junior or senior year in high school.[7] The effect of IQ (or "ability") on educational progress has, not surprisingly, been found to be unambiguously positive, although differences between the sexes have been noted. These sex differences generally suggest a stronger ability—attainment or ability—expectations connection for boys than girls (Sewell and Shah 1967; Alexander and Eckland 1974; Marini and Greenberger 1978). In addition differential effects of ability on attainment in comparison with expectations have been noted (Alexander and Eckland 1975).

Our study examines the symmetry or lack of symmetry in the progress of boys and girls with similar IQs through the educational system, after controlling for all other relevant factors. We also briefly examine some of Griliches's (1979) notions about a possible tendency of parents to equalize outcomes for children with different ability levels. If this process is operative, we anticipate that children with low ability who have siblings of greater ability should experience greater educational success than children from households where all siblings have low ability. Furthermore in families where one child is brighter than the other, there may be sibling peer pressures for the less-able youth to accomplish more than in otherwise similar households where there are no higher IQ youth. Our particular interest is whether effects of this type are symmetrical by sex of child. That is, does a higher-ability boy enhance his sister's educational accomplishments to the same extent that a higher-ability girl helps her brother?

Independent of these factors, there is some evidence that parental encouragement of youth to further their education can contribute to higher educational attainment and/or goals (Rehberg and Westby 1967). Most studies do not include measures of such encouragement, but Hout and Morgan (1975) found that parental encouragement had more influence on boys' than girls' educational expectations. Sewell and Shah (1968) found that parental encouragement affected both boys' and girls' college plans, primarily in higher-status families. We will test for differences in the influence of parental encouragement on brothers and sisters and whether the influence of a same or opposite sex parent has more or less impact.[8]

All other factors in our multivariate analyses are essentially controls, although many can be of interest in their own light.[9] Although our models of differences will indicate the relative levels of educational attainment or aspirations among brothers compared with sisters, they are not useful for indicating absolute levels. Separate educational attainment models for the brothers and sisters will make it possible to see how background factors affect the absolute levels of educational attainment and aspirations of young men and women.

The educational progress variables are measured as of 1976 for the men and 1978 for the women, at which time the sample was age 24 to 34. Educational goals are measured at age 18 or at the earliest point available. Appendix 2A gives a detailed description of variable measurement. The full multivariate analyses appear in appendix tables 2A.2 through 2A.8.

Brothers and sisters in our overall sample have approximately equal likelihoods of completing high school (table 2.1); however, the average brother is substantially more likely to have attended college and somewhat more likely to have completed college by the tenth survey year. As of that point about 34 percent of the young men but only 29 percent of the young women have attained a college degree.[10] Virtually all of this discrepancy in college completion between the sexes reflects the greater ability of young men to attend college. In fact if we limit the sample to brothers and sisters who have attended college, the girl gains an edge over the boy in the probability of completing college.

In the aggregate the brothers also have higher educational goals than their sisters, although among both boys and girls substantial proportions have unrealistic aspirations, as may be seen by comparing the percentage aspiring to a certain level of education with the percentage actually completing that level. Whereas 34 percent of the young men have attained a college

Table 2.1
Educational attainment and educational goals of brothers and sisters

Educational attainment and goals	Brothers	Sisters
Total sample		
Probability of high school completion	0.90	0.88
Probability of college attendance	0.67	0.51
Probability of college completion	0.34	0.29
Mean educational attainment (years)	13.9	13.3
Number of respondents	498	498
High school completion sample		
Probability of college attendance	0.74	0.57
Probability of college completion	0.37	0.33
Number of respondents	.444	440
College attendance sample		
Probability of college completion	0.50	0.57
Number of respondents	333	253
Total sample		
Proportion with college attendance goal	0.70	0.58
Proportion with college completion goal	0.60	0.45
Mean educational goal (years)	14.8	14.1
Number of respondents	469	485
Ratio of college completion probability to proportion with college completion goal	0.56	0.65

Source: Appendix tables 2A.2 through 2A.5.

diploma or better, fully 60 percent had indicated at an earlier date that they wished to complete college—a ratio of 0.56. The comparable ratio for the sisters was 0.65. Thus while a smaller percentage of the young women completed college, their aspirations were substantially below those of their brothers; only 45 percent of the women aspired to complete college.

The Educational Attainment Process for Boys and Girls

In order to examine the extent to which our various explanatory variables independently affected the ability of brothers and sisters to complete high school, attend college, and complete college, we use a multivariate procedure, multiple classification analysis (MCA). In this procedure a value is estimated for the dependent variable for each category of each independent variable assuming that the individual is average on all other characteristics. The coefficients may be interpreted as the probabilities of attaining the various educational levels. The full attainment models may be found in appendix tables 2A.2 and 2A.3.

Sibling Effects

Neither family size nor sibling placement appears to have any significant effect upon the ability of brothers to progress educationally. Neither his number of siblings nor his relative age position compared with his sister(s) or brother(s) seems to affect any of the educational attainment probabilities.

On the other hand, while the relationship is not completely linear, there is evidence that sisters who have no more than one sibling (outside of the sibling pair itself) have an educational advantage over their female counterparts who come from larger families. Thus girls from smaller families have higher probabilities of attending and completing college as well as higher levels of educational attainment than girls from larger families, but boys are neither helped nor hindered by this family size dimension. As with the boys, we find virtually no evidence of sibling placement affecting the educational progress of young women. With only one exception our data do not indicate that being the older or younger sibling of the pair or having older brothers or sisters (outside of the pair) has any effect on a young woman's educational success compared with other young women in other sibling placement arrangements.

Parental Education Effects

In contrast with the lack of sibling effects, the extent of parental education does have a major independent effect on young men's and young women's educational progress. That better-educated parents have better-educated children is hardly surprising, but it is interesting to see how parental education differentially affects the success of sons and daughters. Table 2.2 distinguishes among four categories of parental education, examining the consequences of four combinations derived from having a father (mother) with fewer than 12 years of school or 12 years of school or more.[11]

Almost without exception the educational progress probabilities for sons are higher than those for daughters, regard-

Table 2.2
Parental education and child educational progression

Parental education	Probability of				
	High school completion	College attendance	College completion	High school graduate completing college	College attendee completing college
Son					
Grand mean	0.90	0.67	0.34	0.37	0.50
Both parents high school dropouts	0.81(−0.09)	0.49(−0.18)	0.26(−0.08)	0.32(−0.05)	0.53(+0.03)
Both parents high school graduates	0.94(+0.04)	0.82(+0.15)	0.41(+0.07)	0.44(+0.07)	0.50(+0.00)
Father high school graduate, mother high school dropout	0.94(+0.04)	0.54(−0.13)	0.22(−0.12)	0.23(−0.14)	0.41(−0.09)
Mother high school graduate, father high school dropout	0.92(+0.02)	0.64(−0.03)	0.33(−0.01)	0.36(−0.01)	0.52(+0.02)
Daughter					
Grand mean	0.88	0.51	0.29	0.33	0.57
Both parents high school dropouts	0.80(−0.08)	0.36(−0.15)	0.21(−0.08)	0.26(−0.07)	0.58(+0.01)
Both parents high school graduates	0.94(+0.06)	0.67(+0.16)	0.39(+0.10)	0.41(+0.08)	0.58(+0.01)
Father high school graduate, mother high school dropout	0.86(−0.02)	0.37(−0.14)	0.11(−0.18)	0.13(−0.20)	0.30(−0.27)
Mother high school graduate, father high school dropout	0.87(−0.01)	0.41(−0.10)	0.25(−0.04)	0.29(−0.04)	0.61(+0.04)

Source: Appendix tables 2A.2 and 2A.3.
Note: Numbers in parentheses are deviations from the grand mean.

less of the parents' education. This finding largely reflects the fact that the overall educational completion probabilities for males are higher than those for females, and the deviations within each sex due to variations in parental education are not sufficient to overcome the overall absolute gap. At the high school completion level, differences are generally small. Indeed high school completion probabilities for boys and girls are virtually identical where both parents are high school dropouts or both are high school graduates. Where there are differences in parental education, probabilities modestly favor the son.

Overall only 51 percent of the daughters compared with 67 percent of the sons attended college. The parental education factor does not mitigate this disadvantage for young women; daughters fare no better or worse relative to sons across families with different levels of parental education except in situations where the mother is a high school graduate and the father a dropout. In families of this type, daughters show a greater disadvantage.

By the college completion level, young women have overcome a substantial proportion of their overall educational disadvantage. In nearly all instances, the boy-girl gap in college completion is much narrower than the gap in college attendance. Indeed the brother-sister difference in college completion in those families where both parents have at least completed high school is quite small. It is likely that the greater egalitarian ethic found in higher-status families has some bearing on the sex equality in college completion for this group. This finding is of some consequence since the subset of families where both parents have at least a high school diploma represents the dominant education group in American society. Among most of the generation of young adults now marrying, both partners have high school diplomas.[12] Thus the equality evidenced for daughters in such families bodes well for the future.

The particular importance for young women of at least gaining a college foothold may be seen in the last column of table 2.2, where college completion probabilities are presented for young men and women who have attended college. Sisters in the sample who have attended college have higher college completion probabilities than their brothers in all instances except where their father has more education than their mother.

In families where parental education levels differ, the relative effects of parental education levels are most profound. Daughters are particularly disadvantaged relative to sons in their chances of attending college when the mother has 12 or more years of schooling and the father is a high school dropout, but young women in this family situation who enter college are not less likely than their brothers to complete college. In contrast young women from families where the father has 12 or more years of schooling and the mother is a high school dropout are not particularly disadvantaged relative to their brothers in the probability of attending college, but they do fare worse in the probability of completing college.

These contrasting results can perhaps be interpreted as follows. In families where the mother has more education than the father, on average the mother is likely to have less traditional values than the father, but she is still relatively powerless. Although she has more education than her husband, the association between education and earnings (and therefore power) for women of that generation was relatively low. Thus while the better-educated mother may have had high educational values with regard to her daughter's education, she was less able to subsidize the daughter to attend college, particularly in the face of opposition from a father who on average had more traditional values. However, in situations where a daughter is able to gain college entry, it is likely that both parents have less traditional values. In these situations the less traditional orientation of the mother may enhance the young women's likelihood of completing college.

In contrast families where the father has more education than the mother would on average have different parental traits. The father is likely to be less traditional than the mother and have significantly higher earnings and power within the family. Young women from this type of background would probably be as financially able as their brothers to enter college since the parent in the position of power is likely to be the parent with positive educational values. However, for these same young women, the more traditional value orientation of their mother may translate into a lower probability of completing college.

The data noted in table 2.2 also show one other interesting finding: when the mother's education exceeds that of the father, both the son and daughter complete substantially more education than in families where the father has more education than the mother. This variation suggests that the transmission of educational values across generations is more likely to be a mother-to-child phenomenon.

Ability Effects

It is not surprising to find that greater ability for boys and girls is associated with higher probabilities of educational completion at both the high school and college level. Focusing first on high school completion, table 2.3 shows that in families where both the brother and sister have measured IQs below 100, only about two-thirds of the boys and girls complete high school. Conversely where both have IQs of 100 or greater, 98 percent of the brothers and 93 percent of the sisters graduate. The two asymmetric ability pairs are of particular interest. In families where the boy has a higher IQ than the girl, high school completion probabilities are very high for both sexes, but where the girl is more intelligent, the boy has a probability somewhat below that of the girl. The striking fact is that in both of these asymmetric situations, the youth with less ability in a family where a sibling has above-average ability is much more likely to complete high school than the otherwise comparable youth who has a low-ability sibling.[13] Possible reasons for this phenomenon were suggested earlier. The above-average sibling possibly creates peer pressure, acts as a role model, and provides intellectual support for the less-endowed sibling. In addition parents in these families may strive harder to equalize educational outcomes for their children.

Table 2.3
The effect of IQ on the educational completion of brothers and sisters

IQ	Probability of completing high school		Probability of completing college	
	Brother	Sister	Brother	Sister
Grand mean	0.90	0.88	0.34	0.29
Both have IQ equal to or above 100	0.98(+0.08)	0.93(+0.05)	0.47(+0.13)	0.39(+0.10)
Both have IQ below 100	0.67(−0.23)	0.67(−0.21)	0.10(−0.24)	0.12(−0.17)
Brother equal to or above, sister below 100	0.98(+0.08)	0.95(+0.07)	0.38(+0.04)	0.15(−0.14)
Brother below, sister equal to or above 100	0.86(−0.04)	0.92(+0.04)	0.19(−0.15)	0.28(−0.01)

Source: Appendix tables 2A.2 and 2A.3.
Note: Numbers in parentheses are deviations from the grand mean.

At the college completion level, similar patterns were noted. Where both siblings had IQs equal to or above 100, brothers and sisters had the highest college completion probabilities. Where both had IQs below 100, college completion probabilities were equally low—around 10 percent—for both sexes. The two asymmetric categories were not mirror images of each other, however. Higher IQ boys who had lower IQ sisters did substantially better than higher IQ girls who had brothers with lower ability, although the ten-point difference between 0.38 and 0.28 equally reflects the overall differences in the grand means and deviations of each sex from their grand mean. In addition for the boys there was more of a spinoff effect from having a brighter sister than was true for the converse situation;[14] a low-ability boy who had a high-ability sister was about twice as likely to complete college as a low IQ boy who had a low IQ sister (19 percent compared with 10 percent). On the other hand a low IQ girl gained little (15 percent compared with 12 percent) from having a brighter brother. The substantial sibling spinoff effects noted at the high school completion level suggest the considerable importance of social environments for compensating for limited ability.

Parental Encouragement Effects

Table 2.4 shows that in families where the son felt he was encouraged by a father or mother to attend or complete higher education and a daughter felt she was encouraged less, college completion probabilities strongly favor the son.[15] Where the daughter felt encouraged and the son felt encouraged less, daughters and sons have equal chances of completing college (analogous to the situation where both parents had 12 or more years of education). In general the most favorable situation for both sexes was where encouragement was felt equally or not at all by either sibling. The vast majority (83 percent for the father and 90 percent for the mother) of these cases are where both siblings felt encouraged and in all likelihood represent the family units that were inculcating more general values about the importance of education for everyone.

A comparison of the educational outcomes for sons and daughters indicates that mother's encouragement in comparison with father's encouragement does not provide children of

Table 2.4
The effect of parental encouragement on college completion
probabilities of sons and daughters

Parental encouragement	Probability of college completion	
	Son	Daughter
Grand mean	0.34	0.29
Father encouragement		
Son perceives more than daughter	0.33(−0.01)	0.20(−0.09)
Daughter perceives more than son	0.30(−0.04)	0.31(+0.02)
Equal encouragement (or lack of encouragement)	0.39(+0.05)	0.32(+0.03)
Mother encouragement		
Son perceives more than daughter	0.36(+0.02)	0.21(−0.08)
Daughter perceives more than son	0.26(−0.08)	0.26(−0.03)
Equal encouragement (or lack of encouragement)	0.36(+0.02)	0.35(+0.06)

Source: Appendix tables 2A.2 and 2A.3.
Note: Numbers in parentheses are deviations from the grand mean.

either sex with any particular advantage. Perhaps a more significant general finding (from appendix tables 2A.2 and 2A.3)
is that if a youth perceives less encouragement than does his
or her sibling, in virtually all instances that youth is below average in educational progression compared with others of his or
her sex.

Congruence between Aspirations and Behavior

In general youths' aspirations about their educational attainment exceed their actual attainment by a considerable margin.
Table 2.5 highlights the general relationship between college
completion goals and attainment and shows how they are differentially related to selected characteristics of brothers and
sisters. The full goal models may be found in appendix tables
2A.4 and 2A.5.

Reflecting the fact that boys' educational goals are generally
substantially above those of their sisters but their attainment is
only modestly higher, boys have a much poorer congruence
between aspirations and actual accomplishment than do the
young women. The young men have the most realistic aspirations regarding the likelihood of completing college when
their mother has dropped out of high school, regardless of

Table 2.5
Comparison of college completion goal and actual college completion probabilities for brothers and sisters, by selected characteristics

Selected characteristics	Brother			Sister		
	Actual	Goal	Difference	Actual	Goal	Difference
Parental education						
Both parents high school dropouts	0.26	0.45	−0.19	0.21	0.34	−0.13
Both parents high school graduates	0.41	0.75	−0.34	0.39	0.59	−0.20
Father high school graduate, mother high school dropout	0.22	0.43	−0.21	0.11	0.28	−0.17
Mother high school graduate, father high school dropout	0.33	0.56	−0.23	0.25	0.32	−0.07
Sibling IQ						
Both have IQ equal to or above 100	0.47	0.75	−0.28	0.39	0.56	−0.17
Both have IQ below 100	0.10	0.28	−0.18	0.12	0.24	−0.12
Brother equal to or above, sister below 100	0.38	0.74	−0.36	0.15	0.33	−0.18
Brother below, sister equal to or above 100	0.19	0.43	−0.24	0.28	0.42	−0.14
Father encouragement						
Son perceives more than daughter	0.33	0.64	−0.31	0.20	0.35	−0.15
Daughter perceives more than son	0.30	0.52	−0.22	0.31	0.47	−0.16
Equal encouragement (or lack of encouragement)	0.39	0.65	−0.26	0.32	0.44	−0.12
Mother encouragement						
Son perceives more than daughter	0.36	0.60	−0.24	0.21	0.36	−0.15
Daughter perceives more than son	0.26	0.58	−0.32	0.26	0.48	−0.22
Equal encouragement (or lack of encouragement)	0.36	0.63	−0.27	0.35	0.55	−0.20

Source: Appendix tables 2A.2 through 2A.5.

their father's level of education, primarily because college aspirations are very low for this group of brothers. In a mirror image situation, girls are most realistic when their father has dropped out of high school regardless of their mother's level of education.

Somewhat paradoxically the greatest lack of reality is in those families where one would presume to find the most rational behavior patterns: families where both parents have at least completed high school. While both brothers and sisters in these families are most likely to complete college, they have acquired extremely optimistic aspirations. This is particularly true for the boys in the family; 41 percent actually have completed college but 75 percent had aspired to do so.

For both the boys and girls a somewhat analogous situation appears with respect to the relevance of ability as a predictor of actual college completion and college goals. High IQ boys are the most likely to complete college, but they also have by far the highest aspirations. As a result many actually accomplish less than they had originally intended to (at least as of the tenth survey year). For the sisters the pattern was generally similar though less pronounced because of the young women's generally lower aspirations.

The relationship between parental encouragement and the siblings' college goals closely parallels the pattern of college completion. The encouragement factor produces no particularly pronounced variations in the siblings' degree of realism. Indeed more often than not, for all the variables and for both sexes, greater attainment and higher goals went hand in hand. Educational goals are systematically overoptimistic, although the generally narrower gap for the young women speaks to the greater awareness that they probably have about the likelihood of extensive educational progress.

Determinants of Sex Differences in Educational Progression

We now directly test the extent to which the same background factors are related to the differential ability of the brother or sister to succeed. These difference models do not permit interpretation of whether a boy or girl does well in an absolute sense because we do not distinguish between brother-sister equality where both do poorly or both do well.

In these models the dependent variables are differences between brothers and sisters in whether they completed high school, whether they attended college, and whether they completed college. Because the models have qualitative dependent variables that include more than two categories, we use a multiple choice logit estimation procedure to test for the significance of the various explanatory factors.[16] Appendix tables 2A.6 through 2A.8 include full multiple choice logit models.

For each level of educational completion three models are estimated that permit calculation of the independent effect of various explanatory factors on the probabilities of the brother and sister being in each category of the dependent variable. That is, with respect to the likelihood of having completed high school, the possibilities allowed for in the model are (1) brother has completed but sister has not, (2) either both or neither sibling have completed, or (3) sister has completed but brother has not.[17] The three high school completion multiple logit models included in appendix table 2A.6 compare 1 with 3, 2 with 3, and 1 with 2. Parallel models for the differential probability of college attendance and the probability of college completion are also included in appendix tables 2A.7 and 2A.8, respectively. We focus on the models that compare the possibilities of (1) the brother having more education than the sister with (3) the sister having more education than the brother. This polar comparison should indicate the maximum extent to which the explanatory variables of interest differentially affect the relative success of brothers and sisters. Positive coefficients in the model imply that the brother has an advantage, and negative coefficients favor the sister.

Just as the separate attainment models did not suggest any major association between sibling placement or family size and educational completion, no significant differences in attainment at any educational level may be attributed to these variables. Neither the number of siblings nor their sex or relative position in the family seems to affect the relative success of the boy compared with the girl since none of the logit coefficients approaches significance. The only exception to these findings is that boys are helped modestly at the high school completion level compared with their sisters when he is the oldest in the pair.

With respect to the relative importance of the educational attainment of the youth's parents on the siblings' differential educational progress, similar nonsignificant results were obtained. Unequal levels of parental educational attainment (in comparison with the situation where both parents have at least completed high school) while leading to positive coefficients (boys completing more education than girls) do not significantly favor males.

In the earlier attainment analysis, which focused separately on the young men and women, almost all the sons had higher probabilities of high school completion, college attendance, and college completion than did daughters. The results here suggest that the different parental education categories are not significant predictors of the difference between the brothers' and sisters' attainment, even though the levels of attainment may vary across parental education categories. That is, if the sons have relatively equal advantages in all the parental education categories, a brother-sister difference variable does not attain significance.

It is also somewhat surprising that the parental education category where the father had 12 or more years of education and the mother completed fewer than 12 years does not systematically predict a significantly higher probability of college completion for the young men. Sons in this category were much more likely to graduate from college than were daughters. This may be one instance where the within-family relationships measured in the difference model suggest different results from the analogous comparisons made earlier from the separate sex models. Indeed one objective of this research has been to suggest whether analogous results are obtained when comparing within-family results with separate sex models that do not directly focus on disaggregated differences in attainment. While the two approaches are generally consistent, there is no theoretical reason why they need always be so.

The pattern of association between sibling IQ differences and sibling differences in educational completion generally parallels the earlier separate sex models. Girls who are more intelligent than their brothers have a relative advantage in the likelihood of high school completion over those in homes where both siblings have IQs above 100. Similarly girls in homes where both siblings have low IQ are generally advantaged compared to a situation where both siblings have IQs above 100.

Girls have a similar advantage in the likelihood of college completion when they have greater measured mental ability than their brothers, and boys have a parallel advantage when they have the mental edge. In the earlier separate sex analysis, high IQ for a son appeared to provide him more educational advantage than high IQ for a daughter. This is not inconsistent with the results noted here in the difference models; where both have above-average ability, boys have significantly higher college completion probabilities than girls.

Sons have a high college completion probability in comparison with daughters when they are encouraged to continue their education, whereas the daughters do not feel equally encouraged. In contrast daughters who perceived more encouragement than the son from either parent were only able to hold their own with regard to the probability of completing college. That is, sons' and daughters' college completion probabilities were the same in those families where the daughter felt more encouraged. This finding is generally supported by the difference models. In addition the logit models indicate that with respect to high school completion and college attendance, youth who perceive more encouragement from their same-sex parent have an advantage over their opposite-sex sibling. The same general pattern is evidenced at the college completion level, although the coefficients usually are not significant.

In general the separate sex attainment models are more satisfying in the sense that the results are easier to interpret; in addition they provide measures of absolute accomplishment. On the other hand the intrafamily difference models provide useful indicators of how within-family variations are affected by the various explanatory factors. However, although the intrafamily models indicate the relative positions of the brothers and sisters, they tell little about how much they achieve in an absolute sense. While the difference models theoretically could handle both the difference and absolute level considerations by including appropriate interaction terms, a far larger sample size would have been required to incorporate all the necessary interaction terms.

The substantive interpretations one can draw from a model where differences are essentially being compared with differences within a dummy variable framework depend considerably on which categories are being excluded from the model for reference purposes. For example, the exclusion of the category where both youths had IQs above 100 led to a different interpretation of the other IQ variables than might have been true if the low IQ category had been omitted. In the situation where both youths have IQs over 100, the brother has a substantially greater likelihood of completing college than the sister. In the converse situation where both siblings have low IQs, they both have equally low college completion probabilities. Shifting the reference group might well have altered the relative significance of the other two IQ categories.

Family Background and Work Orientation

A number of factors from a young woman's background directly translate into relative impediments or advantages in her educational accomplishment. Additional preliminary results of other research suggest the continuing importance of background factors as linkages to the broader career orientations of women. Because many young women in this study do not at the present time have strong ties to a job because they have recently had a child, we consider the work intentions of young women as a more satisfactory measure of life-long work commitment. We have examined (appendix table 2A.9) the association between 24-year-old women's work plans for when they will be age 35 and the same background factors in the young women's educational attainment models, including an additional explanatory variable measuring the women's educational attainment.

For the most part there is strong evidence that young women who perceived more encouragement to continue their education than their brother perceived were not only more likely to expect to be working at age 35 but in addition were more likely than other women to anticipate employment in an occupational area less typically occupied by women. Also daughters who had mothers employed during the young woman's adolescence (at age 14) were slightly more likely to anticipate future employment and significantly more likely to expect to be employed in an atypical occupation. In addition and somewhat surprisingly young women who were older than their male sibling were much less likely to anticipate future work and perhaps slightly more likely to expect to be employed in a traditional occupation.

The impact of parental encouragement is of particular interest because it suggests a direct link between educational motivation and employment outcome. In some instances a daughter's educational progress is directly related to the amount of educational encouragement she perceives coming from her mother. Further evidence suggests that this encouragement to carry one's education beyond the high school level has direct employment implications independent of educational attainment.

The intergenerational connection of mothers' to daughters' work is not only of interest in its own light but has implications for women's future work activity in this country. Given the relatively low level of work participation by these young women's mothers, the aggregate impact on the daughter's generation at this time is somewhat limited. However, if this work transference effect continues on to the next generation, its importance will be enhanced because of the much greater level of work participation by this generation of young women (the question of how work attitudes and behaviors can be transferred across generations is considered more extensively in chapter 4).

The evidence regarding the lesser prospective working propensity for young women who were the older of the sibling pair runs counter to some preconceived notions regarding sibling effects. Other research suggests that young women who were the older sibling in a family were more likely to receive more parental attention and resources and thus more likely to succeed as adults, but our evidence suggests the opposite. We hypothesize that being an older child can have negative career implications for a woman to the extent that older boys can provide less traditional work-oriented role models. This conjecture would explain a lack of consistency between the education and employment effects of sibling placement variables. Being an older child may well lead to a young woman's receiving an above-average amount of educational resources but still retaining traditional employment values.

The young woman's educational attainment has a direct and powerful effect on her work and occupational intentions. The substantive implication of this strong direct education effect is that some of the explanatory variables central to this study, in particular the mother's encouragement factor, ultimately affect adult working propensities both as direct predictors and indirectly by the effect on the intervening education variable.

Conclusions   Regardless of the model young men apparently are advantaged in their educational progress compared with young women. In many instances there is an imbalance between the extent to which brothers and sisters are helped or hurt within presumably mirror image situations. Situations that on the surface should favor a young man favor him substantially, whereas situations that should favor a young woman favor her modestly, if at all.

We find little, if any, influence of sibling position or the sex of other siblings on the relative educational progress of youth. On the other hand parental encouragement affects the ability of youth to succeed, and there is some evidence that siblings are helped more often than not by parents of the same sex. Furthermore there is no doubt that a youth's perceptions about parental support (in comparison with his or her sibling's perceptions) are important determinants of educational success.

The parental education factor suggests that from a long-term perspective, much of the educational discrepancy between sons and daughters reflects an intergenerational phenomenon, which is probably short-lived. Most of the sex discrepancy in educational progress reflects the much greater probability for young men to continue their education to the college attendance level. In most instances a young woman who is able to enter college is much more likely to graduate. The sole exception is where the father has graduated from high school but the mother has dropped out, a category of decreasing numerical importance in our society. In addition families where both parents have at least completed high school appear to be relatively egalitarian in terms of sons' and daughters' educational payoffs. Since most young family units now fall into this category, future sex differences in educational attainment are likely to diminish in importance.

Finally the mechanisms behind the connection between children's IQ or mental ability and their educational progress raise some intriguing questions about how social forces can help youth overcome intrinsic academic or ability disadvantage. It is clear that a sibling with less measured ability receives an advantage when he or she has a higher-ability sibling. Low-ability youth with high-ability siblings make substantially better educational progress than youth with low ability who have equally disadvantaged siblings. Because the models have controlled for other socioeconomic factors, this finding is likely related to other forms of intrafamily pressures. It may be, as Griliches (1979) has suggested, that parents strive to equalize outcomes. It may also reflect intrafamily social and psychological support systems whereby higher-ability siblings and parents provide academic assistance. Also educational values, aspirations, and accomplishments may be transferred from one youth to another in subtle ways. A family environment where one youth has more ability may be more sensitive to academic achievement. In this regard having at least one youth with higher measured IQ may simply be another way of operationalizing a family with higher educational goals for their children. The data show that in families with mixed IQs, the educational goal of the less-intelligent sibling is not substantially different from the family units where both siblings have above-average IQs. In fact where the lower-ability child is a son, his educational aspirations are identical to those of high IQ sons in families where both siblings have high IQs.

Although the focus of this chapter has been on educational outcomes, an employment note is in order. It appears that parental educational encouragement has a more generalized impact on the adult life-style intentions of youth. Parental encouragement to further one's education has also been shown to have a direct effect on a young woman's career intentions. This is but one of many pieces of evidence in this book supporting the close connection between familial background factors and adult attitudes and behaviors.

Notes

1. This study examines a subset of these matched pairs. Since it was possible to have multiple pairs from a single household, only one pair per household was chosen. To maximize the likelihood that the sibling pair was raised in a common environment if more than two sibling pairs were available in one home, the pair closest to each other in age was selected. When this choice was ambiguous, pairs of high school age when first interviewed were chosen in an effort to maximize their background data and to increase the likelihood that they grew up in a common environment. The sample was additionally restricted to brother and sister pairs where both siblings were still being interviewed at the ten-year interview point.

Because the young man had to be in his parental household in 1966 and the young woman in her parental household in 1968, many of our matched pairs were of high school age when they were initially interviewed. About 50 percent of the girls and two-thirds of the boys were below age 18 at first interview. Also because the young men were first interviewed on average about 18 months before the young women, the matched pairs are much more likely to include pairs where the brother is older than the sister. This age bias was compensated for by selecting pairs where the girl is older than the boy. For this reason the young women's sample in 1968 had a mean age of 17.8 compared with 16.9 for the young men in 1966.

2. The only characteristic where the matched pairs and the overall sample differed significantly was on the urban-rural dimension, where the matched pairs were somewhat more likely to be of rural origin.

This discrepancy reflects the fact that the sibling pairs, by definition, come from larger households (there must be at least two youth in the family), and larger households are somewhat more likely to be of rural origin. It is important to emphasize that even though this urban-rural discrepancy existed, it was not manifested in any significant socioeconomic differential between the samples. Possible additional sources of bias are noted where appropriate at later points in the discussion.

3. While the status attainment literature has examined differences in educational progress to some extent, data constraints have been a limiting factor in much of the research. Most studies have focused on only one sex, usually males. Few of the samples have been nationally representative, and to our knowledge none has involved a cross-sex sample of pairs from the same household drawn from larger nationally representative cohorts.

4. First, it can be more safely assumed that background factors not measured by the variables in our model will more likely be the same between sibling pairs as opposed to unrelated individuals (Sewell and Hauser 1977). Second, the background factors that do appear in our models are much more likely to be similar among brothers and sisters than among unrelated individuals; that is, any interpretation attached to 12 years of schooling for a father within a family (in terms of family status or quality of the father's education) can unambiguously be assumed to mean the same from the perspective of the children in the family. In contrast a comparison of two youth from different families where both fathers had 12 years of schooling requires one to assume that the operational meaning of 12 years of schooling is the same across families, a more tenuous assumption.

Some researchers would argue, however, that certain family level factors, such as parental education, may vary over time with regard to different siblings. For instance, father's education may have different meaning for the youngest child as opposed to the oldest due to the additional time elapsed since the parent completed his education (Olsen and Wolpin 1980). Since our sibling pairs were selected with a bias to keeping them as close as possible together in age, we reduce the magnitude of this problem.

5. We use a measure of educational aspirations rather than expectations in our research, although some of the literature we refer to is concerned with educational expectations.

6. See appendix to chapter 2 for a more detailed discussion of this variable. Family income was not included in our analysis as a status background measure for several reasons. First, it was difficult to obtain a measure of family income that referenced a point in time during the respondents' childhood or even a point prior to college attendance for some. Second, the income variable has a substantial number of missing data cases, which could pose additional problems of bias.

7. See appendix to chapter 2 for further discussion of this variable. Without belaboring the nature-nurture argument, we assume that this IQ score to some extent measures inherent intelligence independent of acquired ability. It is in all likelihood measuring effects similar to those measured by other researchers who have included IQ measures in their studies.

8. Our encouragement factor is admittedly post hoc. For many of the youth, the encouragement questions were not asked until a number of years after the surveys began. It is extremely likely that in many instances the youth's response regarding parental encouragement could have represented a rationalization for actual behavior patterns. We are not concerned with this complex causality issue here because our in-

tent is not to measure the independent effects of parental encouragement but rather the extent to which brothers and sisters are differentially affected by this encouragement. In this regard our results would be biased only if there were reason to believe that boys were more or less likely than girls to rationalize. Consult appendix 2A for further discussion on this variable.

9. We hypothesize that independent of the family's socioeconomic status, whether the sibling pair was raised with both parents in the home may have a differential effect on their educational progression. Aside from income constraints associated with having only one parent present, it is likely that one-parent households present different role models to youth, particularly since most one-parent families include only a mother and frequently the mother is, of necessity, in the labor force. We also hypothesize that youth who grew up in the South or in rural areas will probably have been socialized in a more traditional milieu, particularly with respect to the role of women in society. Finally our analyses will include a dummy variable indicating whether the young man served in the military. To the extent possible, we would like to remove this effect from our models because it is a factor that impedes the relative educational progression of the brother in comparison to his sister.

10. Our estimates of educational progression probabilities are generally higher than those derived from national statistics for comparable age groups of young men in March 1977 and young women in March 1978 (see U.S. Bureau of the Census 1980a, 1980b). This is particularly true for young women in the probability of attending or completing college. These higher estimates are in part due to attrition biases in the larger NLS young women's cohort over the ten-year period. Girls of high school age who were not enrolled in the initial survey year, divorced, were living in a standard metropolitan statistical area or who came from a family where the father was a blue-collar or service worker tend to be overrepresented among those who attrite. One implication of these biases may be that, at least in the later stages of the educational career path, we may tend to underestimate the positive sex differences in favor of males.

11. Due to the limited number of parents of that generation who attended college, we were not able to break out separately the group of youth whose parents had attended college.

12. In 75 percent of all married couples 25 to 44 years of age in March 1979, both partners had at least a high school diploma. See table 4 in U.S. Bureau of the Census (1980b).

13. One could argue that boys and girls do better when their siblings are brighter simply because, even if their own IQ is low, they still on average have higher ability than individuals with low IQs whose siblings also have low ability. To test this idea, we generated mean IQ scores separately for brothers and sisters for each category of the combined IQ variable. Although we found some evidence in support of this suggestion, the magnitude of the pattern differs little by sex.

14. Consistent with this sex difference and the possible role modeling effect mentioned earlier, additional analyses not presented here indicate that low IQ boys gain the most in terms of college completion when their higher IQ sister is the older in the sibling pair.

15. Our encouragement measure is a comparison of boys' and girls' perceptions. Questions on parental encouragement were asked independently of boys and girls and separately for each parent. Therefore these variables are not youth's perception of their siblings receipt of encouragement relative to their own but rather a comparison of sib-

lings' perceptions across cohorts. To the extent that perceptions do not accurately reflect actual influence and that boys and girls may have different judgments with regard to each level of influence, our variable will not measure the true effect of differential parental encouragement by sex. While ideally we should include in our models for each sex the individual's perception of parental encouragement, problems of collinearity between each parent's influence and with the variable comparing brother's perception to sister's precludes such analysis. It is clear, however, that higher levels of parental encouragement (regardless of sex of parent) go hand in hand with significantly higher levels of attainment.

16. See Schmidt and Strauss (1975) for a brief summary and application of this technique.

17. We chose not to subdivide further the no-difference category such that our dependent measure would contain a total of four rather than three categories primarily because our focus is on explaining the likelihood of a difference.

References

Adams, B. N. 1972. Birth order: a critical review. *Sociometry* 35:411–439.

Adams, B. N., and Meidam, M. T. 1968. Economics, family structure, and college attendance. *American Journal of Sociology* 74:230–239.

Alexander, K. L., and Eckland, B. K. 1974. Sex differences in the educational attainment process. *American Sociological Review* 39:668–682.

————. 1975. Basic attainment processes: a replication and extension. *Sociology of Education* 48:457–495.

Blau, P. M., and Duncan, O. D. 1967. *The American Occupational Structure.* New York: Wiley.

Griliches, Z. 1979. Sibling models and data in economics: beginnings of a survey. *Journal of Political Economy* 87:S37–S64.

Hout, M., and Morgan, W. R. 1975. Race and sex variations in the causes of the expected attainments of high school seniors. *American Journal of Sociology* 81:364–394.

Lin, S. S., and Oliver, P. 1979. The absent brother: the effect of sex of siblings on aspirations and parental encouragement of young women. Paper presented at the annual meeting of the Midwest Sociological Society.

McClendon, M. J. 1976. The occupational status attainment processes of males and females. *American Sociological Review* 41:52–64.

Marini, M. M. 1978. The transition to adulthood: sex differences in educational attainment and age at marriage. *American Sociological Review* 43:483–507.

Marini, M. M., and Greenberger, E. 1978. Sex differences in educational aspirations and expectations. *American Educational Research Journal* 15:67–79.

Olneck, M. R., and Bills, D. B. 1979. Family configuration and achievement: effects of birth order and family size in a sample of brothers. *Social Psychology Quarterly* 42:135–148.

Olsen, R. J., and Wolpin, K. I. 1980. The influence of exogenous child mortality on fertility and educational investments: an example of waiting time regressions with time varying regressors. Working paper, Yale University, October 1980.

Rehberg, R. A., and Westby, D. L. 1967. Parental encouragement, occupation, education and family size: artifactual or independent determinants of adolescent educational expectations? *Social Forces* 45:362–374.

Rosen, B. C., and Aneshensel, C. S. 1978. Sex differences in the educational-occupational expectation process. *Social Forces* 57:164–186.

Schmidt, P., and Strauss, R. P. 1975. The prediction of occupation using multiple logit models. *International Economic Review* 16:471–486.

Sewell, W. H., and Hauser, R. M. 1972. Causes and consequences of higher education: models of the status attainment process. *American Journal of Agricultural Economics* 54:851–861.

————. 1977. On the effects of families and family structure on achievement. In *Kinometrics: Determinants of Socioeconomic Success Within and Between Families,* ed. P. Taubman. Amsterdam: North-Holland Publishing Co.

Sewell, W. H., and Shah, V. P. 1967. Socioeconomic status, intelligence, and the attainment of higher education. *Sociology of Education* 40:1–23.

————. 1968. Social class, parental encouragement, and educational aspirations. *American Journal of Sociology* 73:559–572.

Sutton-Smith, B., and Rosenberg, B. G. 1970. *The Sibling.* New York: Holt, Rinehart, and Winston.

Treiman, D. J., and Terrell, K. 1975. Sex and the process of status attainment: a comparison of working women and men. *American Sociological Review* 40:174–200.

U.S. Bureau of the Census. 1980a. Educational attainment in the United States: March 1977 and 1976. *Current Population Reports.* Series P-20, No. 314. Washington, D.C.: U.S. Government Printing Office.

————. 1980b. Educational attainment in the United States: March 1979 and 1978. *Current Population Reports.* Series P-20, No. 356. Washington, D.C.: U.S. Government Printing Office.

Chapter 3

Fertility
Expectations
and the
Changing
Roles of
Women

Lois B. Shaw
and
Anne Statham

Since the late 1960s there have been sharp decreases in the number of children that women in the United States expect to have and the number they actually have had. Many reasons have been given for these declines, ranging from societal level interpretations focusing on the changing roles of women in American society and overall economic conditions to more individualistic interpretations relating to the increasing need for some women to work in order to maintain an adequate standard of living. Although the NLS data set cannot resolve all aspects of these sometimes conflicting interpretations, it can be used to evaluate at least some of the more important theoretical considerations. In particular the data set permits clarification of some of the causal interrelationships between levels and changes in fertility expectations and women's work attitudes and behaviors and, in a wider sense, general views of women in society.

Women in this NLS sample, who were born between 1943 and 1953, are among the age groups with declining birth expectations. According to the Current Population Survey, women born between 1943 and 1947 expected 2.9 children when they were 20 to 24 years of age (in 1967) but only 2.4 children at ages 25 to 29 (in 1972), while smaller decreases occurred for younger women (Campbell 1981:296). Here we use data on birth expectations from the 1973 and 1978 surveys to examine additional changes in the number of children that these young women expect and to seek reasons for these changes.

Between 1973 and 1978 the economic climate worsened. Average unemployment rates increased from 4.9 percent in 1973 to 6.0 percent in 1978 with a peak of 8.5 percent in 1975; the cost of living increased by an average of 8 percent per year; and housing prices increased rapidly, making home ownership increasingly difficult for young couples. In addition as the baby boom cohorts reached their twenties, increases in the number of young people may have caused some decreases in job opportunities and in average wages, especially among young men the ages of the husbands of the younger women in the NLS sample.[1] During this same period attitudes toward women's roles, including attitudes toward the appropriateness of women working, changed quite dramatically.[2] Along with these changes in attitudes went a rapid increase in the labor force participation of women with preschool children.

In addition divorce rates increased, and the age at first marriage was rising. In a period of such rapid social and economic change it is not surprising that many women changed their plans for childbearing. Of particular concern here is the extent to which changing ideas about childbearing are related to women's changing attitudes and behaviors toward work outside the home.

Changes
in Birth
Expectations,
1973–1978

Table 3.1 shows changes in birth expectations for women who were married in both 1973 and 1978. Although in the aggregate white women expected the same number of children in 1973 and 1978, these figures conceal the revisions many individual women made. About 45 percent of the married sample revised their birth expectations over the five years; about one-quarter expected fewer children in 1978 than 1973 and one-fifth expected more. White women who had not had children previously were most likely to revise their expectations downward; only in this group did average expectations actually decline. Upward revisions in birth expectations were most likely among women who already had children. Once they had at least two children, fewer women revised their birth expectations downward, since increasing numbers had already achieved their expected family size.

Overall the number of children expected by black women increased over the five years. Like their white counterparts, however, black women who had no children in 1973 expected

Table 3.1
Mean birth expectations of married women and percentage increasing, decreasing, and not changing birth expectations between 1973 and 1978, by number of children in 1973

Number of children in 1973	Decrease	Same	Increase	Mean expected 1973	1978	Number of respondents
Whites						
0	34	47	19	2.1	1.9	501
1	27	50	23	2.2	2.2	493
2 or more	14	65	22	2.9	3.0	642
Total	24	55	21	2.4	2.4	1636
Blacks						
0	38	32	30	2.1	1.9	61
1	24	45	31	2.0	2.3	100
2 or more	8	53	39	3.4	3.9	172
Total	18	47	35	2.8	3.1	333

fewer children in 1978 than in 1973. Upward revisions were most common among women who already had two or more children. Although the average number of children expected was similar for black and white women who had no children or only one child in 1973, black women with two or more children expected more children in 1973 than their white counterparts and also had larger increases in their expectations between 1973 and 1978. It is among women who already had children in 1973 that substantial increases in expectations occurred.

Like married women who had no children in 1973, women who were married for the first time between 1973 and 1978 revised their fertility expectations downward during this period. The average number of children expected fell from 2.4 to 2.0 for newly married white women and from 2.4 to 2.2 for black women. The changes in expectations among women who had not already begun childbearing by 1973 are especially interesting: whereas many women with children had already completed their families or were close to their goals, the full effect of any economic or social forces that had a negative influence on women's plans for children would be felt by those couples without children.

Perspectives on Fertility Research

Fertility expectations may be affected by a wide range of factors. Most research on both actual fertility and birth expectations has been influenced by the economic theory of fertility (Becker 1960), which hypothesizes that the husband's income will have a positive effect and the wife's earnings potential a negative effect on fertility. Although most research finds that women with higher earnings potential have or expect to have fewer children, results on the effect of the husband's earnings have been mixed.[3] The most commonly proposed reason for the lack of a positive income effect on fertility is the notion of child quality. The cost of raising each child may be greater as income increases, either because high-income families prefer to spend more in order to produce a "high quality" child (Becker 1960; Willis 1973) or because social norms dictate standards of child rearing that involve larger expenditures at high-income levels (Turchi 1975). In either case as long as costs are higher for high-income families the relationship between husband's earnings and fertility may not be positive unless it is possible to control for these costs.[4]

Easterlin (1966) hypothesized that the standard of living of one's parents should have a direct impact on fertility expectations. His argument is that tastes concerning what constitutes an adequate standard of living are acquired from one's family of origin, especially from living standards acquired during the teenage years when plans for adulthood are being formed. Since children compete with other expenditures, individuals who come from families with high standards of living should prefer fewer children.

Although Easterlin recognizes the importance of tastes for a particular standard of living, he follows the Becker economic tradition in holding other types of tastes suspect. On the other hand a body of sociological literature emphasizes the impact of changes of women's roles on fertility. As women come to see their role as less exclusively family oriented, they will want fewer children. Researchers have found that women's work experience (Cramer 1980), plans to work (Waite and Stolzenberg 1976), and sex-role attitudes (Scanzoni 1978) affect their fertility behavior even after controlling for their earnings potential. Easterlin does not recognize the independent importance of these role changes but sees economic factors as being ultimately responsible. He apparently believes that women's roles, particularly their orientation toward work, have changed only because they have been forced to work by the worsening economic climate experienced by their husbands as a result of a surplus of young men in the labor market (Easterlin 1978). While research suggests that work experience does cause women to change their views of women's roles (Macke, Hudis, and Larrick 1979; Mason, Czajka, and Arber 1976), it is questionable whether women would alter their tastes for working outside the home if economic conditions improved. These role modifications may be more or less permanent; certainly women may be reluctant to give up the expanded horizons, the income they personally control, and the more egalitarian marriages (Scanzoni 1978) that are but a few of the results of their labor force participation.

Plan of Analysis We want to determine the importance of both economic circumstances and women's role perceptions on their childbearing plans. We look first at the effects of these two sets of variables on 1973 birth expectations and then at their effects on upward or downward revisions in expectations between 1973 and 1978. Two measures of family background are used:

first, the Duncan index of socioeconomic status (Blau and Duncan 1967), based on the occupation of the head of household when the respondent was 14 years of age; and second, the number of siblings of the respondent. If desired standards of living are learned during the teenage years, as Easterlin believes, then the relationship between parents' socioeconomic status and birth expectations should be negative. Number of siblings could affect people's own desires for children in two ways. First, at any given level of income, the more children their parents had, the lower the material standard of living. Therefore family size would be a factor along with socioeconomic status affecting the formation of ideas about an acceptable standard of living. However, if tastes for life-styles are formed to a great extent in one's family of origin, coming from a large family might also impart a pro-familial orientation or a preference for large families, regardless of the implications for the family's socioeconomic level.[5] In either case we expect number of siblings to have a positive effect on birth expectations.

The family's current economic situation, another potential determinant of birth expectations, depends to a large extent upon the husband's economic progress. Economic theory argues, however, that major consumer and fertility decisions are based on the family's permanent economic position rather than on current earnings. Since husbands of women in our sample are of different ages, their actual earnings will reflect in part the stage they have reached in their work careers rather than their eventual level of attainment. Therefore we use the husband's education in 1978 as a proxy for permanent income.

Education and past work experiences are used as measures of the wife's earnings potential and therefore of the opportunity cost of interruptions in her employment. However, the effects of education on birth expectations are not clear-cut when increasing numbers of women continue to work after children are born (Shapiro and Mott 1979). Families with two earners may actually be better able to afford the children they want than those with one earner. Nevertheless if a woman wants to work, especially at a demanding job, she may be less likely to want more children than the current norm of two. The conflict between children and work may be not so much between having one or two children and continuing to work as between having a large family and working, as the research of Hout (1978) suggests.

Several measures of women's attitudes toward their social roles are available in the NLS data. Two scales constructed from 1972 items measure the woman's general approval of women's employment. The first scale comprises three items concerning the utilitarian benefits of women's employment, particularly the economic benefits to the family but also the fact that working women feel more useful. For simplicity, we refer to this scale as the economic necessity of women working. The second scale comprises six items concerning the social acceptability of women's working, particularly the extent to which it is harmful to the family (causing juvenile delinquency, neglect of home and family, and similar considerations).[6] Hence the first scale is an indicator of the economic considerations of women's employment, which may influence fertility expectations, and the second represents the influence of changing social perceptions of those women's roles that are particularly related to work and family behaviors. We expect that women who approve of women working for either reason will be more oriented toward working themselves and so will be likely to expect fewer children; these women may also be less likely to see women's identity as tied to the family and might expect fewer children for that reason as well. If Easterlin is correct—that fertility and social role perceptions are primarily a function of economic contingencies—the first scale should have a stronger impact on fertility expectations.

We also have a direct measure of a woman's plans to work: responses to a question asking whether the individual respondent plans to be working at age 35. The direction of causality between work plans and birth expectations is open to question. Waite and Stolzenberg (1976) present evidence that the major effect runs from work plans to fertility expectations. While it is probable that there are reciprocal effects (Cramer 1980), our primary interest here is to determine the extent to which there is an interrelationship between work and fertility plans and whether this varies among different groups.

We first look at the entire group of married women to examine the factors that determine which ones now have the highest and lowest birth expectations and what might have caused them to modify their expectations. These will be our current best estimates of the factors that will affect completed fertility for this cohort of women. Analyzing these women as one group may conceal what is happening to different subgroups, however, previous research suggests that different factors may influence the plans of women with different numbers of children (Hout 1978; Larrick 1981; Namboodiri 1974). Particularly interesting are married women with no children in 1973 and women married between 1973 and 1978, since they were the only groups of women still married in 1978 to have had a net downward revision in birth expectations. We estimate separate regressions for these groups and compare the results with those obtained for women who already had children in 1973.[7]

Interpretation of the results for subgroups must be qualified by the knowledge that the number of children the women had by 1973 was influenced in part by the same factors that influence their expectations. Women who married for the first time after 1973 and women who were already married in 1973 but had no children differed significantly from women who already had two or more children by that date (table 3.2). In addition to being younger, women who were newly married or without children had considerably higher educational attainments (14 years for the newly married as compared to 11 for women with three or more children); they also came from

Table 3.2
Means of explanatory variables, by marital status and number of children in 1973

Explanatory variables[a]	Whites					Blacks
	Single 1973, married 1978	Married both years, by number of children in 1973				
		0	1	2 or more	Total	Total
Duncan index	41.0	39.0	34.0	31.5	34.7	17.0
Number of siblings	2.8	2.6	3.1	3.2	3.0	5.4
Husband's education	14.1	14.0	13.1	12.4	13.1	11.4
Wife's education	14.1	13.7	12.6	11.8	12.7	11.8
Years worked before 1973	2.1	3.2	3.7	3.2	3.4	2.6
Wife's age	21.2	23.0	24.3	26.1	24.6	24.0
Economic necessity of working[b]	9.7	9.8	9.8	9.5	9.7	11.1
Propriety of working[b]	20.2	20.1	19.5	18.4	19.3	19.9
Plans to work at age 35	0.51	0.46	0.49	0.53	0.50	0.61
Number of respondents	265	427	390	513	1,337	251

a. Husband's and wife's education in 1978; other variables in 1973 (1972 for attitudes).
b. Higher scores indicate less traditional attitude.

families with higher socioeconomic status and had husbands with more education than women who already had children.

We might expect women who marry later and have more education to be well established in good jobs so that work-family conflicts might be especially significant for them; their opportunity costs may be higher and their interest in careers stronger. But the economic climate of the mid-1970s was not so favorable as that in the late 1960s and early 1970s when many of the older women in the sample—and younger women who married at an early age—were making plans for and having most of their children. Thus women who already had two or more children in 1973 and those who had not had children by this date might have been changing their expectations for quite different reasons.

Determinants of 1973 Birth Expectations

Before looking at the causes of the changes in birth expectations between 1973 and 1978, we first examine the determinants of the number of children that the women expected as of 1973. Perhaps most important the more education and work experience a woman had, the fewer children she expected in 1973 (table 3.3). This finding supports the view that the earnings that a woman might forgo to have children influences the number of children she will want. However, future work plans did not affect birth expectations of the married group as a whole, perhaps because women who already had several children in 1973 may have felt that they would be free to work by the time they were 35, when their children would be in school.

Black women who stressed the economic necessity or usefulness of working expected fewer children than women who did not. However, there was no significant association between fertility expectations and the noneconomically based women's role items for these women. Since historically the earnings of both parents have been essential to many black families, it is not surprising that for black women economic necessity rather than the appropriateness of working should affect their plans for children.

Conversely the views of white women about the economic necessity of working had no effect on their birth expectations, but their views about the propriety of working had a strong effect. This impact of attitudes suggests that white women who feel they may appropriately play active roles outside the home have reduced their desire for traditional family involvement.

Table 3.3
Determinants of number of children expected in 1973 for respondents
married in 1973 and 1978, by race: regression results

Explanatory variables	Whites	Blacks
Duncan index	0.002	−0.009
	(1.21)	(−1.22)
Number of siblings	0.040	−0.027
	(2.77)***	(−0.84)
Husband's education	−0.014	−0.017
	(−1.08)	(−0.49)
Wife's education	−0.046	−0.112
	(−2.54)***	(−2.10)**
Years worked before 1973	−0.057	−0.092
	(−4.80)***	(−2.25)***
Wife's age	0.050	0.095
	(4.41)***	(2.47)**
Economic necessity	−0.011	−0.078
	(−0.74)	(−1.73)*
Propriety	−0.035	−0.030
	(−3.64)***	(−0.85)
Plans to work at age 35	−0.001	−0.136
	(−0.02)	(−0.69)
Constant	2.777	4.080
	(7.26)***	(2.85)***
Adjusted R^2	0.058	0.071
Number of respondents	1337	251

Note: Numbers in parentheses are t values.
* Significant at the 0.10 level.
** Significant at the 0.05 level.
*** Significant at the 0.01 level.

Perhaps they have come to recognize the conflicts between
work and family life.[8] Blake and del Pinal (1981:260) found that
sex-role traditionality was strongly correlated with awareness
of costs and benefits of child rearing; less-traditional women
were most aware of these costs.

Among white but not black women family background influenced expected family size to some extent. White women
who came from large families themselves wanted more children than those from small families. However, neither the socioeconomic status of her family of origin nor her husband's
education had an influence on the woman's own expected
family size. Thus Easterlin's hypothesis that higher socioeconomic status of a person's family of origin will decrease her
own desired family size while her husband's higher earnings
capacity will increase the number of children she expects is
not borne out by our analysis.

When we look at birth expectations of women who were not married in 1973 but who subsequently did marry and compare these with married women with differing numbers of children, we see that different factors affect birth plans at different stages in the family life cycle. Education and work experience no longer have a negative impact on fertility plans within these two groups (table 3.4).[9] On the other hand, before any children are born, work plans do affect expected family size. Both single women and married women without children expect fewer children if they plan to be working when they are 35 years old. But once families are more nearly complete, work plans no longer affect the number of children expected. In fact women with two or more children who expect the largest families are more likely to plan to work than those who

Table 3.4
Determinants of number of children expected in 1973 for white respondents by marital status and number of children: regression results

Explanatory variables	Single in 1978, married in 1973,	Married Number of children in 1973		
		0	1	2 or more
Duncan index	−0.001 (−0.48)	−0.003 (−1.77)*	0.005 (2.41)***	0.003 (1.32)
Number of siblings	0.070 (2.13)**	0.061 (2.47)***	0.006 (0.32)	0.052 (2.05)**
Husband's education		0.022 (1.08)	0.004 (0.22)	−0.033 (−1.43)
Respondent's education	−0.013 (−0.19)	0.040 (1.26)	0.079 (2.86)***	−0.027 (−0.80)
Years worked before 1973	−0.053 (−0.89)	−0.004 (−0.16)	0.020 (1.11)	−0.024 (−1.24)
Respondent's age	−0.057 (−0.88)	−0.075 (−3.11)***	−0.092 (−4.66)***	0.043 (1.89)*
Economic necessity	−0.056 (−1.63)	0.011 (0.48)	−0.022 (−1.01)	−0.001 (−0.44)
Propriety	−0.035 (−1.41)	−0.035 (−2.38)***	−0.024 (−1.74)*	−0.028 (−1.63)
Plans to work at age 35	−0.517 (−3.48)***	−0.417 (−4.45)***	−0.093 (−1.09)	0.222 (2.03)**
Constant	5.23 (5.30)***	3.73 (6.58)***	3.83 (7.05)***	2.79 (3.78)***
Adjusted R^2	0.121	0.107	0.090	0.021
Number of respondents	276	431	390	516

Note: Numbers in parentheses are t values.
* Significant at the 0.10 level.
** Significant at the 0.05 level.
*** Significant at the 0.01 level.

expect fewer children. Perhaps these women's work plans are due to economic pressures caused by their large families rather than their work plans having affected their expected family size.

Married women with no children in 1973 are the only group for which the Easterlin hypothesis is even modestly confirmed. For this group only, socioeconomic status of family of origin exerts a negative influence on birth expectation, while number of siblings and husband's earnings potential have positive (though in the case of earnings nonsignificant) effects. However, it is at the beginning of the childbearing period that the women's own work plans and attitudes also exert strong influence on birth expectations, contrary to Easterlin's view that the couple's economic circumstances relative to those of their parents are the only important influence.[10]

Determinants of Upward and Downward Revisions in Birth Expectations

We next look at how the variables that affected original 1973 birth expectations influenced changes in expectations between 1973 and 1978.[11] At this point we do not attempt to look at circumstances that changed between the two years. Rather we ask which characteristics of the women and their husbands in 1973 influenced them to change their plans for children by 1978. Later we look at the woman's actual work experience and changes in her husband's earnings during the five years to see whether there are any associated changes in birth expectations. We use multinomial logit analysis to allow for the possibility that upward and downward revisions may be subject to somewhat different influences.[12]

Previously we saw that for the married group as a whole, women with the most education and work experience expected the fewest children. Between 1973 and 1978 women with considerable prior work experience were also more likely to revise their birth expectations downward than were women with little experience (table 3.5). Higher educational attainment, however, did not influence women to revise their expectations in either direction.

Family background had little effect on revisions in birth expectations. If anything white women coming from higher socioeconomic backgrounds were more likely than those from lower-status backgrounds to revise their expectations upward. The husband's earnings ability also had no influence on birth expectations in 1973 or on changes in expectations between

Table 3.5
Some determinants of downward and upward revision in birth expectations for women married in 1973 and 1978, by race: logit results

Explanatory variables	Whites		Blacks	
	Down	Up	Down	Up
Duncan index	0.002 (0.56)	0.006 (1.78)*	−0.005 (−0.36)	−0.013 (−1.07)
Number of siblings	0.001 (0.01)	0.029 (0.84)	−0.005 (−0.07)	0.057 (1.12)
Husband's education	−0.021 (−0.58)	0.006 (0.20)	0.067 (0.80)	−0.020 (−0.34)
Years worked before 1973	0.133 (3.99)***	−0.000 (−0.01)	0.236 (2.57)***	0.017 (0.24)
Wife's education	0.063 (1.34)	−0.023 (−0.53)	0.159 (1.35)	0.012 (0.14)
Propriety	0.049 (1.86)*	−0.046 (−1.96)**	−0.117 (−1.52)	−0.114 (−1.97)**
Economic necessity	0.018 (0.44)	−0.035 (−0.97)	−0.178 (−1.82)*	0.012 (0.15)
Work plans at age 35	−0.204 (−1.26)	−0.041 (−0.28)	0.510 (1.18)	0.442 (1.39)
Number of respondents	1,330		257	

Note: For complete equations see appendix table 3A.1.
    Asymptotic t values are in parentheses.
* Significant at the 0.10 level.
** Significant at the 0.05 level.
*** Significant at the 0.01 level.

1973 and 1978. Easterlin's hypothesis is supported neither here nor in the results for the 1973 equations for the entire sample.

White women's nontraditional orientation toward women's roles was associated with smaller expected family size in 1973. For both races women with nontraditional sex-role attitudes were less likely to revise their birth expectations upward between 1973 and 1978; white nontraditional women were also more likely to expect fewer children in 1978 than in 1973. Our hypothesis that less traditional women will have fewer children for reasons other than simply the economic cost of staying home with children receives support from these results. Although black women who perceived that women work from economic necessity wanted fewer children in 1973, they were less likely than other women to make further downward revisions in their birth expectations, perhaps because their expectations were already below those of other women.

Table 3.6
Determinants of downward and upward revisions in birth expectations: white women single in 1973 and married in 1978 and white married women, by number of children in 1973: logit results

Explanatory variables	Single to married	Married both years Number of children in 1973		
		0	1	2 or more
Downward revision				
Husband's education	−0.148	−0.095	−0.007	−0.036
	(−2.07)**	(−1.67)*	(−0.10)	(−0.47)
Own education	−0.040	−0.130	−0.293	0.371
	(−0.34)	(−1.71)*	(−2.81)***	(3.28)***
Years worked before 1973	0.091	0.017	−0.128	0.166
	(0.68)	(0.25)	(−1.86)*	(2.49)***
Propriety of working	0.020	0.075	0.060	0.035
	(0.32)	(1.83)*	(1.12)	(0.62)
Work plans	0.598	0.320	0.015	−0.772
	(1.67)*	(1.21)	(0.05)	(−2.15)**
Upward revision				
Husband's education	−0.094	0.018	0.005	0.026
	(−1.06)	(0.26)	(0.09)	(0.52)
Own education	0.247	−0.059	−0.033	0.033
	(1.49)	(−0.62)	(−0.39)	(0.47)
Years worked before 1973	0.335	0.031	−0.066	0.045
	(1.68)*	(0.38)	(−1.12)	(1.03)
Propriety of working	−0.324	−0.001	−0.090	−0.038
	(−1.72)*	(−0.03)	(−2.04)**	(−1.03)
Work plans	0.437	0.041	0.049	−0.318
	(0.91)	(0.31)	(0.18)	(−1.35)

Note: Complete logit results are shown in appendix table 3A.2.
     Asymptotic t values are in parentheses.
* Significant at the 0.10 level.
** Significant at the 0.05 level.
*** Significant at the 0.01 level.

Among women who were married after 1973 and married women who had no children by that date, those whose husbands had higher educational attainment were less likely to revise their birth expectations downward (table 3.6). At this early stage in family formation but not later, the husband's earnings ability does appear to be important in insuring that the family can afford to carry out its childbearing plans. Being able to afford more children was not associated with an upward revision of plans, however.

Among women who had no children or only one, greater educational attainment by the woman also decreased the chances that downward revisions would be made, but among women with two or more children, education increased the chances that plans would be revised downward. The effects of work experience before1973 roughly parallel educational effects; women with one child or none were either unaffected or showed mildly positive effects as their work experience increased, whereas women with two or more children were significantly more likely to revise their plans downward the greater their work experience in the past. Our findings for both the education and work experience variables agree with those of Hout (1978), who found potential wage effects more important at higher parities. Hout interprets his findings as indicating that until the two-child norm is reached, women do not curtail their families because of the earnings that might be forgone. After this point the woman's potential earnings are more likely to be considered.

The importance of women's role attitudes is greater among women who have not yet had more than one child. Plans to work at age 35 caused downward revisions in birth expectations only among women who were first married between 1973 and 1978. These women already had lower than average birth expectations in 1973. We conclude that although education and past work experience do not influence plans for children until the two-child norm is reached, women who want to play more active roles and have definite work plans do expect smaller families and have more propensity to revise their childbearing plans downward than do more traditional women.

Changes in Circumstances between 1973 and 1978

Thus far we have looked at long-term or pre-1973 characteristics of women and their families as they relate to changes in birth expectations between 1973 and 1978. In this section we look at changes in some of these characteristics that were occurring concurrently with changes in birth expectations. Of particular interest are the woman's own work experience over the five years and changes in the earnings of her husband over this period. White women who worked at least three-fourths of the time between 1973 and 1978 were much more likely to revise their birth expectations downward than were women who did not work at all. Women who worked most of the time were also less likely to revise their expectations upward than were women who worked a lesser amount or not at all (table 3.7).

Some of the relationship between work and changes in fer-

Table 3.7
Percentage of women changing birth expectations between 1973 and 1978, by percentage of weeks worked and whether any children were born in the interval, by race

Birth expectations	Whites			Blacks		
	Percent of weeks worked					
	0	Less than 75	75 or more	0	Less than 75	75 or more
All women married both years						
Down	18	24	30	16	22	17
Same	58	52	56	37	44	56
Up	24	24	14	47	34	27
Number of respondents	345	793	484	51	131	149
Birth between 1973 and 1978						
Down	15	24	21	15	21	14
Same	51	41	52	21	25	42
Up	34	35	27	65	53	44
Number of respondents	208	466	168	34	75	55
No birth between 1973 and 1978						
Down	23	22	35	a	23	18
Same	68	69	58	a	70	64
Up	9	9	8	a	7	18
Number of respondents	137	327	316	17	56	94

a. Percentage distribution not shown when base represents fewer than 25 respondents.

tility plans reflects the fact that women who did not have a birth between the two dates were more likely to revise their plans downward and much less likely to revise their plans upward than were women who had a child in the interval. At the same time women who did not have a birth were, as expected, more likely to work continuously and less likely not to work at all than were women who had a baby. Looking at changes in plans within the group of women who did not have a birth, we can see that those who worked fairly continuously were considerably more likely to revise their plans downward than were women who worked a lesser amount or not at all. However, none of the groups was likely to revise their plans upward. Within the group that did have a birth, women who worked the most were least likely to revise their expected family size upward and were more likely than those who did not work at all to revise their plans downward. Therefore actual work experience appears to have had a somewhat negative effect on birth

Table 3.8
Percentage of married women who changed their birth expectations between 1973 and 1978, by percentage change in husband's earnings in the interval, by race

	Changes in husband's earnings					
	Whites					
	Total			No children in 1973		
Change in birth expectations	Large decrease	Inter-mediate change	Large increase	Large decrease	Inter-mediate change	Large increase
Down	24	21	27	42	31	34
Same	56	55	52	40	48	50
Up	20	23	21	17	21	16
Number of respondents	237	498	664	52	130	244

Note: Husband's earnings change calculated in constant 1978 dollars. Large changes are greater than 20 percent; intermediate changes include increases and decreases of less than 20 percent. Sample limited to respondents married in 1973 and 1978.

expectations over the five years even apart from the lower probability that women who worked steadily would actually have had a birth.

For black women the effect of work experience on birth expectations operates mainly on upward revisions. Women who worked steadily were much less likely to revise their expectations upward; this was true even among women who had a child in the interval. Among women who did not have a child, the fairly continuous workers were somewhat less likely to revise their plans downward and more likely to revise upward than were those who worked discontinuously.

While the woman's own work experience over the interval was related to changes in her birth expectations, changes in her husband's earnings had no discernible effect for the sample as a whole (table 3.8). Women who had no children in 1973 were somewhat more likely to revise their expectations downward if their husband's income declined, but even this difference is not statistically significant. Although it is possible that the worsening economic climate over the five years did contribute to downward revision of birth expectations in some cases, we are not able to detect such an effect in the NLS data.[13]

Conclusions and Implications

Among white married women there was virtually no change in average birth expectations, while black married women expected slightly larger families in 1978 than in 1973. A good

Blacks					
Total			Two or more children in 1973		
Large decrease	Inter- mediate change	Large increase	Large decrease	Inter- mediate change	Large increase
23	18	21	16	11	17
46	53	46	65	64	60
31	29	33	19	25	23
61	83	129	124	218	216

deal of individual revision of plans occurred, however. Generally these revisions were related to the women's own work experience or work plans and to their perceptions of women's proper social roles rather than their husband's earnings potential or changes in their husband's earnings. Easterlin's hypothesis that husbands' earnings potential relative to that of their parents' generation is the major force behind recent fertility trends receives little support from the sample as a whole. However, there is some evidence that newly married couples and others who had not begun having children by 1973 were less likely to revise their plans downward the higher the educational attainment and earnings potential of the husband. Even for these groups women's nontraditional attitudes, plans for working, and actual work experience all contributed to their decisions about expected family size. Women's own educational attainment, representing the amount of earnings they forgo if they stay at home with the children, caused downward revisions in birth expectations only after the two-child norm was reached.

Easterlin has predicted an upturn in fertility in the coming years when the smaller post–baby boom cohorts reach maturity and job opportunities improve for young men. Butz and Ward (1979) have criticized Easterlin's prediction because it fails to take into account women's job opportunities. Our analysis supports the conclusion of Butz and Ward that women's opportunities are important and in fact goes beyond it to emphasize that women's changing perceptions of the roles they want to play are an additional dimension that should be considered. Only if men's job opportunities improve while women's opportunities worsen and women go back to traditional role orientations would a second baby boom be possible; such a combination of events appears extremely unlikely.

Notes

The authors thank Alice Simon for her expert research assistance.

1. Easterlin's view that a large cohort causes depressed wages finds support in data from the NLS young men's cohort. Hills (1981) found a real wage decrease of 6 percent between 1971 and 1976 among succeeding cohorts of young men age 24 to 27 and a larger decline of 12 percent in their average weekly earnings.

2. Decreasing agreement with the view that a woman's place is in the home—from 45 percent in 1972 to 32 percent in 1977—was also found in the NLS mature women's sample (Shaw and O'Brien 1981). This indicates widespread support for less-traditional roles from the young women's own mothers who are approximately the ages of the women in the mature women's sample.

3. Cramer (1980) found a positive effect of husband's earnings on birth expectations in only some of his models. Hout (1978) found positive effects at low parities but negative effects at higher parities. Insignificant effects are frequent (Turchi 1975).

4. Thornton (1979) found that perceived costs of child rearing were negatively related to fertility. Blake and del Pinal (1981) suggest that low-income families may perceive children as protecting against poverty and loneliness in old age to a greater extent than do high-income families with more social and economic resources. Low-income families may value children as long-term investments as well as for short-term satisfactions.

5. Evidence for the effect of number of siblings on fertility is mixed. Potter and Kantner (1955) found only a weak relationship between number of siblings and actual fertility in the Indianapolis survey of white Protestant families. However, the birth expectations of young adults may be more strongly influenced by their families of origin than their eventual fertility will be. Mott and Mott (1982) and Hirsch, Seltzer, and Zelnik (1981) found a strong relationship between number of siblings and numbers of children desired or expected by teenagers.

6. These scales were derived from a factor analysis of a nine-item scale indicating that these items formed two separate dimensions. The items in the first scale were: a working wife feels more useful than one who does not hold a job; working wives help to raise the general standard of living; employment of both parents is necessary to keep up with the high cost of living. The items on the second scale were: modern conveniences permit a wife to work without neglecting her family; a women's place is in the home, not in the office or shop; a job provides a wife with interesting outside contacts; a wife who carries out her full responsibility does not have time for outside employment; the employment of wives leads to juvenile delinquency; working wives lose interest in their homes and families. Values have been coded so that nontraditionality is the high point on each scale. The responses to these items were then summed to form the scales. The reliability of the scales is 0.446 and 0.786, respectively.

7. Sample sizes are not sufficiently large to permit analysis of these subgroups for the black sample. Analysis of changes in birth expectations among women who divorced or remained single would require somewhat different models from those for married women and are thus beyond the scope here.

8. While at face value our items suggest that less traditional women perceive less conflict between work and family—that a wife's employment need not be harmful to the family—less traditional women are likely to feel more time pressure as the result of trying to fulfill both roles.

9. In fact for women with one child, education is positively correlated with expected family size. This result appears to be due primarily to the fact that one-child families are expected considerably more frequently among women who did not complete high school than among high school or college graduates. College graduates with one child are not overrepresented among those expecting more than two children.

10. Another difference between the total sample and women with a specific number of children is that older women expect fewer children than do younger women at the same stage in the family formation process. For the total sample older women expected more children than younger women, reflecting a cohort effect.

11. Two additional control variables are included in the analysis. Birth expectations in 1973 are controlled for because it seems probable that extremely high expectations are more likely to be revised downward, while couples who plan to remain childless or to have only one child may be under more social pressure to conform to social norms and revise their plans upward. We control also for whether the couple already had children in 1973 since those without children are more likely to revise downward because of infertility. These hypotheses are borne out for the most part as shown in appendix table 3A.1.

12. Multinomial logit is an extension of ordinary binomial logit analysis to cases in which there are more than two choices (Schmidt and Strauss 1975). In the present case with three choices there are two dichotomous dependent variables; one variable takes a value of 1 if expectations were revised downward and 0 if no revision occurred, while the second takes a value of 1 for upward revision and 0 for no revision. The coefficients on the explanatory variables are constrained so that the probabilities of being in each of the three categories will sum to 1.

13. In addition to the percentage change in husband's earnings shown in table 3.8, we examined changes in dollar amounts of earnings and changes in actual earnings compared with earnings that would have been expected on the basis of the husband's characteristics in 1973. In no case could we find a consistent relationship between earnings changes and changes in birth expectations.

References

Becker, G. S. 1960. An economic analysis of fertility. In *Demographic and Economic Change in Developed Countries*. National Bureau of Economic Research. Princeton: Princeton University Press.

Blake, J., and del Pinal, J. H. 1981. The childlessness option: recent American views on nonparenthood. In *Predicting Fertility*, ed. G. E. Hendershot and P. J. Placek. Lexington, Mass.: Lexington Books, D. C. Heath.

Blau, P. M., and Duncan, O. D. 1967. *The American Occupational Structure*. New York: Wiley.

Butz, W. P., and Ward, M. P. 1979. The emergence of countercyclical U.S. fertility. *American Economic Review* 69:318–328.

Campbell, A. A. 1981. Needed research on birth expectations. In *Predicting Fertility*, ed. G. E. Hendershot and P. J. Placek. Lexington, Mass.: Lexington Books, D. C. Heath.

Cramer, J. C. 1980. Fertility and female employment: problems of causal direction. *American Sociological Review* 45:167–190.

Easterlin, R. A. 1966. On the relation of economic factors to recent and projected fertility changes. *Demography* 3:131–153.

————. 1978. What will 1984 be like? Socioeconomic implications of recent twists in age structure. *Demography* 15:397–432.

Hills, S. M. 1981. Introduction and overview. In *Career Thresholds, Vol. 7: Ten Years of Labor Market Experience for Young Men*. Columbus, Ohio: Center for Human Resource Research, The Ohio State University.

Hirsch, M. B.; Seltzer, T. R.; and Zelnik, M. 1981. Desired family size of young American women, 1971 and 1976. In *Predicting Fertility*, ed. G. E. Hendershot and P. J. Placek. Lexington, Mass.: Lexington Books, D. C. Heath.

Hout, M. 1978. The determinants of marital fertility in the United States, 1968-1970: inferences from a dynamic model. *Demography* 15:139–159.

Larrick, D. 1981. Having children: an analysis of white American wives' fertility in the early 1970s. Ph.D. dissertation, The Ohio State University, 1981.

Macke, A. S.; Hudis, P. M.; and Larrick, D. 1979. Sex-role attitudes and employment among women: dynamic models of continuity and change. In *Women's Changing Roles at Home and on the Job*. Washington, D.C.: National Commission for Manpower Policy, Special Report No. 26.

Mason, K. O.; Czajka, J. L.; and Arber, S. 1976. Change in women's sex-role attitudes, 1964–1974. *American Sociological Review* 41:573–596.

Mott, F. L., and Mott, S. H. 1982. Prospective life style congruence among adolescents: sex and ethnic variations in the association between fertility expectations and ideas regarding women's roles. Paper presented at the 1982 meeting of the American Sociological Association.

Namboodiri, N. K. 1974. Which couples at given parities expect additional births? An exercise in discriminant analysis. *Demography* 11:45–56.

Potter, R. G., and Kantner, J. F. 1955. The influence of siblings and friends on fertility. *Milbank Memorial Fund Quarterly* 33:246–267.

Scanzoni, J. H. 1978. *Sex Roles, Women's Work, and Marital Conflict*. Lexington, Mass.: Lexington Books, D. C. Heath.

Schmidt, P., and Strauss, R. P. 1975. The prediction of occupation using multiple logit models. *International Economic Report* 16:471–486.

Shapiro, D., and Mott, F. L. 1979. Labor supply behavior of prospective and new mothers. *Demography* 16:199–208.

Shaw, L. B., and O'Brien, T. 1981. An overview of changes in the lives of mature women, 1967–1977. In *Dual Careers, Vol. 5: A Decade of Changes in the Lives of Mature Women*. Columbus, Ohio: Center for Human Resource Research, The Ohio State University.

Thornton, A. 1979. Fertility and income, consumption aspirations, and child quality standards. *Demography* 16:157–176.

Turchi, B. A. 1975. *The Demand for Children*, Cambridge, Mass.: Ballinger.

Waite, L. J., and Stolzenberg, R. M. 1976. Intended childbearing and labor force participation of young women: insights from nonrecursive models. *American Sociological Review* 41:235–252.

Willis, R. J. 1973. A new approach to the economic theory of fertility. *Journal of Political Economy* 81:S14–S64.

Chapter 4

From Mother to Daughter: The Transmission of Work Behavior Patterns across Generations

Frank L. Mott,
Anne Statham,
and
Nan L. Maxwell

Chapters 5 and 6 examine the relationship of women's work attachment to demographic forces such as marriage and fertility and the sensitivity of these forces to standard economic influences. This chapter combines an economic and a sociological perspective on women's work attachment. This interdisciplinary perspective should enhance our understanding of the mechanisms through which women are either encouraged or dissuaded from maintaining extensive work ties. The two perspectives offer different but complementary insights into how women make decisions about allocating time between home and the labor market.

Sociologists and economists agree that the amount of work a woman does outside the home reflects her balance between orientations toward work and home; they differ, however, about the basis for making these decisions. From the economic perspective the woman's decision depends upon a balance between the market value of her work and nonmarket considerations: the amount of time she spends in the labor market depends upon a balance between what are termed income and substitution effects. For instance, the higher a family's income, everything else being equal, the less necessity for a woman to be employed and the greater the opportunities for her to use her time outside the market in nonpaying activities; this is generally termed the *income effect*. Conversely the greater her potential utility to employers and her potential earnings (as measured in this instance by her level of education), the greater the likelihood that she will be employed. Stated differently the greater her potential earnings, the greater the opportunity cost of not working. This is generally termed the *substitution effect*.[1] These income and substitution effects generally operate in opposite directions, and their net effect on a woman's likelihood of being employed is an empirically observable phenomenon, varying among women in different situations and at different points in time.[2]

In positing income and substitution effects, economic theory assumes that women are operating within a rational economic sphere, that they generally are knowledgeable about the advantages and disadvantages of different courses of action, and that they will behave rationally from an economic perspective in making any economic decision. In reality other seemingly rational factors impinge on those decisions. From a sociological perspective the woman's decisions about work attachment reflect her attitudes about work and about family. The amount of conflict the woman perceives or experiences between work and family will determine her commitment to work. If she has been socialized to believe it is inappropriate for married women to work, she is less likely to work regardless of her potential wage rate or the income level of her family. If she is in a situation where family demands are high and working would make it difficult for her to meet these demands (as when she has a young child), she will also be less likely to work, although her sensitivity to working or nonworking in this situation may well be affected by her taste for market activity.

Economic theories have considered the importance of tastes as a factor that influences the work decision, and they have considered current family demands (such as the presence of young children) as deterrents to working. However, they have not considered the impact of early socialization influences that may differentially affect work behavior regardless of current economic or family situations. The NLS young and mature women's data sets enable us to consider the importance of the woman's background experiences. Past research has shown that a young woman's mother's work behavior and preferences are important determinants of her own orientation toward work (Hartley 1961; Almquist and Angrist 1971; Macke and Morgan 1978; Macke and Mott 1980). From a role theory perspective, women acquire their basic orientations toward working by modeling the behavior and verbalized motives for the behavior of significant others (Kemper 1968), and the mother is certainly one of the most significant others when a young girl is forming her attitudes toward work.

From a sociological perspective we expect the mother's influence to affect the woman's work attachment in two ways. First, we expect daughters of highly work oriented mothers to be more likely to work themselves. Second, we expect the influence of the mother to interact with other influences. For instance, women who have been socialized to feel that working is inappropriate for married women with children may be less likely to work, regardless of the economic demands of their situation. If this is the case, income and substitution effects may operate most strongly for those women who have not been socialized to feel any hesitancy about working—that is, women whose mothers were highly work oriented.

A major objective of this research is to suggest that non-

67

economic factors can differentially affect the likelihood that women will run true to economic form. We anticipate that neoclassical economic theory (in terms of income and substitution effects) will have the strongest effects when a young woman feels no pressure to refrain from working. On the other hand, we anticipate that young women who come from more traditional backgrounds will be more likely to refrain from working if they have a young child in the home than will their counterparts who have mothers with less traditional views and with less-traditional work behavior patterns. Thus we hypothesize that results anticipated from traditional neoclassical labor supply models will be substantially mediated by the forces usually examined in noneconomic disciplines.

The Data Set

We use a special matched set of mothers and daughters from the mature and young women's cohorts of the NLS. In the sample selection process for the four original cohorts, the Census Bureau permitted more than one respondent to be selected from any given household as long as they fell within the particular age constraint of one of the cohorts. Thus if a household included a mature woman who was 30 to 44 as of April 1967 and a young woman who was 14 to 24 as of January 1968, they were included in the mature and young women's samples, respectively. In the vast majority of these cases, the matched pairs were mothers and daughters. Because a major concern of this research is the extent to which daughters model their behavior according to expressed attitudes or behaviors of their mothers, we limit the sample to daughters who were known to be living with their mothers at age 14.

Also because we have only a small sample of black young women, this particular analysis is limited to white women. Finally we focused on those who were married and living with their husbands as of the tenth survey year in 1978. As of 1978 the daughters in the sample were 24 to 34 years old. Most of them had begun childbearing if they intended to, and they are generally representative of a cross-section of white married American women in the principal childbearing ages.[3] Appendix table 4A.1 demonstrates the comparability of our mother-daughter sample to the nationally representative NLS sample of white married young and mature women. Although our sample of daughters is slightly younger than the overall sample and the mothers are slightly older, the only variable in our model that appears to be affected is the one specifying the age of youngest child: the younger daughters have younger children. Thus from the perspectives of both economics and sociology, this subset of white married women who were age 24 to 34 in 1978 should be an appropriate group for evaluating the theoretical orientations already outlined. Our overall sample includes between 550 and 600 women, the exact number depending on the specific variables included in a model and their respective nonresponse rate.

The Research Plan

We examine the general compatibility of some economic and noneconomic perspectives and compare their usefulness in providing insights into the work behavior patterns of adult women. To do this we join a standard neoclassical labor supply framework with role modeling considerations, drawing on the notion that women's behavior is conditioned to some extent by their background—that is, ideas regarding appropriate behavior that are transmitted from mothers to daughters by both the mother's expressed notions about appropriate women's roles (Macke and Morgan 1978; Macke and Mott, 1980) and by the mother's work behavior, which we presume influences the daughter to seek gainful employment (Almquist and Angrist 1971; Hoffman 1975). We are able to view these disciplinary approaches jointly because our matched sample of mothers and daughters enables us to quantify both the work and personal characteristics of the daughters as of 1978, their mothers' attitudes regarding appropriate roles for women, and the mother's work history between the birth of the first child and 1967.

According to standard neoclassical economic theory, a woman's participation in the work force is likely to be positively associated with her level of education because better-educated women on average are more productive workers and can draw a higher wage. Thus everything else being equal, women with more education will be more attracted to the job market because of greater pecuniary incentives; the cost of not working for a woman with more education is greater than the cost for a woman who has less schooling (substitution effects). From a noneconomic perspective better-educated women are more likely to be career oriented and are more likely to seek employment for nonmonetary psychic benefits (Scanzoni and Scanzoni 1976). From this perspective too, better-educated women are also likely to earn higher incomes (Sweet 1973).

From an economic perspective, the greater the income that other family members (primarily husbands) provide, the less the necessity for the woman to work, and the greater the likelihood that she would spend her time on nonmarket activities (income effects). These two variables, education and husband's earnings, are the principal economic variables examined in this study. (For a precise specification of all the variables included in this study, see appendix 4A.)

This analysis also includes control variables indicating the size of the labor force in the area where the young woman lives and whether her residence is in the South. Both of these factors are often found to influence demand: a large labor market is associated with the ability of an individual to find employment of her choosing, and the southern region is negatively associated with the ability of individuals to find employment (Bowen and Finegan 1969). Large labor markets and nonsouthern residence have also been associated with higher wage rates (Fuchs 1971). These control variables are included in this study only because they may directly impinge on the predictive ability of other explanatory variables central to our hypotheses.

Our models also include a dichotomous variable indicating whether the respondent has a preschool-age child in the home, a variable generally found to be a powerful predictor of women's work activity and a key variable in our analysis.[4]

The mothers in the mother-daughter matches were defined as workers if they were employed six months or more in at least one-third of the years between the time their first child was born and 1967. Approximately one-third of the women were employed at least to that extent and two-thirds less than that.

The traditional-nontraditional classification was based on the women's responses to six items regarding their attitudes about appropriate social roles for women.[5] A scale was constructed with high values implying more-traditional views and low values implying less traditional views. A woman was defined as nontraditional if her score was below the median on this scale and traditional if her score was above the median. A complete specification of this scale is included in appendix 4A.

In the following analyses we examine the extent to which

the number of weeks a young woman worked in 1977 is related to the explanatory factors specified above. In 1977 the young women were 23 to 34 years of age and in most instances had been out of their parental household for a number of years. They were all married, and most had children. For the most part they had been bombarded by a variety of nonfamilial influences for some time, and there is every reason to believe that from a work perspective they were responsive to standard economic stimuli such as income and substitution effects.

In this research we look at the effect of the explanatory factors as predictors of weeks worked in 1977 to test directly five hypotheses.

1. Daughters who have mothers with a generally nontraditional attitude about the role of women should, all else being equal, be more likely to work themselves, as shown by the number of weeks worked in 1977.[6]

2. Mothers who worked more extensively themselves are also, all else being equal, more likely to have working daughters.

3. The impact of the mother's work behavior might not be as straightforward as the impact of her attitudes toward working. For instance, a woman may hold very negative feelings toward women working but out of economic necessity work herself. For this reason, we anticipate that the influence of the mothers' sex-role attitude should be greater than the influence of the mothers' work behavior. In addition the relaxing of conservative mores as time passes should produce many mothers who did not have extensive post–first birth work experience even though they may have desired to be employed. We anticipate that young women who have mothers with nontraditional attitudes and extensive work behavior would be most likely to work (independent of other factors), whereas young women with traditional-nonworking mothers would be least likely to work. Within the other two possible combinations of traditionality and work behavior, the attitude aspect should be more influential than the work behavior component since a nontraditional attitude has an unambiguously nontraditional and positive impact on a daughter's likely work behavior, and the effect of a mother's work behavior on a daughter's activity is more ambiguous.

4. According to economic theory we anticipate that standard income and substitution effects should be operative, and they

should be particularly strong when the mother has not transmitted any hesitancy about working. In that case outside forces should interfere less with a young woman's ability to operate within an economically rational framework. Where a young woman's mother has nontraditional views and worked herself, standard income and substitution forces should be strongly operative; the young women will work or not work depending to a considerable degree on such factors as other income available in the family and the potential wage she can obtain in the labor market because her ability to respond rationally to these forces will not be encumbered by conflicting familial (or at least parental) pressures, whether overt or perhaps more subtle internalized psychological constraints. Conversely where a young woman is subject to negative work pressures because of traditional background orientations, we hypothesize that standard income and substitution effects will be less strong. Operationally we expect to find the strongest effects in the model where the mother was a nontraditional worker and the least powerful effects where the mother was a traditional nonworker. Between the other two possibilities, we expect stronger economic effects in the situation where the mother was nontraditional but did not work.

5. Economic theory posits that having a small child should be a strong deterrent to female employment; however, as with the income and substitution effects, this factor is unlikely to affect all women equally.[7] Women whose background is more traditional should be more disposed toward filling the home work role when they have small children than women from less traditional backgrounds. For this reason we hypothesize that the age of the youngest child variable will be more of a deterrent to the labor supply of young women with traditional mothers who did not work. Conversely young women whose mothers have nontraditional values and worked should be the least reluctant to work themselves when they have a small child in the home.

The absolute sizes of both the income-substitution effect and youngest child effects are empirical questions dependent on a wide range of factors that go far beyond the scope of this study. Our intention here is merely to suggest that the noneconomic factors are not only important in their own light; they are of crucial significance for interpreting the standard economic effects. Indeed failing to account for role model considerations may lead to serious misspecifications of economic factors if those factors do not predict well for a substantial subset of women.

Results

Overall there are differences in 1977 weeks worked by the daughters in the sample that are related to their mothers' work role orientation (table 4.1). The average daughter worked about 28 weeks in the year; daughters who had nontraditional mothers worked about 30 weeks compared with 25 weeks among those whose mothers were more traditional. This difference is statistically significant and consistent with our first hypothesis. However, the mother's actual work activity was a significant predictor of work activity only if the mother held traditional attitudes; but it operated in the wrong direction: daughters whose mothers had not worked extensively worked more weeks themselves. Thus the mother's work activity is not nearly as important as her attitudes, at least as both are measured in this study.

In order to consider directly the independent effect of mother's work orientation on a daughter's work tendency, we regressed the daughter's weeks worked in 1977 on our full range of relevant explanatory variables in a multiple classifica-

Table 4.1
Mean weeks worked in 1977, by mothers' work role orientation and pre-1967 work behavior

Mother's characteristic	Mean weeks worked	Number of respondents
Total	27.73	532
Mother traditional*·**	25.29	245
Worked***	23.65	63
Did not work	25.86	182
Mother nontraditional**	29.82	287
Worked	29.78	102
Did not work	29.83	185
Mother worked	27.44	165
Mother did not work	27.86	367

Note: The sample consisted of white, married, spouse-present women 24 to 34 years old in 1978 who were interviewed in 1978 and lived with their mother at age 14.
* Statistically significant ($p \leq 0.05$) from the nontraditional sample.
** Statistically significant ($p \leq 0.01$) from the total sample.
*** Statistically significant ($p \leq 0.001$) from the traditional nonworker sample.

tion framework. With this technique one can determine for each category of the explanatory variable of interest the mean weeks worked for a woman who is assumed to be average on all other variables included in the analysis. For example, women whose mothers had nontraditional values and worked between first birth and 1967 and who are treated as average on all the other factors would have worked an average of 30.1 weeks in 1977 (table 4.2). This compares with 30.4 weeks for daughters of nontraditional nonworkers, 28.4 where the mother was a traditional nonworker, and 27.9 for the remaining traditional worker category. These results, which controlled for all the other factors considered relevant, suggest that nontraditional attitudes of mothers are translated into a greater propensity for daughters to work independent of other considerations and that the mother's work activity was not important.

Table 4.2
Mean weeks worked between 1977 and 1978 for white women, by selected characteristics: multiple classification analysis results

Characteristic	Mean weeks worked
Daughter's education	*
0–11 years	17.6
12 years	26.4
13 years or more	31.0
Husband's earnings[a]	*
Less than $5,000	27.0
$5,000–$9,999	32.3
$10,000–$12,999	29.6
$13,000–$17,999	28.9
$18,000–$22,999	22.1
$23,000 and over	16.1
Age of youngest child	*
Under 6	21.0
6 and over	37.9
Mother's attitudes and work behavior	*
Mother nontraditional worker	30.1
Mother nontraditional nonworker	30.4
Mother traditional worker	27.9
Mother traditional nonworker	28.4

Note: See appendix table 4A.2 for complete model and table 4.1 for sample definition.
* Significant at the 0.01 level.
a. In 1977 dollars.

We had anticipated the greater importance of the less ambiguous verbalized women's role attitude dimension, but the total lack of significance of the behavioral component is somewhat surprising; it may reflect an inadequate operationalization of the background work factor. It may also be associated with our premise that the ambiguity of the nature of the mother's work attachment might make it a less important predictor of daughter's work. The importance that the mother attached to her work activity, her satisfaction with that work, and the somewhat limited nature of that attachment, even for many women whom we defined as workers, may have limited its operational effectiveness.[8]

Also in table 4.2 (using multiple classification analysis) and in table 4.3 (using ordinary least squares regression techniques), strong substitution and income effects for the overall sample of white married women appear. Women with higher education worked many more weeks and women whose husbands had higher earnings worked far fewer weeks than their less-educated and poorer counterparts, controlling for all the other factors in the model.

These significant substitution and income effects mask the fact that both economic factors are operative only for certain subsets of women. By stratifying the sample separately by mother's attitudes regarding the appropriate roles for women or by mother's work activity, it may be seen in table 4.3 that the variable of daughter's education and husband's earnings are both significant only in the models limited to where the mother is nontraditional or where she worked during the earlier years. Further when we consider jointly the mother's attitude and behavior, the income and substitution factors are both significant only in the model where the mother has nontraditional attitudes and worked. Thus as we hypothesized earlier, income and substitution factors are significant in the situation where the woman is free of familial conflict situations, whether covert or overt. Where her mother is supportive of nontraditional women's roles and in addition worked extensively herself, the daughter was less constrained in making rational economic decisions; thus the daughter is free to weigh carefully and balance the utility of her home and work time and to strike a balance based on her current situation rather than on beliefs that working is not good.[9]

Finally it may be seen in table 4.3 that regardless of which

Table 4.3
Estimated mean weeks worked between 1977 and 1978 for white women, by mothers' work orientation for selected characteristics: regression results

Characteristic	All women	All women	Mother non-traditional	Mother traditional
Daughter's education	2.086**	2.019**	2.253**	1.784**
Husband's earnings	−0.0003**	−0.0003**	−0.0003*	−0.0003
Youngest child under 6	−16.752**	−16.551**	−15.486**	−17.748*
Mother non-traditional worker		2.04		
Mother non-traditional nonworker		3.12		
Mother traditional worker		−.535		

Note: See appendix table 4A.3 for complete model and table 4.1 for sample definition.
* Significant at the 0.05 level.
** Significant at the 0.01 level.

subset one focuses on, having a child under the age of 6 in the home is a clear and strong deterrent to a woman's ability to work extensively outside the home. However, the model in table 4.3 with the smallest coefficients for age of youngest child also has, as hypothesized, the strongest income and substitution effects. In other words the conditioning factors conducive to a freedom to act rationally in the labor market are the converse of those that would constrain the work activity of a woman with a small child. Once again a mother who has untraditional ideas about women's work and has worked herself is likely to pass on to her daughter similar liberalized notions. This transference will make it psychologically easier for these daughters to work when they have a small child in the home. Operationally this should and has translated into a somewhat less negative coefficient for age of youngest child.

Conclusions

The results suggest the importance of incorporating noneconomic factors directly into labor supply analyses. The results in the neoclassical models in our analysis varied substantially depending on the characteristics of the women's mothers. In-

Mother worker	Mother nonworker	Mother non-traditional worker	Mother non-traditional nonworker	Mother traditional worker	Mother traditional nonworker
3.023**	1.604**	3.928**	1.232	1.674	1.837*
−0.0005**	−0.0003	−0.0005*	−0.0003	0.004	−0.0003
−15.237**	−17.141**	−11.244**	−18.548**	−21.57**	−16.682**

deed focusing only on the overall model would suggest results that are misleading for most women. From a broader perspective the secular importance of this finding lies in the knowledge that in our society we are witnessing radical changes in the views of both men and women about appropriate activities for women, and these changed attitudes are being passed on from generation to generation. As attitudes continue to be transformed, we expect a spiraling impact on the behaviors of subsequent generations of women. Women who have adopted these newer attitudes no longer will be dissuaded from working because of traditional family pressures, such as the presence of young children. These same women will also become freer to think of maximizing their own economic gain in the labor force and, if this continues to happen and women win complete freedom to choose rationally, traditional neoclassical models will again become more appropriate for interpreting their work activity.

Notes

1. For a fuller discussion of income and substitution effects as applied to time allocation, see Becker (1965). This model assumes that women have full information about their worth in and out of the labor

market, and their decision to supply labor is an economically rational decision. That is, the motivation to supply labor is based on a woman's potential wage in the market and the value of her time outside the market. If her time outside the market is more valuable than the wage she would receive in the market, she will devote most of her time to activities outside the paid labor market. Since leisure is a normal good, any increase in income will lead to an increase in the consumption of her time outside the market and a decrease in the amount of labor she supplies to the market. This is called the income effect. On the other hand, higher wages will draw her into the labor market because she will substitute the more valuable market time for leisure time.

2. This issue is considered directly in chapter 6.

3. See chapter 5 for a more extensive discussion of the relationship between work and fertility.

4. A variable indicating the number of children in the household was not included partly because the constrained age of our sample limits the parity range of the respondents and partly because the literature generally suggests that it is the age of the youngest child that dominates most labor supply analyses (Sweet 1973; Bowen and Finegan 1969). Women who have no children are coded as having no child under the age of six.

5. Although nine sex-role attitude statements were asked, only six dealt with social roles; the other three dealt with economic roles and were deleted because a factor analysis indicated that they formed a separate scale.

6. This attitude series was asked of the mothers in 1972, which post-dates when most of their daughters left home. On average it is likely that the mothers had more-traditional views earlier in time. However, using the 1972 scale should not introduce any significant bias as long as the women who were more traditional later were also more traditional earlier, a reasonable assumption. Also in terms of impact on their daughters' behavior, it can be argued that the closer proximity in time between 1972 and 1978 probably increases the impact of the mother's attitudes on the daughter's behavior.

7. This is due to the increase in work in the home once a child is born. If a woman's wage rate in the market is not high enough to cover the loss of her productivity in the home while working, she will reduce the amount of time she spends in the paid labor force once a child is born. For a more detailed discussion of this phenomenon see Gronau (1973).

8. We defined as working mothers all mothers who worked six or more months in at least one-third of the years between their first birth and 1967. We could not define the working mother category more generously because of sample size constraints.

9. One could argue that inserting mother's attitude and work behavior into a standard labor supply model could sufficiently control for these background factors. However, including the variables in the models (instead of stratifying the models by the variable) assumes that the income, substitution, and child effects are the same for all groups and that the mother's effect on the daughter's labor supply is a direct effect. We are arguing that a mother's effect operates by changing the relative magnitude of the income, substitution, and child effects, and thus it is inappropriate to assume that these effects are the same for all groups of women. This is shown by the differing coefficients on the education, husband's earnings, and age of youngest child variables when the models are stratified by the mother's characteristics.

References

Almquist, E., and Angrist, S. 1971. Role modeling influences on college women's career aspirations. *Merrill-Palmer Quarterly* 17:263–279.

Becker, G. S. 1965. Theory of the allocation of time. *Economic Journal* 75:493–517.

Bowen, W. G., and Finegan, T. A. 1969. *The Economics of Labor Force Participation.* Princeton: Princeton University Press.

Cain, G. C. 1966. *Married Women in the Labor Force: An Economic Analysis.* Chicago: University of Chicago Press.

Fuchs, V. R. 1971. Hourly earnings differential by region and size of city. In *Readings in Labor Market Analysis*, ed. J. F. Burton, L. K. Benham, W. M. Vaughn III, and R. J. Flanagan. New York: Holt, Rinehart and Winston.

Gronau, R. 1973. The intra-family allocation of time: the value of the housewives' time. *American Economic Review* 63:634–651.

Hartley, R. E. 1961. Sex roles and urban youth: some developmental perspectives. *Bulletin of Family Development* 2:1–12.

Hoffman, L. W. 1975. Effects on child. In *Working Mothers*, ed. L. W. Hoffman and F. I. Nye. San Francisco: Jossey-Bass.

Kemper, T. D. 1968. Reference groups, socialization, and achievement. *American Sociological Review* 33:31–45.

Macke, A. S., and Morgan, W. R. 1978. Race, maternal employment and work orientation among adolescent girls. *Social Forces* 51:187–204.

Macke, A. S., and Mott, F. L. 1980. The impact of maternal characteristics and significant life events on the work orientation of adolescent women: a longitudinal look. *Research and Labor Economics* 3:129–146.

Sweet, J. A. 1973. *Women in the Labor Force.* New York: Seminar Press.

Scanzoni, L., and Scanzoni, J. 1976. *Men, Women and Change: A Sociology of Marriage and the Family.* New York: McGraw-Hill.

Frank L. Mott
and
David Shapiro

The traditional view of women as secondary workers who may take a part-time job to supplement family income or to buy nonessential consumer durables has become largely outdated. The American woman in 1980 is a partner in the family's income-producing process. Although they do not yet have equal footing with men in the labor market, more and more women are seeking permanent attachments to the work place for a full range of reasons, as is true with men. One dramatic indicator of this rapid transition in the NLS is that in 1968 only 22.4 percent of young women 14 to 22 years of age said they expected to be working when they reached age 35, but by 1979 this percentage grew to 67.8 (Shapiro 1980). Within one decade the percentage of women anticipating attachment to the work place during the prime adult years more than tripled.

Although many more women are now employed than in the past, several important questions about the strength of their work commitment remain. Do the higher female employment rates mean that most women are working, but only sporadically and part of the time, or do they indicate that smaller percentages are working most of the time? Is there a substantial segment of the adult female population who maintain a fairly continuous attachment to the work force regardless of their personal circumstances?

In our society men are generally expected to work during their adulthood, at least until they reach an age where it is socially acceptable to retire. A man not following this pattern without a "legitimate" excuse (such as serious illness or an inability to find work) is generally discredited. The employment of women is not yet so institutionalized, but there may already be large numbers of women in American society who have effectively internalized the work ethic; for them working constitutes a major life activity. Family and other personal considerations are important, just as they are for many working men. We hypothesize that work has the same major meaning in the lives of these women as it does in the lives of many men.

To test this hypothesis we focus on the life-cycle stage where traditionally women have the least work attachment: the years when they have young children in the home. There is evidence of substantial work attachment among young women in the periods immediately before and after the birth of the first child, the time when women traditionally withdrew from gainful employment (Shapiro and Mott 1979). The observed work attachment of a substantial proportion of women at this critical first birth life-cycle point is symptomatic of a substantial and continuing work attachment and suggests a major social change (Shapiro and Mott 1978; Mott and Shapiro 1978). Here we try to document that work before and after the first birth shows a strong positive association with work at later points independent of other demographic and economic considerations. In other words we predict that many women work and continue working regardless of children and regardless of income and other economic considerations, just as is true for men.

The Research

We hypothesize that the substantial proportions of young women working immediately before and after the first birth will follow fundamentally different life-style paths from those prevailing in their mothers' generation, for whom work outside the home and child rearing were substitute and not complementary activities.

Increasing proportions of women will show a fairly continuous pattern of attachment to the labor force, for many reasons. Given our hypothesis of a strong association between market work at the first birth and subsequent work independent of child rearing, we examine the nature and extent of work activity in 1978 of women who had their first child between 1968 and 1973. We observe at least five years between the first birth and 1978, hypothesizing that those who showed more work attachment at the earlier life-cycle point will also show more in 1978 (as measured by weeks worked in the year preceding the 1978 interview or by work activity during the 1978 survey week), regardless of whether they have had additional children.

Work commitment is motivated by social and psychological as well as economic considerations. As fertility has continued the secular decline that was interrupted by the baby boom, smaller family size has contributed to the development of more favorable norms and attitudes toward women working outside the home, and it has also made such work activity easier. In addition we believe that women increasingly are perceiving market work and careers as sources of rewards, psychic as well as financial, that can be complementary to rather than substitutable for careers in the home. This work commitment will be manifested by a continuity of work behavior that cannot be completely accounted for by standard economic measures and that persists even in the face of competing family considerations.

The Data

Young women who gave birth for the first time between the 1968 and 1973 surveys and who were still in the sample at the 1978 interview had between five and ten years between the birth of their first child and 1978. There are approximately 1,100 women—about 750 white and 350 black—in this sample.

We will examine how different dimensions of work experience in the post–first birth period are related to earlier work commitment. Our measure of work commitment is whether a woman was employed immediately before and/or immediately after having her first child. All references to employment before or after the first birth refer to the interval between six months before the first birth and the birth month itself and the interval between the birth month and six months later.

Work
Attachment
in the Years
Following a
First Birth

About two-thirds of all young mothers are employed at some point within six months of their first child's birth, and almost one-third are employed both before and after the birth (table 5.1).

The largest portion of these women employed shortly before or after their first birth were high school graduates; women who had completed high school showed a much stronger work attachment. No work attachment in the intervals under consideration was shown by almost half of the white and black high school dropouts compared with only about a quarter of their graduate counterparts. As we will see, both educational attainment and early work attachment are impor-

Table 5.1
Work attachment before and after the first birth, by race
(percentage distribution)

Work attachment pattern	Whites	Blacks
Before and after	28.8	32.6
After only	6.5	16.6
Before only	35.0	17.0
Neither	29.7	33.9

Note: Universe: Women who had a first birth between 1968 and 1973 and who were interviewed in 1978.

tant predictors of subsequent work activity, and they partly proxy for work commitment.

Overall the white women in our sample worked 6 months or more in 38.4 percent of their postbirth years (up to 1978), and the black women worked 6 months or more in 50.2 percent of the years (table 5.2).[1] Thus work attachment in this postbirth span, which averaged about seven years in length, was quite substantial. Only slightly over 10 percent of the white and slightly less than 20 percent of the black women worked six months or more in all of their postbirth years, evidence that in the aggregate the work patterns of women with young children still differ substantially from those of men.

A more careful examination of table 5.2 suggests substantial variations among different subsets of women, however. At one extreme, women who did not complete high school and showed no work attachment around their first birth worked six months or more in fewer than 20 percent of their postbirth years. This same group had no instance where a woman worked in all her postbirth years, and almost half did not work six months or more in any year. This group represents a noncommitted subset of women who still follow the traditional pattern of female work activity and choose to refrain from paid work activity, at least during this life stage.

At the other extreme are women who have completed high school and were employed in both the months before and after the first birth. White women in this category worked six months or more in 63 percent of their postbirth years, and their black counterparts worked 77 percent of the time. Substantial proportions—30 percent of the whites and 40 percent of the blacks—worked in all postbirth years, and only insignificant proportions never worked.

Thus these better-educated highly committed and less-educated uncommitted women set the limits for defining the range of work activity of women with young children. Many women still follow the traditional path of labor force withdrawal when their children arrive, but many are also showing patterns of almost continuous work participation.

Not surprisingly women who have additional children are less likely to have continuous working patterns, although early work commitment (that is, working before or after the first birth) continues to be an important independent determinant of later attachment (see table 5.3). That is, even among the

Table 5.2
Percentage of post–first birth years working at least 6 months or more, by race, educational attainment, and work attachment before and after first birth

Work attachment pattern	Percent of postbirth years worked 6 months or more	
	Whites	Blacks
All women	38.4	50.2
Before and after	60.1	70.5
After only	49.0	58.8
Before only	31.2	39.0
Neither	23.5	30.5
Fewer than 12 years school	22.8	37.3
Before and after	37.8[a]	54.5[a]
After only	23.2[a]	55.3[a]
Before only	20.9	31.5[a]
Neither	19.2	17.8
12 or more years school	41.8	56.1
Before and after	62.5	76.8
After only	62.8	61.0
Before only	32.4	42.2
Neither	25.3	39.2

a. Sample sizes are small.

subset who have additional children before 1978, substantial proportions continue to show extensive attachment during the principal childbearing years. Overall white women who have no additional children by the 1978 survey date work six months or more in about 55 percent of their post–first birth years compared with 33 percent of their counterparts who have at least one additional child. The comparable statistics for blacks are 70 percent and 40 percent, respectively.

Within the subset who have a second child (and represent about three-quarters of the sample), the extent of postbirth work activity is quite sensitive to earlier work attachment. Among both white and black women, those who worked before and after their first child was born (as well as those who worked after the birth only) showed the highest levels of postbirth work activity according to the measures of work activity used in this study. Thus regardless of a woman's subsequent fertility behavior in the years following the first birth, women

Percent of women working 6 or more months in all postbirth years		Percent of women not working 6 or more months in any postbirth year		Number of respondents	
Whites	Blacks	Whites	Blacks	Whites	Blacks
11.5	18.8	30.1	19.8	758	321
28.1	37.7	8.9	3.9	218	95
20.0	20.5	22.4	10.3	50	55
5.0	7.5	37.0	23.8	260	52
1.0	5.0	44.4	38.5	230	119
1.2	13.3	38.4	34.3	135	105
1.1	33.3[a]	11.4[a]	12.8[a]	22	22
0.0[a]	25.0[a]	47.1[a]	5.0[a]	17	15
4.4	5.9[a]	38.5	17.6[a]	31	15
0.0	0.0	44.9	58.2	65	53
13.6	21.0	28.4	13.4	623	216
30.9	40.4	8.7	0.9	196	73
29.6	17.2	9.9	12.1	33	40
5.1	7.9	36.7	23.8	229	37
1.5	8.7	44.4	23.9	165	66

who showed stronger earlier work commitment continued to manifest greater attachment in the later years.

Conversely those women who continued their childbearing by 1978 and those who have, so far at least, stopped at one child show only modest differences in early attachment (table 5.4). Early work attachment is not particularly useful as a predictor of subsequent fertility behavior. Women apparently either are committed or not committed, and this commitment seems to have little bearing on their subsequent childbearing behavior.

These results, which may seem somewhat contradictory, are useful for clarifying the importance of distinguishing between longitudinal and cross-sectional thinking. From a longitudinal perspective, the data suggest that work commitment at one life-cycle point translates into greater commitment at later points, regardless of whether a woman has additional children. Of course the levels of attachment for women who have addi-

Table 5.3
Percentage of post–first birth years working at least 6 months or more, by race, educational attainment, work attachment before and after first birth, and 1978 parity

Work attachment pattern or education	Percent of postbirth years worked 6 months or more	
	One child	Two or more
Whites	55.3	33.4
Before and after	74.9	54.5
After only	66.7	45.5
Before only	47.5	26.8
Neither	38.2	19.4
Fewer than 12 years school	30.9	20.6
12 or more years school	55.1	37.4
Blacks	69.9	41.1
Before and after	91.0	60.4
After only	77.6	50.0
Before only	44.3	39.0
Neither	52.8	24.5
Fewer than 12 years school	60.3	30.7
12 or more years school	71.4	47.4

tional children are temporarily lower, reflecting a short-term (cross-sectional) withdrawal from the work force in the period immediately after the birth.

We can also examine these women's post–first birth work activity by following them year by year through the first five postbirth years.[2] Both black and white women gradually increase their work activity in the years following the first birth, as measured by the percentage working six months or more in a given year (figure 5.1). Overall by five years after the birth, about 40 percent of white and 55 percent of black women are working six months or more, a remarkable statistic for a full cross-section of women at a life-cycle point where they have traditionally withdrawn from work.

For those women who earlier had shown the greatest degree of commitment (being employed before and after their first birth), work activity rates continue at quite a high level: 60 to 65 percent for white women and 65 to 75 percent for black women. The activity curve for these women is relatively flat over the five-year interval even though a majority had at least one additional child in the interval. Further about 73 percent of the most committed white women had at least two children

Percent of women working 6 or more months in all postbirth years		Percent of women not working 6 or more months in any postbirth year		Number of respondents	
One child	Two or more	One child	Two or more	One child	Two or more
20.1	9.0	11.9	35.5	177	579
45.1	21.4	5.1	10.3	56	161
25.0	18.7	15.9	24.1	51	178
8.5	4.1	11.9	43.6	11	39
0.0	1.3	21.0	51.0	59	201
4.8	0.2	21.4	43.2	29	106
23.1	11.4	9.9	33.9	148	473
34.0	11.4	12.1	23.5	141	175
58.0	27.0	0.0	6.0	50	42
42.9	8.2	0.0	14.3	28	26
12.5	4.2	34.4	16.7	32	20
16.1	1.6	19.4	43.3	31	87
44.8	5.4	20.7	38.4	29	74
34.6	13.3	10.3	15.1	112	101

Table 5.4
First birth work attachment, by subsequent fertility behavior and race (percentage distribution)

Work attachment pattern	Whites		Blacks	
	One child by 1978	Two or more children by 1978	One child by 1978	Two or more children by 1978
Before and after	34.2	27.4	35.5	30.9
After only	5.9	6.7	19.9	15.1
Before only	31.7	36.0	22.7	14.8
Neither	28.2	29.9	22.0	39.2

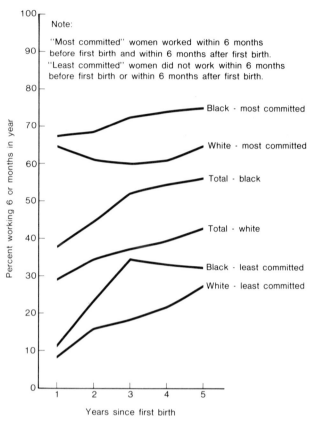

Figure 5.1
Percentage of women working 6 or more months in year, by years since first birth, extent of work commitment, and race

by 1978 (table 5.5). The relatively flat work activity curve for these women is consistent with the idea that for at least some young women, childbearing does not substantially alter working patterns. Indeed the pattern of early work attachment for white women had no discernible influence on their longer-term fertility behavior (table 5.5). Among black women, however, that small percentage of women who never worked are somewhat more likely to have had an additional child by 1978.

Just as early work commitment leads to a pattern of above-average work activity in the following years, noncommitment has the opposite effect. The least-committed black and white women have continuing (although gradually increasing) low levels of work activity in the five years following the first birth (figure 5.1). The least-committed black group does show some

Table 5.5
Percentage with two or more children in 1978, by first birth work attachment, educational attainment, and race

Work attachment or education	Whites	Blacks
Total	77.2	69.7
Before and after	72.8	66.7
After only	79.0	63.6
Before only	79.1	60.0
Neither	78.0	80.3
Fewer than 12 years school	77.6	79.4
12 or more years school	77.1	67.1

decline after the third year, as is consistent with our earlier evidence of noncommitted black women being the only group that had distinctly higher post–first birth fertility behavior.[3]

The association between earlier and later work commitment is not reduced in any way when parity controls are introduced (figures 5.2 and 5.3; see also table 5.3). Both white and black women who have had only one child by the 1978 survey and women who have had additional births show an enormous disparity in work activity over the five postbirth years between the "most" and "least" work-committed women. Among white and black women who do not have any additional births by 1978, work activity rates reach 90 percent. The activity curves for the women who have at least one additional child are lower, but the disparities between the least- and most-committed groups are just as large, providing further support for our hypothesis of a strong continuing work association for many women regardless of intervening fertility behavior.

The following multivariate analysis focuses on the association between earlier work commitment and the level of work activity in 1978. It is useful first to examine in summary fashion the extent of work attachment in the 1978 survey week in relation to earlier work attachment, controlling for intervening fertility behavior. There is a strong association between earlier and later work attachment even after controlling for intervening fertility behavior (table 5.6). Women who have had fewer children show higher levels of 1978 work activity, which suggests a short-term influence of having had a child on the ability of a woman to participate in gainful employment. The subset of women who have had no additional children by 1978 and

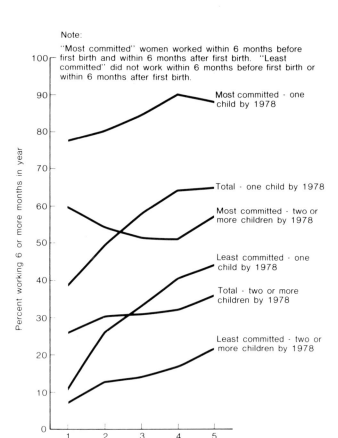

Note:

"Most committed" women worked within 6 months before first birth and within 6 months after first birth. "Least committed" did not work within 6 months before first birth or within 6 months after first birth.

Most committed - one child by 1978

Total - one child by 1978

Most committed - two or more children by 1978

Least committed - one child by 1978

Total - two or more children by 1978

Least committed - two or more children by 1978

Percent working 6 or more months in year

Years since first birth

Figure 5.2
Percentage of white women working 6 or more months in year, by years since first birth, extent of work commitment, and number of children by 1978

who worked soon after their first birth have a 1978 level of activity not substantially different from that of men their age—almost 91 percent. Overall women who have had only one child by 1978 have a 74 percent employment rate compared with about 50 percent among those who have had one additional child and about 33 percent among those women who have had at least two additional children.

Several important results will be tested more thoroughly in the multivariate analyses that follow. For both white and black women, we must distinguish between relationships that have short- and long-term implications. The results strongly suggest that a young woman's prospective fertility behavior is largely

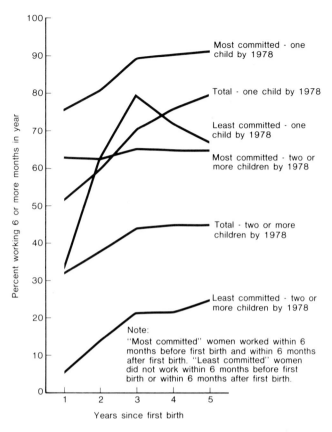

Figure 5.3
Percentage of black women working 6 or more months in year, by years since first birth, extent of work commitment, and number of children by 1978

independent of her earlier (around first birth) work behavior. For reasons largely independent of her observed employment behavior, she either will or will not have additional children in the long run. There is also in the long run a clear, strong association between earlier and later work activity regardless of intervening fertility behavior, although intervening fertility events may offset work activity in the short run. The principal implication is that substantial proportions of women show relatively continuous patterns of work activity regardless of whether they have additional children. As human capital analyses suggest, this continuity bodes well for their ability to succeed economically in their long-term employment efforts. The more

Table 5.6
Percentage employed in 1978, by first birth work status and
1978 parity

	Worked before first birth	
1978 parity	Yes	No
Total	59.1 (612)	41.3 (418)
One child	81.1 (179)	61.7 (111)
Two children	56.7 (330)	39.8 (216)
3 or more children	38.7 (147)	27.6 (157)

Note: Number of respondents in parentheses.

continuous their work, the larger their long-term earnings,
work stability, and access to higher-status occupations.

**A Multivariate
Perspective**

We have documented the close association between work
commitment before and after the first birth and the extent of
work commitment in the years that follow. This association is
not surprising. It is commonly assumed that the link between
earlier and later work activity is mediated by intervening fertility behavior (Cramer 1980; Waite 1980; Smith-Lovin and
Tickamayer 1978). That is, work at the earlier point in time is
associated with subsequent lower fertility, which in turn leads
to a higher level of later work activity.

This common assumption suggests that women working before and/or after their first birth will be less likely to have a second birth, and not having a second birth should lead to a higher
level of later work activity. From a modeling perspective, this
interaction implies, first, that first-birth work behavior should
be a significant predictor of post–first birth fertility behavior,
after controlling for other relevant factors, and, second, the
post–first birth fertility behavior should be a significant independent predictor of later (1978) work activity. Further, because of these implied work-fertility interactions, there is a
third implication that first-birth work behavior should no longer
be a major independent predictor of later work behavior when
we control for intervening fertility.[4]

We have examined these implications to some extent in our
tables. In contrast to the first implication, we found that post–
first birth fertility behavior was quite insensitive to pre– and
post–first birth work behavior. This finding supports our idea
that, at least in this sample of young mothers, women's views
of work operate independently of their family plans. Our find-

Returned to work			
0–6 months	7–11 months	Never or 12 or more months	Total
70.7 (390)	56.9 (112)	38.7 (400)	52.3 (134)
90.6 (113)	76.7 (25)	63.1 (103)	74.3 (290)
69.3 (177)	54.6 (55)	37.5 (214)	50.5 (546)
48.6 (90)	41.7 (32)	21.3 (143)	33.7 (298)

ing that later (1978) levels of work attachment are sensitive to whether a second birth had taken place supports the second implication that (independent of work commitment) having additional children does inhibit subsequent labor force attachment, at least in the short run. Finally, contrary to the third implication, we found evidence of a strong association between earlier and later work activity, even after controlling for intervening fertility events. This evidence is consistent with our hypothesis that a continuing work commitment obtains among many women irrespective of their fertility intentions and behavior. The tabular results thus suggest that substantial numbers of women have strong career intentions, as shown by a relatively continuous work history during those years when traditionally women were most likely to withdraw from the labor force.

We now focus on measuring the independent association between earlier and later work attachment, controlling not only for intervening fertility behavior but also for a variety of other factors usually considered to be important determinants of work behavior. For example, the strength of association between early and later work may be at least partly due to other economically motivated variables. Further to the extent that the standard economic-demographic explanatory factors do measure the economic need and financial incentive to work, the power of the early work attachment perhaps can be attributed to other dimensions of an individual's attachment to work, such as the psychic benefits that many people derive from their job, independent of the direct financial benefits. In effect, then, the early work attachment variable may well be reflecting longer-term aspects of an individual's tastes or psychological need for work activity and career satisfaction. For these reasons a thorough test of the strength and nature of the association among the work factors requires a more complete model that regresses later work activity on early work activity, including as independent predictors a full range of appropriate other factors. If the strength of the early to later work association remains relatively unchanged even with these variables in the model, it will enhance our ability to interpret the work-to-work association as being independent and as representing something other than a spurious correlation with other explanatory criteria. Including these additional factors makes the explanatory early work variable less ambiguous.

In the following multivariate analyses, we attempt to measure how earlier work attachment affects later work attachment independent of fertility and these other explanatory factors. We do this by examining current (1978) work attachment, controlling for other influences on work activity and for whether the respondent was in the labor force just prior to and just after the first birth. Equations will be estimated both with and without controls for fertility as of 1978. Without controlling for fertility, the coefficients of the first-birth work variables will measure the gross effect of early work attachment on later work attachment; once fertility is explicitly controlled for, the coefficient(s) for work activity around the birth event will measure the net effect of earlier attachment on later attachment (that is, net of intervening fertility behavior and other relevant factors). The degree to which the net coefficients differ from the gross coefficients will reflect the extent to which intervening fertility mediates between early and later work activity.

Economic theory suggests that current or recent labor force participation will depend on a comparison of the individual's market wage with her "home wage," or shadow price of time.[5] The individual's market wage will depend on both personal characteristics that reflect her human capital accumulation (such as schooling, work experience, and job tenure) and labor market characteristics (such as size and geographic region). The individual's home wage—the value that the household places on units of the wife's time spent in nonmarket activities—should depend on assets, other household income, number and ages of children, tastes, and education.[6]

Since we focus on the link between early and later work attachment and on the mediating effects of intervening fertility behavior on that link, it is not necessary to generate separate estimates of functions determining the market wage and the shadow price of time. Instead we use a reduced-form approach, estimating labor supply functions in which current work attachment is related to observable determinants of the market wage and of the home wage.[7] Also included are two variables measuring work attachment immediately before and immediately after the first birth. Empirically, then, we estimate regressions where work attachment in 1978 is a function of education, husband's income, size of the local labor force, South/non-South residence, interval since last birth, additional children since the first birth, and previous work attachment.[8]

The equations were estimated both with and without controlling for subsequent numbers of children. In addition our earlier analyses were conducted separately by race, and we found evidence of racial differences that we interpreted as perhaps reflecting the effects of greater upward mobility among blacks (Mott and Shapiro 1978). Hence the analyses here are also stratified by race, our expectation being that early work attachment would be more strongly associated with later work attachment among blacks, other things equal, due to the persistence over time of upward mobility effects.[9]

The results of this estimation are provided in appendix table 5A.2.[10] The coefficients of the control variables generally have the signs that one would expect on the basis of theory and previous empirical work: other things equal, current and recent work activity is significantly lower for women with a high-income husband and with more children and significantly higher for women with more schooling and with a greater time span since the birth of the last child (this latter variable controls for the age of the youngest child in the household).

Table 5.7 shows the estimated coefficients and partial derivatives for the early work attachment and intervening fertility variables, drawn from the complete equations reported in appendix table 5A.2. The coefficients of the two dichotomous variables measuring work activity just before and just after the first birth are always positive and in almost every case highly significant. The evidence of a link between early and later work attachment is thus clear and strong. At the same time there is no clear pattern of racial differences in the importance (net or gross) of early work attachment on later work activity. Examination of the coefficients of the two variables measuring early work activity in each pair of equations (with

Table 5.7
Estimated coefficients and partial derivatives of the work attachment and fertility variables, by race

| Independent variables[a] | Dependent variables | | | |
| | Weeks employed during preceding year | | Employment status as of 1978 survey | |
	Coefficient (*t* value)	Coefficient (*t* value)	Partial derivative (*t* value)	Partial derivative (*t* value)
Whites				
BEFORE	5.364 (3.10)	5.628 (3.23)	0.098 (2.25)	0.108 (2.49)
AFTER	9.175 (5.39)	9.413 (5.49)	0.269 (6.14)	0.267 (6.15)
KIDS	−4.540 (−3.42)		−0.135 (−3.86)	
Blacks				
BEFORE	7.983 (3.24)	8.391 (3.39)	0.118 (1.81)	0.125 (1.95)
AFTER	5.783 (2.32)	6.265 (2.50)	0.177 (2.76)	0.182 (2.85)
KIDS	−4.169 (−2.48)		−0.072 (−1.62)	

Note: The first two columns show ordinary least-squares regression coefficients, and the last two columns give partial derivatives (evaluated at the mean) based on probit analysis. For the complete equations from which these estimates are obtained, see appendix table 5A.2. The asymptotic *t* values reported for the last two columns refer to the corresponding probit coefficients.
a. See note 8 to this chapter for definitions of all variables.

and without controlling for fertility) reveals that the mediating effect of intervening fertility behavior that we expected to find is essentially negligible for both whites and blacks. That is, in all cases the decline in the coefficients of the variables measuring early work attachment concomitant with introduction of the fertility variable is small, and usually the decline is trivial in size and not statistically significant. At the same time the (negative) coefficient of the fertility variable is quite large and highly significant.

Thus fertility has a clear impact on subsequent work behavior. There is a strong link between work attachment as of the time of the first birth and work attachment in 1978 (five to ten years later), virtually independent of intervening fertility behavior. The missing link is between early work attachment and subsequent fertility.[11] Whereas the conventional wisdom suggests that women who were more strongly attached as of the first birth would have fewer additional children, the results indicate no such relationship.[12]

In view of both theoretical considerations and the large body of evidence focusing on trade-offs between fertility and work behavior, the absence of a link between early work behavior and subsequent fertility is quite surprising. It should be emphasized that this finding was made possible by the longitudinal nature of the data analysis. From a cross-sectional perspective, the 1978 data do indicate a significant adverse impact of fertility on employment activity. By tracking the same individuals over time, however, we are able to establish that although there is a strong link between fertility and subsequent work, there is no corresponding link between early work (as of the first birth) and subsequent fertility. In brief those women with strong work attachment as of the first birth do not differ from their weakly attached counterparts in the likelihood of having additional children, and independently of the number of children in 1978 (and given the values of other relevant variables such as educational attainment and husband's income) the strongly attached women are consistently and considerably more likely to work.

Apparently early attachment to work reflects at least in part an unmeasured commitment to work (that is, a motivation or taste for work) that influences attachment throughout the life cycle. The distinctly larger coefficients for postbirth as compared to prebirth work activity are consistent with this interpretation, since working while mothering an infant represents a stronger commitment to work than working while pregnant.[13]

Although our failure to find a link between early work activity and subsequent fertility could be an anomaly, this finding probably reflects fundamental changes in the way that increasing numbers of young women view their participation in the labor market. In the past women frequently regarded themselves as secondary workers, and they exhibited casual and intermittent labor force activity over the life cycle, but increasing numbers of women now manifest close and continuous work attachment. The secular increase in female labor force activity is suggestive of this phenomenon at a crude aggregate level.[14] In a similar vein, a recent analysis of labor force participation of successive cohorts of American women concludes, "The shift in the age patterns of labor force participation for women over the 20th century has been so pervasive that the participation profile of the female cohorts now entering the labor force will closely resemble the traditional worker profile of men" (Gregory 1980).

Conclusions

The past two decades have witnessed a marked decline in both fertility and fertility expectations of American women.[15] Concomitant with this decline has been a considerable reduction in the duration of the life-cycle span during which child-raising activities occupy a principal portion of the time and energy of married women. Increasing numbers of young women approach and begin adulthood with fertility expectations significantly lower than those of their mothers and with a growing awareness that the bearing and raising of young children will take place during a relatively short portion of their adult lives. Because they have more time over the life cycle available for employment, growing proportions of women see employment and careers as both feasible and desirable activities. In sociopsychological terms, one might argue that from a long-term, life-cycle perspective, declining fertility has reduced the role conflicts and tensions inherent in combining a career with motherhood.

Given the labor market penalties associated with discontinuous labor force participation, there is considerable incentive for women with expectations of strong lifetime attachment to the work force to have less-frequent and shorter labor force withdrawals.[16] The frequency of withdrawals will depend largely on fertility behavior, which will of course be influenced by a number of other factors in addition to the opportunity cost of the mother's time.[17] The duration of labor force withdrawals associated with childbearing will depend on child-care practices (more formally, on the technology of production of child services). The labor market imposes pressures on women with a strong work orientation to remain continuously attached to employment over the life cycle, and such women will thereby be induced to substitute the labor services of the spouse, other relatives or friends, and day care centers for their own time in caring for their children.

Notes

The authors thank Jean Haurin for her outstanding research assistance.

1. See appendix to chapter 5 for detailed discussion of how post–first birth cumulative work behavior was determined.

2. Because of the biennial interviewing pattern between 1973 and 1978, the sample reported on here does not include the same respondents for all years reported.

3. Other evidence not presented here shows that the over-the-years work activity levels for all groups except the black, least-committed group follow similar patterns even after introducing controls for educa-

tional attainment. Only black noncommitted women with 12 or more years of school follow a pattern dissimilar to the overall black noncommitted group. Their activity level is substantially above that for all black noncommitted women, reflecting a radically different fertility behavior pattern for that group.

4. We do not mean to imply that this chain is the only route whereby earlier and later work behavior may be associated. It is, however, the most commonly suggested mechanism, and this data set is ideally suited for testing its plausibility. There are other possible hypotheses: work and fertility (at both the later and earlier life cycle points) may have a common causation, work at both points in time may have a common causation, independent of fertility, and work at the later point may be causally determined (at least partly) by work at the earlier point. To varying degrees these hypotheses are interrelated.

5. The home wage or shadow price of time of an individual is the value the household places on units of the individual's time spent in nonmarket activities. Thus a woman's home wage represents the value of her time in household production. For a more formal discussion of the theoretical underpinnings here, see Shapiro and Mott (1978), pp. 572–576.

6. Empirical work indicates that the shadow price of a woman's time is positively related to household assets, other family income, the woman's education, and the number of children, and negatively related to the ages of children. For example, see Gronau (1973) and Heckman (1974).

7. This approach has been used elsewhere by Heckman and Willis (1977) and by Shapiro and Mott (1978).

8. ATTACH measures the respondent's current or recent work attachment. It is a dichotomous variable equal to 1 if the respondent was employed as of the 1978 survey date and 0 otherwise (current attachment), and a continuous variable measuring the number of weeks worked in the year preceding the 1978 survey (recent attachment).

EDUC equals the highest grade of school completed by the respondent.

INCHUS measures the respondent's husband's income (in thousands of dollars) in 1977.

LFSIZE measures the size of the labor force (in millions) in the respondent's 1978 area of residence.

SOUTH is a dichotomous variable equal to 1 if the respondent resided in the South in 1978 and 0 otherwise.

SPAN measures the number of months between the birth of the respondent's last child and the 1978 interview date.

KIDS equals the number of additional children the respondent has had since her first child through 1978.

BEFORE is a dichotomous variable equal to 1 if the respondent was employed within six months prior to the birth of her first child and 0 otherwise.

AFTER is a dichotomous variable equal to 1 if the respondent was employed within six months after the first-birth event and 0 otherwise.

9. To the extent that our mobility hypothesis is correct, it implies that in comparing strongly attached and weakly attached women as of the first birth, there will be a difference among blacks associated with striving for upward mobility that will be absent or at best considerably attenuated among whites. This additional factor (which we assume will continue to be relevant as of 1978) led us to anticipate larger coefficients for blacks for the two variables measuring work attachment as of the first birth.

10. Ordinary least-squares regression analysis was used to analyze weeks worked during the year preceding the 1978 survey date, and probit analysis was employed to analyze 1978 survey date employment status. Probit analysis was used to avoid the econometric problems associated with using ordinary least-squares regression analysis with a dichotomous dependent variable. See Theil (1971).

11. In order to examine this missing link more directly, we regressed fertility after the first birth on virtually the same independent variables used in the previous analysis. Consistent with economic models of fertility, educational attainment was negatively related and husband's income was positively related to subsequent fertility, and the duration since the first birth was also positively related to fertility. Both the pre-birth and postbirth work attachment variables had negative coefficients, but the coefficients were small and insignificant (usually with t statistics inferior—in absolute value—to unity).

12. In addition to the estimates reported here, we have done similar analyses focusing on those respondents who had a second birth between the 1968 and 1973 interview dates. The resulting estimates are quite similar to those reported here, suggesting that our findings can be generalized beyond the one-parity group.

13. More formally, presence of an infant sharply increases the woman's home wage or shadow price of time, thereby reducing considerably the probability of work immediately following the birth. Those women who nonetheless work during this period are thus likely to have a particularly strong commitment to work. In our earlier work, variations in work activity during the interval immediately following the birth event proved generally least amenable to explanation using standard labor-supply variables, while the one variable that attempted to measure tastes for market work (and which was not usually significant) did help explain variations in work activity during this particular interval (Mott and Shapiro 1978).

14. This is particularly so in light of analyses of sequential labor force participation, indicating that the probabilities of women being in the labor force are not well approximated by the overall female labor force participation rate but rather tend toward the extremes (for example, see Heckman and Willis 1977). Such analyses suggest that the secular growth in participation may be viewed as a consequence of a growing proportion of women with a high probability of being in the work force at any point in time and a correspondingly diminishing proportion of women with weak work attachment.

15. See chapter 6 for a more comprehensive discussion of this phenomenon.

16. Withdrawals from the work force result in forgone work experience, human capital accumulation, and wage increases. There may also be an additional penalty in the form of depreciation of previously accumulated human capital, although the size and even existence of this depreciation effect is subject to debate. See Mincer and Polachek (1974); Sandell and Shapiro (1978); Corcoran and Duncan (1979); and Mincer and Ofek (1980).

17. Actual fertility will often differ from early fertility expectations. Freedman, Freedman, and Thornton (1980) recently found in a longitudinal study that the discrepancy between initial expectations and final parity bore no systematic relationship to early family income or to wife's or husband's educational attainment. Thus for the first-birth and second-birth cohorts examined here, it seems likely that subsequent fertility will differ from early expectations for many. At the same time

our empirical results suggest that early work commitment is maintained and persists regardless of subsequent fertility behavior.

References

Corcoran, M., and Duncan, G. 1979. Work history, labor force attachment, and earnings differences. *Journal of Human Resources* 14:1–20.

Cramer, J. C. 1980. Fertility and female employment. *American Sociological Review* 45:167–190.

Freedman, R.; Freedman, D. S.; and Thornton, A. D. 1980. Changes in fertility expectations and preferences between 1962 and 1977: their relation to final parity. *Demography* 17:365–378.

Gregory, R. J. 1980. Labor force participation rates of cohorts of women in the United States: 1890 to 1979. Paper presented at the annual meeting of the Population Association of America, Denver, Colorado.

Gronau, R. 1973. The effect of children on the housewife's value of time. *Journal of Political Economy* 81:S168–S199.

Heckman, J. 1974. Shadow prices, market wages, and labor supply. *Econometrica* 42:679–694.

Heckman, J., and Willis, R. J. 1977. A beta-logistic model for the analysis of sequential labor force participation by married women. *Journal of Political Economy* 85:27–58.

Mincer, J., and Ofek, H. 1980. Interrupted work careers. National Bureau of Economic Research, Working Paper No. 479.

Mincer, J., and Polachek, S. 1974. Family investment in human capital: earnings of women. *Journal of Political Economy* 82:S76–S108.

Mott, F. L., and Shapiro, D. 1978. Work and motherhood: the dynamics of labor force participation surrounding the first birth. In *Women, Work and Family,* ed. F. L. Mott. Lexington, Mass.: D. C. Heath and Company.

Sandell, S. H., and Shapiro, D. 1978. The theory of human capital and the earnings of women: a reexamination of the evidence. *Journal of Human Resources* 13:103–117.

Shapiro, D. 1980. Aspirations for age 35. In *Pathways to the Future,* ed. M. E. Borus et al. Columbus, Ohio: Center for Human Resource Research, The Ohio State University.

Shapiro, D., and Mott, F. L. 1978. Labor force attachment during the early childbearing years: evidence from the National Longitudinal Surveys of young women. *Annales de L'INSEE* 30–31:565–598.

———. 1979. Labor supply behavior of prospective and new mothers. *Demography* 16:199–209.

Smith-Lovin, L., and Tickamayer, A. R. 1978. Labor force participation, fertility behavior, and sex role attitudes. *American Sociological Review* 43:541–557.

Theil, H. 1971. *Principles of Econometrics.* New York: John Wiley.

Waite, L. 1980. Working wives and the family life cycle. *American Journal of Sociology* 86:272–294.

Chapter 6

Labor Force
Attachment
of Married
Women Age
30 to 34: An
Intercohort
Comparison

David Shapiro
and
Lois B. Shaw

By the age of 30, most women have married and in all likelihood have small children in the home. The ages of 30 to
34 thus perhaps represent the life-cycle stage where many
women feel the greatest conflict between the demands of the
home and those of the marketplace. Much of the research in
this book either implicitly or explicitly assumes that women are
increasingly resolving this dilemma by increasing their market
work involvement at all life-cycle stages, including the time
when young children are in the home. Such a view implies that
women with young children today are behaving differently
from similarly situated women in the past. However, it is not
certain whether true behavioral changes have occurred or
whether differences in the circumstances of women today—
for example, their own increasing educational attainments and
the lessening disapproval of working mothers—account for
their greater labor-market attachment. This chapter clarifies
this issue by contrasting the work attachment of women (from
the NLS mature women's sample) who were 30 to 34 years of
age in 1967 with that of their counterparts from the young
women's sample who were 30 to 34 years old in 1978.

Work Activities
of Women Age
30 to 34

In 1967 about 44 percent of white women and 62 percent of
black women age 30 to 34 were in the labor force. By 1978
the labor force participation of white women at these ages had
risen dramatically to about 60 percent, nearly as high as that of
black women, whose participation had increased only margin-
ally from 62 to 64 percent (table 6.1). An increase in the percentage of white women who were unmarried and had high
participation rates contributed modestly to the overall increase
in labor force participation that occurred, but the primary
source of the increase in participation rates was the large increase among married women, particularly those with children.
In contrast to the situation for white women, the decline in
marriage among black women actually served to keep overall
participation rates down because the participation rates of married black women had surpassed those of unmarried black
women by 1978. Since the important changes in labor force
participation occurred among married women, this group will
be the focus of the rest of this chapter.

Not only were more wives working in 1978 than in 1967, but
those who did were more likely to have full-time jobs (table
6.2). The percentage of women who worked at least 39 weeks

Table 6.1
Labor force participation rates of women age 30 to 34 in 1967 and
1978, by race and marital status

Marital status	1967	Number of respondents	1978	Number of respondents
Whites				
Married, spouse present	37.8	987	54.2	929
Other	81.4	165	86.9	216
Total	43.8	1,152	60.2	1,145
Blacks				
Married, spouse present	59.5	264	70.9	192
Other	66.9	169	57.4	175
Total	62.3	433	64.3	367

Table 6.2
Percentage of married women workers age 30 to 34 who worked
full time and at least 39 weeks in the previous year in 1967 and 1978,
by race

	1967	1978
Whites		
Worked 35 or more hours per week	51	67
Worked 39 weeks or more	53	69
Worked 35 or more hours for at least 39 weeks	37	48
Blacks		
Worked 35 or more hours per week	59	85
Worked 39 weeks or more	67	75
Worked 35 or more hours for at least 39 weeks	51	66

during the year also increased, as did the percentage who
worked full time for at least 39 weeks in the previous year. No
matter what measure of work attachment is used, young
women in 1978 were more involved in employment outside
the home than were their counterparts in 1967.

The decade also saw improvement in the kinds of jobs held
by married women in their early thirties. Changes were especially striking for black women. Although the percentage
employed in professional or managerial jobs increased substantially for both races, black women were also much more
likely to work at clerical or sales jobs in 1978 than in 1967
(table 6.3). Indeed clerical and sales work became the largest
employment category for blacks as well as whites; about one-
third of black wives and about 45 percent of white wives were
employed in these occupations.[1] Equally striking was the decline in private household employment. By 1978 very few mar-

Table 6.3
Occupational distribution and average hourly wages of married women age 30 to 34 in 1967 and 1978, by race (percentage distribution)

Occupation	Whites		Blacks	
	1967	1978	1967	1978
Professional/managerial	19	28	11	19
Clerical/sales	42	45	16	33
Blue collar	19	11	20	24
Private household	2	1	23	3
Other service	14	13	26	20
Farm	4	2	5	1
Average hourly wage (1978 dollars)	4.07	4.75	3.50	4.15

ried black women aged 30 to 34 were still employed in the private household sector, whereas eleven years previously nearly one-quarter of black wives had been so employed. For both races the improvement in the kinds of jobs held was also reflected in average hourly wages in 1978. After controlling for inflation, they were about 60 cents per hour higher than in 1967.

Social and Economic Changes over Eleven Years

Many social and economic changes contributed to this increased work attachment. Previous research has shown that higher levels of education, smaller families, and more favorable attitudes toward women working outside the home all lead to increases in employment, while higher levels of husband's earnings and high unemployment rates cause decreases in labor market activity.[2] The increasing educational attainment of married women in their early thirties is shown in table 6.4. College attendance and graduation nearly doubled in eleven years, and the percentage of women who had not completed high school decreased considerably. On average women in their early thirties in 1978 had completed in excess of one more year of school than women of the same age in 1967. Higher educational attainment contributed to the better jobs and higher wages noted for the 1978 sample. These higher wages and better jobs in turn provide incentives to women to remain employed and to spend less time at home with children.

On average married women in the late 1970s had about one fewer child than married women of the same age in the late 1960s (table 6.5). Because their families were smaller, fewer women still had preschool children by the time they reached

Table 6.4
Educational attainment of married women age 30 to 34 in 1967 and 1978, by race (percentage distribution)

Highest grade completed	Whites		Blacks	
	1967	1978	1967	1978
Less than 9	10	3	23	7
9–11	18	14	27	28
12	52	46	39	38
13–15	10	18	7	17
16 or more	10	19	4	9
Mean	11.7	12.8	10.4	11.8

Table 6.5
Age of youngest child and average number of children of married women age 30 to 34 in 1967 and 1978, by race (percentage distribution)

Age of youngest child[a]	Whites		Blacks	
	1967	1978	1967	1978
0–2	32	26	38	18
3–5	29	27	26	20
6–11	28	35	20	45
12 or more	4	4	8	8
None	7	9	8	9
Mean number of children[a]	2.8	2.1	4.0	2.6

a. Living at home.

Table 6.6
Changes in attitudes toward women's roles: married women age 30 to 34 in 1967 and 1978, by race (percentage distribution)

Attitudes[a]	Whites		Blacks	
	1967	1978	1967	1978
Traditional	32	4	24	9
Moderate	55	49	53	63
Nontraditional	13	42	24	28
Mean score	10.1	12.0	11.0	11.9

a. Scale runs from 3 to 15: traditional = 3–9, moderate = 10–12, nontraditional = 13–15.

their thirties, and the percentage with children in elementary school increased.[3] Both the smaller numbers and older ages of their children made it easier for married women in this age range to work.[4]

Striking changes in attitudes toward women working outside the home also took place during the 1970s. We have a measure of these changes in responses to three questions asking whether it is all right for a woman with children to work under certain circumstances.[5] Table 6.6 illustrates the magnitude of the change in these views. The percentage of women who are nontraditional (measured by their view that it is all right or at least not wrong to work in all three circumstances) increased dramatically for white women, and in both races fewer women held completely traditional attitudes. Thus over the span of eleven years the view that women with children should not work became much less of a barrier to women's employment.

Unlike these changes in attitudes, educational attainment, and family size, economic changes during the eleven years may have retarded women's labor force participation. The unemployment rate increased from about 4 to 6 percent. Some women who might otherwise have worked probably could not find jobs and dropped out of the labor force. The average earnings of husbands (in constant 1977 dollars) increased from about $15,000 to $17,000 for white women and from about $9,000 to $11,000 for black women. Since higher earnings of husbands generally cause reduced work in the labor market among wives, this increase might also have depressed women's employment somewhat, especially since the financial pressures to work might be mitigated with smaller families.

Determinants of Women's Work Activity

We now turn to a more formal examination of the effects of these and other changes. We begin by analyzing the determinants of labor supply of married women age 30 to 34 in a multivariate framework. Labor supply equations are estimated separately for women in each cohort, controlling for wife's educational attainment, husband's earnings, number of children, age of youngest child, the unemployment rate in the local labor market, and several other variables frequently used in labor supply analyses.[6] Preliminary estimates indicated that there were distinct racial differences in the determination of labor supply, so we have estimated separate equations for whites and blacks.[7] Two measures of labor supply were used as dependent variables in the analyses: labor force participation as of the survey week and number of weeks worked during the preceding year.[8]

The estimated labor supply equations are provided in appendix tables 6A.3 and 6A.4 for whites and blacks, respectively.[9] The coefficients of the independent variables generally have the expected signs, indicating (other things being equal) that higher educational attainment is associated with greater labor supply, while higher husband's income, higher unemployment rates, greater numbers of children, and the presence of young children in the household all tend to depress labor supply.[10] The coefficients of these key variables of interest are shown in table 6.7, which clearly shows that among whites, these coefficients are almost always highly significant, while among blacks, the husband's income and the unemployment rate are never significant and only the presence of children under age 3 is consistently significant.[11]

Cross-cohort comparisons of coefficients of the key variables reveal that among whites, the effects of educational attainment, husband's income, and unemployment were greater (in absolute value) in 1978. The results regarding the fertility variables are more complex. The total number of children had a significant depressing effect on labor supply in 1978 but not in 1967, while the presence of young children had a stronger impact in 1967. Among blacks educational attainment had a negative though insignificant effect on labor supply in 1967, but by 1978 the effect of educational attainment had become significantly positive. In fact by 1978 the effects of education had become similar for black and white women. As with their white counterparts, the presence of young children had a smaller impact on the labor supply of black women in 1978 than in 1967, but the decline in the effect of young children was much larger for black women than for white women. By 1978 only the presence of children under age 3 significantly reduced the labor supply of black women; the presence of older preschool children had no effect.

In the past ten years dramatic changes have occurred in women's attitudes and expectations about work in the labor market. To assess the impact of these attitude changes on the labor supply behavior of married women, we have reestimated our labor supply equations with a measure of the respondent's attitude regarding the propriety of women working outside the

Table 6.7
Labor supply equations for married women age 30 to 34 in 1967 in 1978, by race: selected coefficients

Independent variables	Labor force participation rate		Weeks worked in preceding year	
	1967	1978	1967	1978
Whites				
Highest grade completed	0.024 (3.3)	0.041 (5.2)	1.1 (3.4)	1.9 (5.4)
Age of youngest child				
Under age 3	−0.327 (−7.7)	−0.277 (−6.3)	−13.4 (−7.5)	−12.4 (−6.2)
Ages 3–5	−0.172 (−4.0)	−0.136 (−3.2)	−8.1 (−4.4)	−5.4 (−2.8)
Ages 12 and over	−0.006 (−0.1)	0.050 (0.6)	−2.5 (−0.7)	6.0 (1.5)
No children	0.193 (2.6)	0.023 (0.3)	8.7 (2.7)	6.0 (1.8)
Number of children	−0.001 (−0.1)	−0.037 (−2.1)	−0.7 (−1.2)	−2.2 (−2.8)
Husband's earned income[a]	−0.011 (−5.2)	−0.011 (−6.6)	−0.4 (−4.7)	−0.5 (−6.1)
Unemployment rate	−0.013 (−1.4)	−0.016 (−2.3)	−0.2 (−0.6)	−0.8 (−2.5)
Blacks				
Highest grade completed	−0.019 (−1.3)	0.044 (2.9)	−0.2 (−0.3)	2.2 (2.9)
Age of youngest child				
Under age 3	−0.354 (−3.8)	−0.191 (−1.9)	−18.7 (−4.6)	−10.7 (−2.1)
Ages 3–5	−0.181 (−1.9)	−0.047 (−0.5)	−7.5 (−1.8)	−3.4 (−0.7)
Ages 12 and over	−0.035 (−0.3)	0.102 (0.7)	−0.2 (−0.0)	3.3 (0.5)
No children	−0.085 (−0.6)	−0.093 (−0.7)	0.8 (0.1)	−2.5 (−0.4)
Number of children	−0.025 (−1.5)	−0.014 (−0.5)	−1.0 (−1.4)	−1.4 (−1.1)
Husband's earned income[a]	−0.004 (−0.5)	0.002 (0.3)	−0.4 (−1.2)	−0.1 (−0.5)
Unemployment rate	−0.001 (−0.1)	0.005 (0.4)	0.1 (0.1)	−1.0 (−1.3)

Note: Complete equations shown in appendix tables 6A.3 and 6A.4; *t* values are in parentheses.
a. In thousands of 1977 dollars.

home. The resulting equations are provided in appendix tables 6A.5 and 6A.6 for whites and blacks, respectively; and coefficients of the education, fertility, income, unemployment, and attitude variables are shown in table 6.8.

Each of the four equations shows that among whites, attitudes toward women working are significantly related to labor supply in the expected direction. White married women with relatively favorable attitudes toward women working have labor force participation rates about 20 percentage points higher and work roughly 7 additional weeks per year than their counterparts with relatively unfavorable attitudes toward women working.[12] Among blacks the coefficients of the attitude variable have the expected sign in every case, but in only one of the four equations is the coefficient highly significant.

Comparing the remaining coefficients in table 6.8 with those in table 6.7, we see that in general, controlling for attitudes toward women working tends to reduce somewhat the positive impact of educational attainment and the negative impact of total numbers of children on labor supply and to increase slightly the strength of the depressing effect of young children on labor supply. These changes in the magnitudes of the estimated coefficients are all fairly small and reflect the correlations between the attitude scale and each of the variables. For example, women with more schooling also have more favorable attitudes toward working, so controlling for the latter reduces the estimated effect of the former.

To summarize, then, our evidence indicates that both in 1967 and 1978 educational attainment, husband's earnings, family structure, and attitudes toward women working were consistently and significantly related to the labor supply of 30- to 34-year-old married white women. Over the course of this period of sharply increased work activity of white married women, both the positive effects of schooling and the negative effects of the unemployment rate on labor supply became larger. The changes in the effects of family structure were more complex and to some degree offsetting, while the measured impacts of attitudes toward women's roles and husband's earnings were essentially unchanged.

The empirical evidence for blacks was much weaker. Neither their husband's earnings nor the local unemployment rate affected their labor supply. Between 1967 and 1978 education

Table 6.8
Labor supply equations controlling for attitudes toward women working for married women age 30 to 34, by race: selected coefficients

Independent variables	Labor force participation rate		Weeks worked in preceding year	
	1967	1978	1967	1978
Whites				
Highest grade completed	0.017　(2.4)	0.035　(4.5)	0.8　(2.7)	1.7　(4.7)
Age of youngest child				
Under age 3	−0.320 (−7.8)	−0.269 (−6.2)	−13.2 (−7.4)	−12.1 (−6.1)
Ages 3–5	−0.174 (−4.2)	−0.138 (−3.3)	−8.1 (−4.6)	−5.5 (−2.9)
Ages 12 and over	0.011　(0.1)	0.056　(0.6)	−1.9 (−0.5)	6.2　(1.5)
No children	0.228　(3.1)	0.040　(0.6)	9.9　(3.2)	6.7　(2.1)
Number of children	0.002　(0.1)	−0.027 (−1.6)	−0.6 (−1.1)	−1.8 (−2.2)
Husband's earned income[a]	−0.010 (−5.1)	−0.011 (−6.6)	−0.4 (−4.6)	−0.5 (−6.1)
Unemployment rate	−0.015 (−1.6)	−0.016 (−2.3)	−0.3 (−0.7)	−0.8 (−2.5)
Attitudes toward women working	0.043　(6.5)	0.039　(5.1)	1.5　(5.4)	1.6　(4.7)
Blacks				
Highest grade completed	−0.016 (−1.2)	0.043　(2.8)	−0.1 (−0.2)	2.1　(2.8)
Age of youngest child				
Under age 3	−0.353 (−3.9)	−0.191 (−1.9)	−18.7 (−4.6)	−10.7 (−2.1)
Ages 3–5	−0.169 (−1.8)	−0.035 (−0.4)	−7.3 (−1.7)	−2.0 (−0.4)
Ages 12 and over	0.017　(0.1)	0.010　(0.7)	0.7　(0.1)	3.1　(0.5)
No children	−0.013 (−0.1)	−0.096 (−0.7)	2.1　(0.3)	2.8 (−0.4)
Number of children	−0.017 (−1.0)	−0.012 (−0.5)	−0.9 (−1.2)	−1.2 (−0.9)
Husband's earned income[a]	−0.005 (−0.6)	0.002　(0.3)	−0.4 (−1.2)	−0.1 (−0.4)
Unemployment rate	0.002　(0.1)	0.007　(0.5)	0.2　(0.2)	−0.9 (−1.2)
Attitudes toward women working	0.035　(2.7)	0.013　(0.7)	0.6　(1.1)	1.5　(1.6)

Note: Complete equations shown in appendix tables 6A.5 and 6A.6; *t* values are in parentheses.
a. In thousands of 1977 dollars.

became a stronger influence on their labor supply while the effects of children became weaker. Only the presence of children under age 3 had a consistently significant impact on the labor supply of black wives.

Accounting for Increased Labor Supply of Married Women

We have seen how the determinants of labor supply of 30- to 34-year-old married women changed between the late 1960s and the late 1970s. Earlier we examined changes in the characteristics of married women in this age group during this period (greater educational attainment and lower fertility, for example). Now we bring these two strands of our analysis together in an effort to account formally for the increased labor supply of 30- to 34-year-old married women.

Conceptually the differences in labor supply between women in the two panels can be decomposed into two parts: a portion attributable to changes in the values of characteristics that influence labor supply and a portion attributable to changes in the *impact* of particular characteristics on labor supply.[13] For example, given that more schooling results in stronger attachment to the work force, the greater educational attainment of women in 1978 should result in greater labor supply, other things equal. At the same time the stronger impact of schooling on labor supply in 1978 also contributes, in and of itself, to higher labor force participation rates and greater numbers of weeks worked.

Working with the labor supply equations for whites from the preceding section, we have estimated the percentages of the total observed increase in labor supply of 30- to 34-year-old married women between 1967 and 1978 that can be attributed to changes in the values of those characteristics that influence labor supply.[14] These estimates are provided in the first row of table 6.9.

Greater educational attainment in 1978, as well as lower fertility, higher husband's income, and other differences as compared to 1967 (exclusive of changes in attitudes toward women working) account for very little of the total increase in labor force participation and only about one-fifth of the increase in weeks worked. That is, given the impact that each characteristic had on the labor supply of 30- to 34-year-old married women in 1967, our estimates indicate that if women in 1967 had had the characteristics of their counterparts in 1978, their labor force participation rate would have been higher by

Table 6.9
Estimated effects of changing characteristics on the 1967–1978 increase in labor supply of 30- to 34-year-old white married women, with and without controls for attitudes toward women working

Contribution to change in labor supply due to changes in:	Not controlling for attitudes	
	Labor force participation	
	Absolute	Percentage
All characteristics taken as a group	1.1	8
Educational attainment	2.6	18
Family structure	2.7	19
Husband's income	−2.1	−15
Unemployment rates	−2.7	−19
Attitudes		
All remaining variables	0.7	5

1.1 percentage points and they would have worked an additional 1.8 weeks per year (representing approximately 8 and 21 percent, respectively, of the total increases in these two measures that actually did take place between 1967 and 1978).

If we answer the question, What percentage of the observed increases in labor supply of white married women in their early thirties can be accounted for by the changes in the characteristics of such women? using the equations that also controlled for attitudes toward women working, our estimates are distinctly higher—over 50 percent.[15] These global results thus suggest that changes in attitudes toward women working appear to have been a major influence on wives' labor supply.[16]

In order to examine this last point more closely, table 6.9 shows the contributions of each of our key variables in accounting for the increased labor supply, both with and without controlling for attitudes toward women working. The partially offsetting effects of some of the major influences on labor supply can be clearly seen.[17] Thus, for example, in the equation in which attitudes are not controlled for, the overall impact of changing characteristics is to increase the labor force participation rate by only 1.1 percentage points, but this overall figure is the outcome of the positive impact of increased educational attainment (2.6 percentage points) and reduced fertility (2.7 percentage points) offset by the negative impact of higher husband's income (2.1 percentage points) and higher unemployment (2.7 percentage points).[18]

Weeks worked		Controlling for attitudes			
		Labor force participation		Weeks worked	
Absolute	Percentage	Absolute	Percentage	Absolute	Percentage
1.8	21	8.2	57	4.3	57
1.2	14	1.9	13	0.9	11
1.6	19	2.5	17	1.5	18
− 0.8	− 10	− 2.1	− 14	− 0.8	− 9
− 0.5	− 6	− 3.0	− 21	− 0.6	− 7
		8.3	58	2.9	35
0.3	4	0.6	4	0.3	4

From the perspective of the contributions of each key variable in accounting for increased labor supply, the figures in table 6.9 indicate that changes in attitudes toward women working have indeed been the major influence on changes in wives' labor supply.[19] At the same time changes in educational attainment, fertility, husband's income, and unemployment rates have all had important effects in influencing the work attachment of white married women in their early thirties; and in particular, higher husband's incomes and higher unemployment rates prevented wives' labor supply from rising even more than it actually did.

These analyses indicate that overall if the women in 1967 had had the characteristics of their counterparts in 1978 (greater education, lower fertility, and so on), their labor supply would have been greater by amounts representing from up to about 20 percent of the observed increase in labor supply (without controlling for attitudes) to over 50 percent of the observed increase (incorporating attitudes into the analysis). Conversely we may ask, Given the characteristics of 30- to 34-year-old white married women in 1967, what percentage of the observed increases in labor supply can be accounted for by changes in the influence that particular characteristics have on labor supply?

Using the equations that omit attitudes as an independent variable, we find that the answer is approximately 65 to 75 percent. That is, if the determinants of labor supply had been those represented by the coefficients estimated for 1978 rather than those estimated for 1967, the women in 1967 would have had higher labor force participation rates and would have worked more weeks per year, by amounts representing two-thirds or more of the actual increases in labor force participation and weeks worked that took place between 1967 and 1978. Using the equations that control for attitudes, the corresponding figures are of the order of 20 to 30 percent. Thus the portion of the increased labor supply attributable to changes in the determinants of labor supply declines sharply once the impact of attitudes toward women working is incorporated into the analysis. This sharp decline reflects both the importance of changes in these attitudes over time and the stability of the impact of attitudes.

A final point worth noting in the examination of changes over time in the impact of particular characteristics on labor supply concerns changes in the coefficients of educational attainment. These coefficients are considerably larger in 1978 than in 1967, indicating that schooling differences play a more prominent role in generating labor-supply differences in 1978 than in 1967. Some of this increase in the impact of educational attainment may be related to enhancement of job opportunities available to women during the 1970s, particularly with respect to desirable jobs increasingly available to women with relatively high levels of schooling. In addition as social approval of women working becomes more widespread, women may feel freer to consider their own opportunities in deciding whether and how much to work.[20]

Conclusions and Implications

The most important factors contributing to recent increases in labor force attachment of white married women in their early thirties were their increasing levels of education, decreasing family size, and more favorable attitudes toward working outside the home. Increases in husband's earnings and an unfavorable economic climate had a depressing effect; increases in labor force participation and weeks worked might have been even larger in a different economic environment. Educational attainment became a stronger influence on the labor force participation of both white and black women. We did not find evidence for any decrease in the importance of husband's earnings or family structure in affecting white women's labor supply.

Our analyses have taken family structure as given and as an independent determinant of wives' labor-supply behavior. Since the dependent variables in the analyses measure current and recent labor supply (labor force participation during the survey week and weeks worked during the preceding year), this approach seems reasonable. From a longer-term, life-cycle perspective, however, the family structure resulting from previous fertility should perhaps be regarded as endogenous; that is, although family structure will influence current and recent labor-supply behavior, past and prospective labor-supply behavior may also influence fertility and hence family structure. To the extent that such reverse causality is present, the estimated effects of changes in family structure on increases in labor supply will be overstated.[21] We believe that the current and recent nature of the dependent variables minimizes the magnitude of this potential simultaneity bias; but clearly analyses using longer-term measures of labor supply should attempt to take account explicitly of the possible endogenous aspects of fertility behavior.[22]

Finally we can use our results to speculate about the future course of labor supply behavior among married women. It seems unlikely that the observed increases in educational attainment and more favorable attitudes toward women working will be reversed. At the same time continued changes as large as those that occurred over the period of our study appear unlikely. Hence these factors may continue to contribute to greater labor supply in the future, but we suspect that any such increases will be relatively smaller than those that took place during the 1970s. If the real incomes of husbands continue to grow without commensurate growth in women's earnings, this will exert a continuing downward impact on wives' labor supply, further reinforcing our expectation of an end to the rapid increases of the past ten to fifteen years.

The two factors whose future courses are most difficult to predict are fertility and unemployment rates; however, reductions in fertility comparable to those of the 1970s seem highly unlikely. We thus anticipate a slackening of the increase in labor supply associated with changing family structure. The future course of the economy cannot be predicted. Cutbacks in educational, social, and health programs may decrease opportunities for women in some of the jobs that historically have provided major sources of employment. A lesser emphasis on affirmative action programs could have a similar effect. These influences might be offset by a resumption of rapid economic growth, but if this growth is concentrated in heavy industry and the military sectors, women's job opportunities may not expand proportionately. Overall, however, it is probable that the positive influences on the labor force participation of wives in their thirties will continue to outweigh the negative influences although the very rapid increases in work attachment observed between the late 1960s and late 1970s are not likely to be repeated in the 1980s.

Notes

The authors would like to thank Theresa O'Brien, Eva Chen, and Diane Brady-Hahn for their excellent assistance.

1. For both races, the great majority in this category were in clerical work; only 7 percent worked in sales occupations.

2. Research based on the theory of female labor supply developed by Mincer (1962), Cain (1966), and Bowen and Finegan (1969) has consistently shown that education, family structure, husband's earnings, and unemployment affect wives' work activity. Effects of sex-role attitudes on work decisions have been demonstrated by Waite (1979), Macke, Hudis, and Larrick (1978), and Shaw (1980).

3. If women in 1978 were having children at later ages than previously, the percentage with young children might have been as high in 1978 as in 1967; however, any tendency toward later childbearing was apparently offset by the smaller average number of children born.

4. It is also possible that increased work activity led women in the 1970s to desire fewer children than their counterparts in the 1960s. This possibility will be discussed further and has been highlighted in chapter 3.

5. The three questions asked the respondent's opinion of a woman with children working as measured on a five-point scale running from strongly agreeing that working was all right to strongly disagreeing. The circumstances for working included: if it is absolutely necessary to make ends meet; if she wants to and her husband approves; if she wants to even if her husband does not particularly like it. The questions asked in 1967 differed from those asked in 1978 in one way. The 1967 question referred to a married woman with children between the ages of 6 and 12, while the 1978 question referred to a mother, a father who works full time, and several children under the age of 6 with a trusted relative who lives nearby who can care for the children. In assessing changes in attitudes one must weigh the younger ages and possibly greater numbers of the children in the 1978 version against the fact that their adequate care is assured. It is our opinion that on balance the younger ages of the children referred to in 1978 makes this version a more stringent test of attitudes toward women playing an expanded role outside the home than the 1967 version, so that if anything we are understating the attitude shift between the two cohorts of women. If the 1967 version is deemed more stringent, we would be overstating the attitude shift, but probably not substantially. Within-cohort comparisons have consistently shown that attitudes have become less traditional over time and that younger women have

less-traditional attitudes than do older women. See, for example, Mott (1978) and Shaw and O'Brien (1981).

6. The other variables include health status, residence in the South, labor market size, and whether the respondent has been married more than once. These factors constitute a fairly standard set of independent variables in examining labor supply behavior. For a discussion of the rationale underlying this specification, see chapter 5. Although this specification is commonly used, it is also possible that increased labor supply led women to desire fewer children. Thus the direction of causality could have been the reverse of what we are proposing. Alternatively the same forces could have acted both to increase labor supply and to reduce family size. In either case we might be underestimating the true impact of changes in education, husband's earnings, and other factors on women's work activity.

7. Chow tests provide support for this stratification by race; that is, the equations for whites differ significantly from those for blacks in every case. Past research has also found significant differences in the determinants of labor supply for black and white women. See Bell (1974) for a discussion of some of the underlying reasons for these differences.

8. Mean values and standard deviations of the variables used in the analyses are reported in appendix tables 6A.1 and 6A.2. Unemployment rates are calculated from Current Population Survey sampling areas for each year. In 1967 all respondents lived in these areas. In 1978 some respondents had moved to other areas for which no current unemployment rates were available. Missing values on these unemployment rates were imputed by multiplying the 1970 unemployment rate in the same labor market by the ratio of the mean unemployment rate of all labor markets in 1978 to the mean in 1970.

9. In addition to the ordinary least-squares regressions (OLS) reported in the appendix tables, we also estimated probit equations for labor force participation in order to avoid the econometric problems resulting from using OLS with a dichotomous dependent variable. Since the probit results were quite similar to the OLS results, we have presented the latter here, for simplicity and clarity of exposition. Probit results are available on request.

10. The principal exception to this statement occurs in the older panel of blacks, among whom there is no evidence of a positive impact of schooling on labor supply.

11. This pattern is also evident to a lesser degree for the coefficients of the other control variables in the labor supply equations. While half of these coefficients are statistically significant (two-tailed test) among whites, only one-fourth are significant among blacks (appendix tables 6A.3 and 6A.4).

12. "Relatively favorable" and "relatively unfavorable" were defined as being one standard deviation above the mean attitude score and one standard deviation below the mean, respectively.

13. Empirical application of this conceptual approach in a regression context can be traced back to Blinder (1973) and Oaxaca (1973), each of whom examined sex differences in wage rates. In addition Shaw (1980) has utilized this decomposition technique to examine changes over time in female labor supply behavior.

14. The analysis here is confined to whites because the labor supply equations for blacks had so few significant coefficients. Since the estimated coefficients serve as weights in evaluating the impact of changing characteristics, the absence of reliable coefficients for blacks seriously undermined our effort at evaluation.

15. The estimates reported here utilize the coefficients from the 1967 labor supply equations as weights in evaluating the impact of changing characteristics. Alternatively one could use the 1978 coefficients as weights, in which case the changing characteristics are estimated to account for from 25 to 35 percent of the observed increase in labor supply (excluding attitudes) to 70 to 80 percent of the observed increase (including attitudes).

16. The possibility of a simultaneity problem regarding attitudes and labor supply must be acknowledged. This question will be addressed further.

17. An individual variable may account for more of the total change in labor supply than all of the variables taken together. This simply reflects the fact that some variables (for example, husband's income) have changed in ways that would reduce labor supply, so that the net increase due to all variables taken together can be exceeded by the increase implied by one or more individual variables.

18. The net effect of changes in the remaining determinants of labor supply is to add 0.5 percentage points to the labor force participation rate.

19. One might argue that since favorable attitudes toward women working can be an outcome of as well as a contributor to work experience, our failure to take account of this simultaneity problem may have led us to overstate the impact of attitudes on labor supply. That is, in this view, the attitude measure would (at least in part) be serving as a proxy for previous labor supply in "predicting" current labor supply. To address this question, we have estimated a further variant of our labor supply equations in which years of work experience since leaving school are also controlled for. In these equations this experience measure is highly significant, adding considerably to the overall explanatory power of the equations and reducing the coefficients of the attitude variable by about 30 to 40 percent (thereby lending some credence to the argument). However, the attitude variable remains highly significant, leading us to conclude that while perhaps the estimates in table 6.9 do overstate somewhat the independent effect of attitudes on labor supply, it is nonetheless evident that attitudes toward women working are a significant determinant of wives' labor supply and that changes in these attitudes during the 1970s contributed considerably to the observed increase in work attachment of married women.

20. This interpretation is supported by chapter 4 where educational attainment was found to have a much stronger effect on the labor force participation of women whose own mothers were nontraditional working women than it had on the participation of women whose mothers held more traditional attitudes. Although we control for the women's own attitudes in our analysis, these may not adequately reflect the influence of the attitudes of parents, friends, and neighbors. When there is widespread social disapproval of women with children working, women may hesitate to go against public opinion even if they believe personally that working would be desirable for themselves and not harmful for their children.

21. That is, some of the changes in family structure would have to be regarded as reflecting (rather than causing) changes in labor supply.

22. One further point worth noting here is that during the period from 1967 to 1978, a relatively convenient and highly effective method of birth control—oral contraceptives—became increasingly available to women. This phenomenon alone, quite independently of labor supply considerations, would be expected to lead (to at least some degree) to

the lowering of overall fertility and earlier completion of childbearing that in fact took place during the 1970s.

References

Bell, D. 1974. Why participation rates of black and white wives differ. *Journal of Human Resources* 9:465–479.

Blinder, A. S. 1973. Wage discrimination: reduced form and structural estimates. *Journal of Human Resources* 8:436–455.

Bowen, W. G., and Finegan, T. 1969. *The Economics of Labor Force Participation.* Princeton, N.J.: Princeton University Press.

Cain, G. 1966. *Married Women in the Labor Force.* Chicago: University of Chicago Press.

Macke, A. S.; Hudis, P. M.; and Larrick, D. 1978. Sex role attitudes and employment among women: dynamic models of continuity and change. In *Women's Changing Roles at Home and on the Job.* National Commission for Manpower Policy Special Report No. 26.

Mincer, J. 1962. Labor force participation of married women: a study of labor supply. In *Aspects of Labor Economics: A Report of the NBER*, ed. H. G. Lewis. Princeton, N.J.: Princeton University Press.

Mott, F. L. 1978. The National Longitudinal Surveys mature women's cohort: a socioeconomic overview. In *Women's Changing Roles at Home and on the Job.* National Commission for Manpower Policy Special Report No. 26.

Oaxaca, R. 1973. Sex discrimination in wages. In *Discrimination in Labor Markets*, ed. O. Ashenfelter and A. Rees. Princeton, N.J.: Princeton University Press.

Shaw, L. B. 1980. Changes in the work attachment of married women, 1966–1976. Paper presented at the annual meeting of the Population Association of America in Denver, Colorado.

Shaw, L. B., and O'Brien, T. 1981. An overview of changes in the lives of mature women, 1967–1977. In *Dual Careers: A Decade of Changes in the Lives of Mature Women*, ed. L. B. Shaw. Columbus, Ohio: Center for Human Resource Research, The Ohio State University.

Waite, L. J. 1979. Projecting female labor force participation from sex-role attitudes. In *Women in the Labor Force in 1990*, ed. R. E. Smith. Washington, D.C.: The Urban Institute.

Chapter 7

Marital Transitions and Employment

Frank L. Mott
and
Sylvia F. Moore

Except for spinsters and widows who were forced to seek employment for economic reasons, earlier generations of women limited their labor market participation to the years between school leaving and marriage. Because very few marriages in American society terminated for reasons other than death before the early 1900s, the need to seek employment due to a separation or divorce was not a major social or economic consideration. In contrast, divorce and a subsequent remarriage have now become relatively common events in American society. Perhaps 50 percent of young women marrying for the first time will divorce (Weed 1980), and the vast majority will ultimately remarry (U.S. Bureau of the Census 1977).

Partly because of the pervasiveness of this demographic fact and its obvious effect on the economic well-being of young women and their families, many academic and popular writers have focused in recent years on the relationships between changes in marital status and other social and economic events. In various ways, writers have considered whether or not divorced (and to a lesser extent remarried) women are perhaps different from other women. In addition, much attention has been paid to the significant economic traumas associated with marital disruption. Unfortunately, however, most of these studies have been based either on impressionistic evidence or, in the case of the academic literature, on cross-sections that allow comparisons only among women with different marital statuses at one point in time.

We have already documented many of the dramatic changes in women's attitudes and behaviors with respect to family and career. To some extent, we suggest links between these factors, always noting that the causal connections may reflect the process of fundamental social change rather than micro-level links between specific behaviors and attitudes. This chapter carries this philosophical orientation one step further, examining whether changes in marital status at the individual level of analysis are indeed linked to attitudes about the place of women in society. To what extent are marital transitions associated with overt and covert attitudes about employment and actual employment behaviors? Do a woman's ideas about work affect her likelihood of altering her marital status? Perhaps most important, does her employment history and behavior enable her to cope economically with marital transitions? The employment revolution may be central to women's behavior, both as a potential determinant of changes in marital status and as a necessary consequence of those changes.

The association between work attachment and marriage, divorce, and remarriage is quite complex. At the present time a substantial proportion of young women within a first marriage are employed. There is also some evidence that employment within a first marriage is associated with the likelihood of a subsequent marital breakdown. An employed woman dissatisfied with her marriage is in a better economic position to leave her spouse and form an independent family unit (Ross and Sawhill 1975; Mott and Moore 1979). In addition women who have divorced are frequently in need of steady employment in order to support themselves and their families. Following this temporal transition into subsequent life-cycle stages, there is considerable interest in the question of whether employment following a first marital breakdown is related to the likelihood of subsequent remarriage and to economic well-being within the second marriage. It is of some importance to consider whether or not women who remarry (or conversely do not remarry) differ from other women in terms of their demographic, social, and perhaps psychological attributes, because of the ability of a woman to succeed in the job market is closely correlated with her personal characteristics.

Historically women who divorced as well as those who remarried were a very small minority of the population; they followed a nonnormative behavior path and as such could be assumed to be different in many sociodemographic and psychological respects from other women. But today's greater social acceptability of divorce and the large proportion of women who now divorce and remarry lead us to hypothesize that the personal characteristics of divorcees and remarriers may be quite similar to those of other young women.

By the tenth year survey in 1978 the vast majority of the women in the NLS young women's data set had been married at least once; 360 of these divorced for the first time between 1968 and 1973 and thus had at least five postdivorce years as of the 1978 survey. This chapter follows these divorcing women from their first marriage into single life and, for the approximately 60 percent who remarry within five years of their divorce, into a second marriage. Do their personal characteristics contrast with those of women who divorce but do not remarry within five years and with those who are still within their first marriage as of 1978? Is earlier employment experience an important predictor of subsequent remarriage? To the extent that sample sizes permit, separate statistics for black and white young women will be presented.

Sociopsychological Differences between Nonremarriers and Remarriers

Because divorce and remarriage now affect large proportions of the young adult population, we hypothesize that attitudes about appropriate roles for women and behaviors of young women in the different marital statuses may be quite similar to each other. Such similarity would also suggest that aside from the temporary need for special income support sometimes associated with the loss of a spouse, there may not be any significant variations in employment probabilities for women in the different marital statuses.

The results presented in table 7.1 appear to support our initial hypothesis that young women in different marital situations have similar attitudes about the role of women. On only two of the eleven statements relating to women's roles do the once-married women indicate more traditional attitudes than their remarried counterparts, and both of these statements relate to employment. Nonremarrying and remarried women's attitudes differ substantially only on two items. Divorced but not remarried women are more likely to feel that a woman's place is in the home. They are also more likely to agree with the statement that "a working wife can establish just as warm and secure a relationship with her children as a mother who does not work" than their remarried counterparts. Of course this statement may partly represent a rationalization consistent with the fact that divorced nonremarried women must generally handle the home and work roles themselves. Despite these two attitude differences, the results generally support our hypothesis that sex-role attitudes will not differ significantly by marital status.

Shifting from attitudes to their behavioral manifestations, we see in table 7.2 the percentages of women by marital status who have the sole responsibility for different household tasks. While women in second marriages are in some instances less likely to have sole responsibility for certain tasks, the differences are clearly modest. Divorced women who have not remarried are more likely to have sole responsibility for grocery shopping and child care but are not more likely than remarried women to have sole responsibility for other household tasks.

Table 7.1
Attitudes toward women's roles for white women in 1978, by marital status

Attitude item	Percent agreeing with attitude		
	Married once by 1978	Married twice by 1978	Divorced in 1978 following first marriage
Modern conveniences permit a wife to work without neglecting her family	71.6	66.9*	75.3
A woman's place is in the home, not the office or shop	20.5	20.0	30.4
A wife who carries out her full family responsibilities does not have time for outside employment	16.5	18.4	17.6
A working wife feels more useful than one who does not have a job	45.0	54.9**	57.8
The employment of wives leads to juvenile delinquency	25.5	30.4	26.3
Employment of wives is necessary to keep up with the high cost of living	61.7	72.5**	75.0
It is much better for everyone concerned if the man is the achiever outside the home and the woman takes care of the home and family	36.2	38.2	37.8
Men should share the work around the home with women such as doing dishes, cleaning, and so forth	80.3	80.3*	87.5
A working wife can establish just as warm and secure a relationship with her children as a mother who does not work	81.8	76.5***	90.3
Women are much happier if they stay at home and take care of the children	18.3	21.8	18.4
A woman should not let bearing and rearing children stand in the way of a career if she wants it	78.0	79.9	82.9
Number of respondents	2,773	200	159

Note: These women have all been in a first marriage at least five years. They are the same women who were the married-spouse present (MSP) comparison group in our earlier divorce study and were still MSP in a first marriage in 1978. See Mott and Moore (1979).
* Married-twice group significantly different ($p \leq 0.05$) from divorced in 1978 group using one-tailed t test.
** Married-twice group significantly different ($p \leq 0.01$) from married-once group using one-tailed t test.
*** Married-twice group significantly different ($p \leq 0.01$) from divorced in 1978 group using one-tailed t test.

Table 7.2
Percentage of white women with sole responsibility for selected household tasks in 1978, by marital status

Household task	Percent with sole responsibility		
	Married once by 1978	Married twice by 1978	Divorced in 1978 following first marriage
Grocery shopping	67.0	64.7	73.7
Child care	30.0	35.6*	49.0
Cooking	72.3	64.4**	67.3
Cleaning dishes	60.1	57.6	54.3
Cleaning house	61.3	55.3	51.8
Washing	81.8	74.3	75.8
Number of respondents	2,109	160	93

* Married-twice group significantly different ($p \leq 0.01$) from divorced in 1978 group using one-tailed t test.
** Married-twice group significantly different ($p \leq 0.05$) from married-once group using one-tailed t test.

Their greater need to work full time may force them to draw more heavily on outside assistance to cope with household tasks. Thus in general no apparent major differences appear between women in the different marital statuses with regard to how they view their roles and how they distribute tasks within their own homes.

Transitions in Economic Well-Being

The period following a divorce can be difficult, reflecting a woman's loss of a husband's income and the greater probability that she will have the sole responsibility for her children. These difficulties are compounded for women who have limited employment skills and little knowledge about how to find jobs. We examine here the extent to which divorcing women encounter such problems and the speed with which they make adjustments, whether or not they remarry. It is virtually a truism that many women who remarry improve their general economic well-being; however, this is not to imply that divorced women choose a new partner in order to improve their economic status; that issue will be considered separately later.

The NLS data set enables us to follow the divorcing women from their first marriage through divorce and in many instances into a second marriage. Here we focus on a series of personal and family characteristics of the divorcees at several life-cycle points: two surveys before the divorce, one survey before the divorce, the first survey after the divorce, and the first survey following a remarriage.[1] For the nonremarriers we have a refer-ence point paralleling the remarriage point for the remarriers.[2]

Regardless of the proxy used for a young woman's eco-nomic resources, it is clear that prospective divorcees are in transition for some time preceding the divorce, probably be-cause they frequently separate in the year before the divorce. Regardless of remarriage status, mean family income gradually declines over the two-year interval preceding the divorce and is lowest in the first survey after divorce (table 7.3). Percent-ages of both remarriers and nonremarriers in poverty and re-ceiving welfare also increase over the period before divorce and are highest at the first survey after divorce. However, the percentages of nonremarriers in these two categories are ab-solutely higher than the percentages for remarriers at all sur-vey points. This absolute difference is due to the fact that those classified as nonremarriers are more likely to be black and to have their own children present in the household.[3] Not surprisingly the remarriers show a substantial improvement in family income at the first survey after remarriage, with a paral-lel decline in poverty status. The nonremarriers ultimately also show income improvement, reflecting their gradual adjustment

Table 7.3
Selected socioeconomic characteristics of remarriers and nonremarriers at points before and after a first divorce

Characteristic	Two surveys before divorce	One survey before divorce	First survey after divorce	First survey after remarriage[a]
Mean family income[b]				
Remarriers	8,250	6,945	5,663	7,496
Nonremarriers	8,008	6,793	5,610	5,876
Percent in poverty				
Remarriers	12.0	16.1	25.8	20.4
Nonremarriers	20.4	27.4	37.3	29.6
Percent on welfare				
Remarriers	7.0	15.8	20.6	17.4
Nonremarriers	12.4	16.5	28.5	29.1
Percent employed				
Remarriers	49.5	50.5	59.3	48.4
Nonremarriers	58.3	52.9	57.9	63.1
Number of divorcees	297	350	359	341

a. Or reference point for nonremarriers.
b. In 1977 dollars.

Table 7.4
Selected characteristics of the employed at points before and after divorce, by ultimate remarriage status

Characteristic	Two surveys before divorce	One survey before divorce	First survey after divorce	First survey after remarriage[a]
Mean hours worked				
Remarriers	15.8	18.3	21.4	16.8
Nonremarriers	18.6	19.0	20.4	24.1
Hourly rate of pay (1967 dollars)				
Remarriers	0.81	0.88	1.11	1.04
Nonremarriers	0.95	1.05	1.16	1.43
Weeks worked in year				
Remarriers	22.5	24.6	30.5	29.4
Nonremarriers	26.5	27.2	31.3	31.7
Bose occupational status score[b]				
Remarriers	41.6	41.7	43.2	43.5
Nonremarriers	43.0	42.9	45.0	45.8
Number of divorcees	297	350	359	347

a. Or reference point for nonremarriers.
b. The Bose Occupational Index is a status measure used to indicate a woman's relative position in the occupational hierarchy. Unlike the more widely used Duncan Index, it was developed with respect to female rather than male incumbents of census occupational categories. For further details, see Bose (1973).

to their new status. Whereas the overall percentage employed for the remarriers declines when they remarry, the percentage employed among the nonremarriers continues to increase.

A traditional hypothesis states that the chief labor force response of divorced women to diminished financial resources is either to enter the labor force or to increase the intensity of participation. Also according to the traditional view, women's financial resources increase if they remarry, thus reducing the intensity of their participation or permitting them to drop out of the labor force.

As expected upon remarriage women reduce their overall participation and the intensity of their participation (as measured by the number of hours per week worked) relative to those who remain divorced (see table 7.4). These remarriers have consistently lower wages and lower occupational status (as measured by the Bose index) than those who do not remarry. One economic explanation for these differences is that women who remarry do so in part because their potential wage is sufficiently low to make rapid remarriage an attractive alternative to trying to support their families on their earnings.

Even at a point two years preceding divorce, remarriers have lower employment rates and, among those who are employed, lower work intensities than those who do not remarry. This relatively weak attachment of remarriers may partly reflect greater financial resources available in their first marriages, as evidenced by their lower percentages on welfare and smaller percentages in poverty than in the families of nonremarriers. The sample group of divorcees may also include a subset of women who leave a marriage because of psychological pressures associated with their desire to follow a career. Such women are more likely to maintain a high level of labor force commitment while divorced and therefore will be less likely to remarry unless they can find a partner generally sympathetic with their long-term career intentions.

Is the Transition Status Permanent?

Because substantial proportions of women are already undergoing major changes in socioeconomic status at the last survey point before the divorce, it is useful to compare a woman's status as of the second survey before divorce with her status at the survey following divorce. To complete the data on the transition undergone by remarriers, these two points will be considered in conjunction with the first survey point after remarriage. Thus in table 7.5, "always" being in a particular status means that a woman is in that status at three points: at the second survey before divorce, the first survey after divorce, and the first survey after remarriage. "Never" being in a particular status implies the converse, and "sometimes" means the woman was in the status either at one or two points.

Overall about 29 percent of the remarriers are employed at three life-cycle points, and only a very small percentage are always on welfare or in poverty. Little racial difference appears in the percentages of remarriers who are always employed, though black remarriers are much more likely than their white counterparts to be on welfare or in poverty at all three points. Part of the explanation for their greater poverty lies in the fact that black women have over a 60 percent higher likelihood of

Table 7.5
Status continuity between survey points within first marriage, between first and second marriage, and within second marriage, by race (percentage distribution)

	All remarrying women		
Status	Total	Whites	Blacks
Employed			
Always	28.9	28.9	32.4
Sometimes	46.4	46.9	46.5
Never	24.7	24.2	21.1
On welfare			
Always	2.5	1.9	11.2
Sometimes	26.4	26.4	54.9
Never	70.9	71.7	33.9
In poverty			
Always	3.4	1.7	23.5
Sometimes	33.3	33.5	30.2
Never	63.3	64.8	46.3
With own children present			
Always	50.2	48.6	80.7
Sometimes	21.7	21.6	13.2
Never	28.1	29.8	6.1
Number of remarriers	200	160	40

Note: "Always" refers to having status (1) at second to last survey preceding divorce, (2) at first survey after divorce, and (3) at first survey after remarriage (or at reference interview for nonremarriers). "Never" refers to respondents who did not have status at any of the three points, and "sometimes" refers to the residual respondents.

having children continuously present in the household. Only 6 percent of the black remarriers never had children present in the household at any point surveyed during the transition process from first to second marriage.

It is important to emphasize the transitional nature of the divorced status for many of these remarrying women. While about 75 percent of the remarriers are employed at least at one of the three life-cycle points, only about 7 percent are employed only at the transition point between marriages. In other words the extent of overall employment attributed directly to being divorced is minuscule. Similarly while about 37 percent of the remarriers are in poverty during at least one of the three survey points, only about 12 percent are in poverty only while divorced. Analogous percentages for those on welfare are 29 percent and 4 percent, respectively. These figures indicate that caution should be exercised before attributing changes in socioeconomic status entirely to the divorcee's marital status.[4] The vast majority of the women who remarry and/or are employed, in poverty, or on welfare are also in those statuses either before they leave their first marriage or after they enter their second marriage. The relative universality (or conversely absence) of these factors among subsets of women suggests that they may not be useful predictors of either divorce or remarriage.

Theories of Remarriage

Research focusing on the various social, economic, and psychological causes for the breakup of a marriage is quite extensive. Despite this relative wealth of literature, no generally accepted theory of the determinants of divorce has evolved. The economics literature has come the closest to evolving a testable theory of its causes (Becker, Landes, and Michael 1977). Economic factors hypothesized to cement a marriage are termed income effects, while those hypothesized to contribute to marital disintegration are termed independence effects. Such factors as a husband's high earnings or substantial unearned income will tend to create a disincentive for a woman to separate, while high potential personal earnings or access to significant personal assets may provide encouragement to leave an unsatisfactory marriage (Ross and Sawhill 1975; Mott and Moore 1979; Cherlin 1977; Hampton 1975; Becker, Landes, and Michael 1977).

The problems with respect to research on divorce determinants are even more severe when the focus is on remarriage characteristics. Unlike divorce the impact of remarriage on the American family structure is just beginning to receive attention despite the overwhelming numbers of young (and for that matter, older) women who experience the event. Just as little media attention has been given to remarriage, little theoretical or empirical research has been done on its social, economic, and psychological determinants or consequences.

Only a few researchers, particularly economists, have attempted to develop a theory to explain the determinants of remarriage. In the sparse literature on the subject, these determinants are frequently depicted at least partly as the mirror images of the determinants of divorce. Factors that encourage a person to leave one marriage are frequently hypothesized to be the same factors that will inhibit entry into a new marriage.

129

And those factors that deter a person from leaving a bad marriage will tend to promote a quick remarriage (Becker, Landes, and Michael 1977).

According to the remarriage theory, the feeling of economic independence that creates an incentive for a woman to leave a "bad" marriage also reduces the likelihood that she will remarry because there are fewer gains from the marriage. These economists assume a dichotomy between marriage and a career. For low-wage women, the chief gain from a marriage is the ability to stay home, raise the children, and generally maintain the home. Such women will seek out a high-wage partner whose potential earnings are sufficiently high for her to expect that she will be able to become or remain a housewife. The high-wage or "career" woman, on the other hand, will have little incentive to marry unless she decides to search for a low-wage husband who will be willing to pick up the household duties.[5]

This theory (of both divorce and remarriage) tends to ignore the possibility that marriage and a job outside the home can function as complements rather than substitutes. Recent literature in psychology and the popular press talks about the drive among today's young women to combine marriage, career, and family. From such a perspective there is no reason to assume that a career woman has any less desire to be married than one oriented toward becoming or remaining a housewife.

As Jessie Bernard points out, the need for financial support is only one of the many reasons for a divorced or widowed individual to desire remarriage. Many personal, social, and psychological factors such as love, loneliness, habit, or the desire for stability may stimulate remarriage. External pressures from one's family or friends or the need for peer status may inhibit or promote the idea of remarriage (Bernard 1956).

Remarriage on the part of the woman requires a willing partner. There must be opportunities for meeting and courting prospective spouses, and community and family pressures may inhibit or encourage the process of meeting such individuals. Positive personal characteristics such as attractiveness, health status, and emotional stability will tend to increase the number of potential offers. Existing theory ignores the possibility that the women who are most eager to remarry from an economic standpoint, due to few job skills, low job commitment, or little personal income, may face fewer marriage offers because they are less attractive to potential spouses than are women who have more economic independence.

The reasons why individuals decide to marry are extensive and complex, involving a mix of economic and psychological factors, some of which are idiosyncratic. Most research has focused on economic and demographic factors at least in part because these types of variables are the easiest to quantify. Variables that attempt to proxy for the psychological attributes of the individual and his or her family are far more difficult to quantify.

Predicting the Tempo of Remarriage

The vast majority of young adult women who divorce ultimately remarry. The relevant questions to be answered are, How quickly do these women remarry? and What are the significant predictors of the speed with which this process occurs? The tempo of remarriage is estimated by a series of remarriage probability models with different durations since divorce.

Proxies for the young woman's potential earned income that may influence the timing of remarriage include a variable measuring her employment status at the survey following the divorce and whether she is employed full time or part time at the same survey point. We hypothesize, as do other researchers, that greater work intensity will be associated with a greater degree of economic independence and therefore with a lower probability of remarriage. Another proxy for an independence effect is the extent of the young woman's work experience since leaving school, hypothesized to be negatively correlated with remarriage probabilities. Finally a variable measuring the woman's educational attainment is included as a more fundamental proxy for career commitment. Education is expected to be negatively correlated with remarriage, according to existing economic literature on the subject. The inclusion of the proxy for career commitment should offer a good test of the concept that career and marriage more often function as substitutes rather than complements.

The existence of nonportable unearned income (that is, income that a woman cannot take with her into a new marriage) is proxied by measures of whether the divorcee was receiving welfare at the survey after her divorce and whether she perceives her financial situation to have improved, remained the same, or deteriorated since she left her first marriage. Both a theoretical and empirical literature suggests that access to welfare income is negatively associated with the probability of remarriage (Hutchens 1979).[6] Welfare, if viewed as a form of "nonportable" income, will act as an independence effect, creating an incentive for the woman not to remarry. Presumably a woman who perceives her financial situation to have been improved by a divorce will be more reluctant to remarry than her counterpart who cites a deterioration in her economic position over the same period.

We also include a measure of a woman's satisfaction with her job by distinguishing those women who were satisfied with their work at the survey following the divorce from those who were dissatisfied with their jobs at the same point. We hypothesize that women who are satisfied with their jobs will have less need to seek alternative satisfaction through remarriage than those who are unhappy with their work.

Since we also seek to ascertain whether a career commitment operates independently of the economic necessity of working, we include a measure of whether each woman was employed at the point of her first marriage. The direction of this variable with regard to the timing of remarriage is not clear. If marriage and career function chiefly as substitutes, then this variable should be negatively associated with quick remarriage. If, however, they can function as complements as well, their complementarity should diminish the significance of the hypothesized negative relationship.

Shifting away from the economic perspective, we find that certain demographic factors are also seen as impediments to a quick remarriage. The presence of a child in the home traditionally has been viewed as a deterrent to seeking a new spouse, both because a child increases a woman's cost of time spent in such a search as well as reduces her attractiveness as a potential mate (Becker, Landes, and Michael 1977). On the other hand, recent empirical research using panel data has produced disparate results, with the relationship being found to be sensitive to the age of the divorced woman. For divorced women in the age range 25 to 30, other recent research found no significant association between the presence of children and remarriage probabilities (Ross and Sawhill 1975; Hannan, Tuma, and Grueneveld 1977; Koo and Suchindian 1980). The presence of a health problem is presumed to make it more difficult for a woman to engage in a search for a new husband and to reduce the number of potential partners. Women whose first marriage was of relatively long duration are hypothesized to be more marriage oriented and therefore more likely to begin to search fairly quickly after a divorce or even before the divorce for a new spouse (Becker, Landes, and Michael 1977). Finally the age of the divorcee at the time of divorce should be negatively associated with the probability of remarriage, although the fairly narrow age range of our divorcee cohort may negate the potential significance of this variable.

Two other factors are considered to affect the timing of the remarriage. First, women who come from a stable family background (as measured by having lived with both parents at age 14) are hypothesized to search more quickly for a new spouse than their counterparts who do not have such role models.[7] Second, living in a rural environment is hypothesized to be associated with relatively quick remarriage due to few life-style alternatives and a more traditional value structure.[8]

Our method is to regress the probability of remarriage within one, two, three, four, and five years on the list of variables as described (see appendix to chapter 7 for a complete specification of the variables). The longitudinal data set permits examination of the changing importance of these variables as the time since divorce increases and the percentage of divorced young women who have remarried rises. The multivariate technique employed is multiple classification analysis (MCA), a form of regression analysis using dummy variables. With the MCA technique, a determination is made for each category within a given independent variable, of the proportion of women who have remarried, assuming that members of that category have an average value on all other variables included in the model. The dependent variable is dichotomous with a value of 1 given to those young women who divorced between 1968 and 1973 and who remarried within five, four, three, two, or one years of divorce, respectively, and a value of zero if the respondent did not remarry within the same time period.

The full models and a complete specification of the variables can be found in appendix tables 7A.2 and 7A.3 and appendix 7A, respectively. Here the focus will be on a series of graphs (figure 7.1), which indicate the independent (holding all other characteristics constant) effect of certain sociodemographic

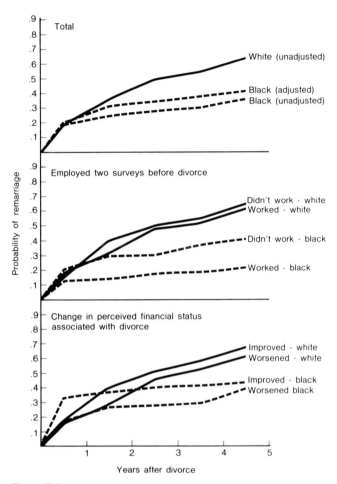

Figure 7.1
Adjusted probabilities of remarriage for selected characteristics, by race

and economic variables on the probability of remarriage as the duration since divorce increases. Thus the remarriage percentages given in these figures are adjusted, where the assumption in each trend line is that the women are average on all other characteristics.

Although white and black women remarry at the same rate in the year after divorce, their patterns subsequently diverge. By five years after the divorce, over 60 percent of the white but only about one-third of the black women have remarried. Only about one-third of the racial difference reflects measurable differences in the characteristics included in the

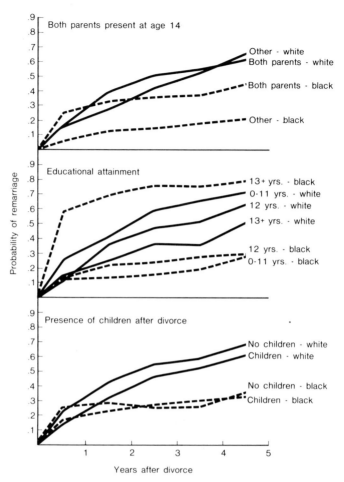

.9 — Both parents present at age 14
.8
.7   Other - white
.6   Both parents - white
.5
.4   'Both parents - black
.3
.2   Other - black
.1

.9
.8 — Educational attainment
.7   13+ yrs. - black
.6   0-11 yrs. - white
.5   12 yrs. - white
.4   13+ yrs. - white
.3   12 yrs. - black
.2   0-11 yrs. - black
.1

.9
.8 — Presence of children after divorce
.7   No children - white
.6   Children - white
.5
.4   No children - black
.3   Children - black
.2
.1

     1   2   3   4   5

Years after divorce

Figure 7.1 (continued)
Adjusted probabilities of remarriage for selected characteristics by race

model. Figure 7.1 documents these continuing racial disparities in remarriage rates for the specific characteristics under
consideration.

Looking first at the economic factors, we see that white
women with extensive work experience do not remarry any
less frequently than their less experienced counterparts, at
least in the first three years after divorce. By five years after
divorce, white women with extensive work experience are
somewhat less likely to have remarried, thus showing a modest independence effect. On the other hand, black women
with more than three years of experience are much more likely
to have remarried than those without such experience. This

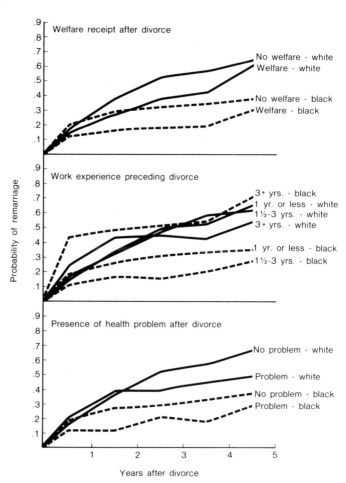

Figure 7.1 (continued)
Adjusted probabilities of remarriage for selected characteristics by race

pattern is established at the first survey after divorce and continues through the entire five years, although after the first year little change appears in the remarriage gap between women in different work experience categories.

Among the black divorcees the differences in remarriage probabilities between those with and without extensive work experience lie in the extremely high remarriage rate during the first year after divorce for those with extensive work experience. But the timing of remarriage with respect to this characteristic is not constant across the years after the divorce: in fact the work experience variable has predictive value only in the first postdivorce year. Research that examined long-term remarriage probabilities would completely miss this key point.

Both white and black women who receive welfare income after divorce are less likely to have remarried, but not to a statistically significant degree. However, the explanatory relevance of this factor also diminishes for both races as the period since divorce lengthens.

Among white women education appears to be a fairly good proxy for the potential wage rate. As we hypothesized, women with less education are much more likely to remarry, and lower education is particularly powerful in predicting rapid remarriage. Among black women, however, the direction of the relationship between education and the probability of remarriage is exactly reversed: more education leads to significantly higher remarriage rates. After the first survey point, however, the remarriage rates by education parallel each other, indicating once again that the predictive value of the variable rests in its utility for predicting quick remarriages.

The attitudes of black divorcees as to their financial status after their divorce is also a significant predictor of remarriage, though the significance of this variable is confined to those who have remarried by the first survey after the divorce. Black women who stated at this point that their financial status had improved since the divorce were much more likely to have remarried. In contrast, for white divorcees the variable has no significance.

A variable measuring predivorce employment status was included to proxy for career commitment independent of economic need. For white divorcees this variable has no significance at any postdivorce point. Among blacks our career commitment hypothesis appears to be borne out: at all postdivorce points, women who were not working during their first marriage (at least at the point at which they were surveyed) were more likely to have remarried. By five years after divorce the adjusted remarriage rate for those who were not working before their divorce is almost 20 percentage points above the rate for their working counterparts.

Moving away from the economic characteristics to demographic and sociological factors, we find mixed results. The presence of children in the home is not a significant predictor of remarriage, a finding consistent with other recent evidence. The exception is that white women with children are more likely to have remarried by the first postdivorce point. Health problems do appear to deter remarriage for white women as the time since the divorce increases, but among blacks health problems show no effect. Finally the fact that a divorced woman lived with both parents when she was age 14 had significant positive effects on her remarriage chances only if she was black and then only with regard to remarrying or not within the first year.

Other variables produce mixed significance levels among white and black divorcees (see appendix tables 7A.2 and 7A.3). No significant difference appears among white women in remarriage rates between women with first marriages of short and longer duration. In contrast among black women the duration of first marriage has a significant effect on the re-marriage rate, but the direction is counter to what has been hypothesized. Black women whose first marriages were short-lived had by the end of five years an adjusted remarriage rate almost 20 percentage points higher than their longer married counterparts.

Living in a nonurban area appears to be immediately condu-cive to remarriage for white women and to a lesser extent for black women. But for both groups, this rural effect becomes significant in the later postdivorce years, consistent with the relatively limited life-style options available outside of metro-politan areas. Finally among white women, working and being dissatisfied with one's job appears to be significantly corre-lated with remarriage in the later years after divorce.

In summary, the results presented in Table 7.6 indicate that the capability of the socioeconomic and demographic variables chosen to predict the tempo of remarriage for our sample of young women is limited. Results vary significantly depending on the postdivorce survey period being analyzed.

The models for white young women, regardless of the time period surveyed, were generally statistically insignificant.[9] However, examination of the separate models does provide some clarification of the relative importance of the chosen so-cioeconomic and demographic characteristics on predicting the timing of the remarriage. For example, the presence of chil-dren, low education, and not being employed appear to be useful predictors of a quick remarriage (most likely indicating that the search for a new spouse had occurred during the first marriage). On the other hand, the urbanness of the woman's residence and her health status become significant predictors of remarriage as the number of years since the divorce increase.

For black women the importance of examining the timing of remarriage is even more stark. The only model with any predictive value is the one predicting a very quick remarriage, within the first year after divorce. The models predicting remarriage after this first postdivorce year are included only to portray their striking contrast in predictive power. One hypothesis to explain the contrast in the statistical significance of the two models is that black women who remarry quickly represent a selected population who in many instances have already made the remarriage decision before or at the time of the divorce. Support for this hypothesis is seen in the characteristics of this population: high education, improved financial status after divorce, a stable childhood, and being employed before the divorce.

Conclusions

The relatively low predictive power of the remarriage models in this study points out once again that economic factors are only one of the reasons why people remarry. It is more difficult to create effective proxies for such personal and psychological demand factors as love, loneliness, the desire for stability, and pressure from family and/or friends, all of which may be contributing factors. On the supply side, the availability of potential spouses may be inhibited or expanded by factors such as community pressures, attractiveness, and emotional stability. Some characteristics promoting remarriage from either the demand or supply side will be idiosyncratic. Most research has focused on a limited number of economic and demographic variables, either because of quantification problems with other variables or because of the limited nature of the data set. Most surveys are not very successful at reaching the psychological characteristics of an individual; even when such questions are included, quantification is difficult.

This study finds no relationship between the tempo of remarriage and many of the easily quantifiable socioeconomic and demographic factors. Data limitations may not be the cause of our lack of success; rather, as is congruent with our original hypothesis, there may be no major measurable socioeconomic and demographic differences between divorced women who remarry and those who do not. The general

Table 7.6
Adjusted remarriage probabilities for selected time intervals following
a first divorce, by race

	White	
	1–5 years after divorce	First year after divorce
Children		
Yes	0.683	0.222
No	0.614	0.144
Education		
Under 12	0.713**	0.258**
12	0.628	0.118
13 and over	0.515	0.156
Ln marriage		
Low	0.635	0.191
High	0.650	0.138
Divorce age		
Under 20	0.670	0.286
20–23	0.669	0.158
24–26	0.597	0.133
27 and over	0.612	0.209
SMSA		
No	0.735**	0.150
Yes	0.591	0.185
Financial improvement		
Better	0.675	0.179
Same	0.617	0.181
Worse	0.602	0.156
Hours worked and satisfied		
Not working	0.640	0.251**
Working/dissatisfied	0.778	0.050
Satisfied/part time	0.645	0.206
Satisfied/full time	0.624	0.094
Health problem		
Yes	0.670**	0.173
No	0.485	0.216
Lived with 2 parents		
No	0.669	0.175
Yes	0.631	0.173

2–5 years after divorce	Black		
	1–5 years after divorce	First year after divorce	2–5 years after divorce
0.461	0.362	0.263	0.099
0.470	0.348	0.169	0.179
0.455	0.280***	0.122***	0.157
0.509	0.291	0.123	0.168
0.360	0.794	0.578	0.218
0.444	0.432**	0.205	0.228**
0.509	0.226	0.143	0.082
0.382	0.295	0.300	−0.005*
0.511	0.293	0.198	0.095
0.463	0.402	0.181	0.221
0.404	0.375	0.071	0.304
0.585***	0.514	0.287	0.227
0.406	0.317	0.159	0.158
0.496	0.431	0.335***	0.095
0.436	0.269	0.055	0.213
0.445	0.395	0.171	0.224
0.389***	0.388	0.263	0.125
0.730	0.533	0.107	0.426
0.438	0.472	0.116	0.356
0.530	0.258	0.096	0.161
0.497**	0.366	0.201	0.165
0.268	0.288	0.121	0.167
0.494	0.215**	0.060***	0.155
0.459	0.444	0.264	0.180

141

Table 7.6 (continued)

	White	
	1–5 years after divorce	First year after divorce
Welfare receipt		
No	0.647	0.182
Yes	0.615	0.140
Worked predivorce		
No	0.650	0.153
Yes	0.614	0.178
Work experience		
1 year or less	0.649	0.156
1½–3 years	0.631	0.175
3½ years or more	0.544	0.256
Adjusted R^2	0.024	0.035
F–ratio	1.264	1.394
Number of respondents	238	238

* Significant at 0.10 level.
** Significant at 0.05 level.
*** Significant at 0.01 level.

social acceptability of divorce and remarriage makes both status changes readily accessible to most people who desire to change status (sooner or later) for a wide range of highly idiosyncratic and individualistic reasons, which we have not measured here. We predict that future remarriage studies that focus on the standard range of factors will also be unsuccessful in predicting at the disaggregated level.

The lack of predictive value in our overall models leads to some general conclusions. First, in the media as well as in the academic literature the prevailing tendency is to portray transitions such as divorce or remarriage as unique and traumatic events in one's life cycle. Employment during marriage is increasingly the norm among younger women in American society. Few of these women appear to work solely because they are in a transition status, either divorced or separated. Similarly poverty and welfare are not unique to these marital transition periods. Very few of our sample of remarried women are in poverty or on welfare only between marriages. Rather poverty and welfare tend to represent a continuous status for a certain subset of these young women. In sum there is little demon-

2–5 years after divorce	Black		
	1–5 years after divorce	First year after divorce	2–5 years after divorce
0.465	0.371	0.211	0.160
0.474	0.313	0.126	0.186
0.498	0.408***	0.199	0.210**
0.435	0.216	0.125	0.091
0.493	0.353	0.193	0.160
0.457	0.282	0.109	0.173
0.289	0.722	0.438	0.285
0.027	0.174	0.285	−0.160
1.295	1.873**	2.647***	0.428
238	92	92	92

strated evidence that the marriage or remarriage event is used as a mechanism for economic improvement.

Second, in the study of life-cycle transitions of younger women, the research issue of principal interest should be the timing of the remarriage rather than overall probability of remarriage. Our research clearly indicates that the particular postdivorce point in time being analyzed significantly alters the sensitivity of remarriage probabilities to (at least) the socioeconomic and demographic variables we have chosen.

Finally caution should be exercised in generalizing about any relationship between more liberal ideas regarding the role of women and divorce or remarriage likelihoods. Commonplace phenomena are not represented only by a particular substrata within the society. Our results on the attitudes of the remarriers and nonremarriers toward the appropriate roles for women as well as toward their household behavior patterns are clearly consistent with the observation that societal views are changing across the board. Although the general liberalizing of American society has contributed to changing mores regarding marriage and divorce, it is frequently unwise to transfer these societal-level generalizations to individual actions and differences.

Notes

The authors thank Nan Maxwell for her excellent research assistance.

1. In many respects, a postdivorce point two surveys following divorce would have been preferable because it would have provided a socioeconomic situation more typical of the divorced state; however, by that survey point about one-third of the divorcees had already remarried and attained the socioeconomic status associated with remarriage. Thus the results would have been difficult to interpret.

2. In order to compare the remarriers at a "post-second marriage" point, we constructed a reference group of nonremarriers by assigning the nonremarriers "reference years" in proportion to the distribution of first post-second marriage year for the remarriers. For example about 20 percent of the remarriers were remarried by the first survey after divorce, so 20 percent of the nonremarrying sample were randomly assigned the first post-divorce survey as their reference year, and so on. This methodology is detailed extensively in the appendix to chapter 7.

3. Only 35 percent of black divorcees have remarried by the end of five years as compared with 60 percent of the whites. In addition 90 percent of black women have a child present in the home at the first survey after the divorce, as compared with about two-thirds of the white women.

4. A cautionary note: the interview point in the first marriage is approximately one and a half years before the divorce. To the extent that the divorcing women are already separated at that point, the economic well-being of the women in their first marriage may be understated.

5. The high-wage husband, on the other hand, will be expected to seek out a low-wage partner who will relieve him of household responsibilities. Correspondingly a low-wage husband will presumably remarry an even lower wage woman or a high-wage woman whose potential earning power would allow him to remain in the home.

6. Hutchens tests the notion that public assistance, by focusing payments on families without husbands, can promote marital separations and discourage remarriage. His results appear to confirm his hypothesis. The general relationship between the existence of welfare assistance, particularly Aid for Dependent Children, and female headedness has been addressed by Ross and Sawhill (1975), Honig (1974), and Duncan (1976).

7. This hypothesis stems from work done on intergenerational transmission of marital dissolution propensities as seen in the work of Mueller and Pope (1977). Empirical work provided partial support for the idea that parental marital instability leads to "high-risk" mate selection outcomes for their children, resulting in higher dissolution rates of their first marriages.

8. In our preliminary runs, a series of variables measuring the woman's sex-role attitudes were included, but they were insignificant in all cases.

9. The intervening models for the first two, three, and four years since divorce are somewhat more satisfactory; see appendix table 7A.2.

References

Becker, G. E.; Landes, E.; and Michael, R. 1977. An economic analysis of marital instability. *Journal of Political Economy* 85:1141–1187.

Bernard, J. 1956. *Remarriage.* New York: Dryden Press.

Bose, C. 1973. *Jobs and Gender: Sex and Occupational Prestige.* Baltimore, Md.: Johns Hopkins Press.

Cherlin, A. 1977. The effect of children on marital dissolution. *Demography* 14:265–272.

Duncan, G. 1976. Unmarried heads of households and marriage. In *Five Thousand American Families—Patterns of Economic Progress IV.* Ann Arbor: Institute for Social Research.

Hampton, R. 1975. Marital disruption: some social and economic consequences. In *Five Thousand American Families—Patterns of Economic Progress III.* Ann Arbor: Institute for Social Research.

Hannan, M. T.; Tuma, N. B.; and Grueneveld, L. P. 1977. Income and marital effects: evidence from an income maintenance experiment. *American Journal of Sociology* 82:1185–2121.

Honig, M. 1974. AFDC income, recipient rates, and family dissolution. *Journal of Human Resources* 11:303–323.

Hutchens, R. 1979. Welfare, remarriage and marital search. *American Economic Review* 69:369–379.

Koo, H., and Suchindian, C. M. 1980. Effects of children on women's remarriage prospects. *Journal of Family Issues* 1:497–515.

Mott, F. L., and Moore, S. F. 1979. The causes of marital disruption among American women: an interdisciplinary perspective. *Journal of Marriage and the Family* 41:355–365.

Mueller, C., and Pope, H. 1977. Marital instability: a study of its transmission between generations. *Journal of Marriage and the Family* 39:83–92.

Ross, H., and Sawhill, I. 1975. *Time of Transition.* Washington, D.C.: The Urban Institute.

Weed, J. A. 1980. National estimates of marriage, dissolution and survivorship. *Vital and Health Statistics*, Series 3, DHHS Publications: No. PHS81-1403, Table A:5.

U.S. Bureau of the Census. 1977. Marriage, divorce, widowhood, and remarriage by family characteristics: June, 1975. *Population Characteristics*, Series P-20, No. 312: 8–9.

Chapter 8

Summary and Conclusions

Frank L. Mott

Changing female work behavior has been intimately inter-twined with changes in how both men and women view the roles of women in society. Women now work more outside the home because it is considered more acceptable and appro-priate for them to do so. Conversely work is viewed by most Americans as more appropriate than it was only a few years ago because paying jobs are now seen by more Americans as psychologically and economically profitable for many women, just as they are for men. In this book we have tried to provide insights into why women choose to work outside the home beyond the approaches usually considered in standard eco-nomic analyses, as most prior empirical research has been rather narrowly focused on economic considerations. Here we have tried to document how the motivations for women's work are much more complex. Currently the motivations be-hind the propensity of women to work or not work are far more complicated than those of men. While the times may be changing, they have not yet changed enough so that an adult male can choose a nonmarket adult life-style unless he is will-ing to risk being held in low esteem by many of his male and female peers. Nonwork activity by adult males is reflexively as-sumed to be nonnormative behavior; if a man is not working, it is assumed that he cannot get a job.

In contrast many women have the option to work or not work because societal norms have shifted toward an almost universal acceptance of women working outside the home. Given the optional nature of employment for many women, the motivations behind their work activity are far more diffuse. Quite a few work because that is the only way they can, with or without spouse, keep their family income above the poverty line. Others work because they are striving to move their families into the socioeconomic mainstream; for the funds essential to purchase a home, educate a child in a way they prefer, or gain access to the wide variety of tangible and intangible assets or commodities they view as desirable. At the other extreme some women work just for the sheer plea-sure of the work, which derives from characteristics intrinsic to the job itself or other prestige or status dimensions associated with the employment. Most women who work do so for a vari-ety of reasons that overlap the above motivations as well as others not considered here; economic motivations are important but obviously not the only rationale for seeking market work.

The motivations for female employment at the individual level encompass economic factors, sociopsychological considerations, and demographics. All these interact with and are effectively constrained by the social structure in which we operate. Most research on female labor force participation has emphasized the economic factors because they are theoretically more developed than other areas of female labor force research and because they have been the easiest to quantify.

Several chapters in this book consider from a multidisciplinary perspective the factors that impinge on women's attitudes toward work and their work behavior. While traditional neoclassical labor supply theory certainly clarifies in important ways how economic considerations affect a woman's propensity to be employed, it does not permit a holistic interpretation. Not all women react to the same stimuli in the same way. Family income levels, a woman's acquired or potential job skills, and her family situation all affect whether she will choose to participate in the marketplace. However, women's responses to these economic factors depend on how they have been conditioned by family background, social environment, and immediate family. Although the available data have not permitted consideration of all aspects of these factors that affect female market work, we have been able to consider somewhat more broadly the motivations behind female employment. For example, two women may have the same economic stimulus but respond in different manners because of psychological constraints related to how their parents, friends, spouse, or children feel about their being in or out of the home.

The extent to which the changing employment profile of the young adult female population has been paralleled by a dramatic demographic transition was highlighted in chapter 1. In recent years young women on average have been staying in school longer, marrying later, and beginning childbearing at much later ages than was true for their mothers' generation. Although these demographic changes have not coincided precisely with the increases in female labor force participation, they have generally paralleled each other. Whereas female employment has been gradually increasing since the 1950s, the average age at first marriage and first birth was declining during the first half of the period before beginning its precipitous rise to current levels. Thus the demographic and economic forces have reinforced each other in recent years. Several of our analyses suggest that any causal links between employment and fertility behavior (except for the obvious cross-sectional association between current work activity and the presence or absence of a small child in the home) are tenuous. This partly reflects the gradual fertility transition from one in which three children were common to one in which two children are the norm. Although a significant number of women are choosing childless or one-child marriages, the dominant pattern remains a desire for two children regardless of whatever plans a couple may have for their own lives. The principal variation in American fertility behavior at this time is in when women will have these children rather than if they have them.

What perhaps needs greater attention is the extent to which women are following life courses that differ from the traditional norms. Substantial proportions of women marry before finally completing their schooling. This trend has major social implications because it implies that permanent attachments are being formed at a life-cycle stage when values, particularly those relating to family and career, are still in flux. This trend undoubtedly has constrained many female (and perhaps male) careers and may well be a contributor to the recent escalation in divorce rates, although it has diminished somewhat in recent years as the average age at marriage has risen. The increase in the average marriage age has not only contributed to the fertility decline but also has enabled increasing proportions of women to gain a foothold on their careers before beginning their families. This career orientation by more women is associated with a delay in the entry into motherhood; more important it permits more rational life-style decisions to be made by young couples before they are faced with parenthood.

Although many women work outside the home, a large proportion still do not, at least while they have small children; if 40 percent of women with children below school age are in the labor force, 60 percent are not. From a philosophical perspective one should consider the social, psychological, and economic implications for society of the fact that for several generations in postindustrial America, women who wished to have jobs outside the home frequently did not because of pressure from family, friends, peers, and the society at large. Indeed these pressures still operate for many women, however, our society may now be in transition to a situation in which increasing numbers of women who do not wish to work may feel pressured into doing so. Here we will not belabor the possible costs and benefits of such a transition, but it certainly heralds major changes in how the average American adolescent can approach his or her adult role responsibilities.

In a society in as great a flux as ours, role conflict situations are inevitable for many people. Institutions such as schools, churches, and youth service organizations cannot solve these problems, but they can help youth enter adulthood better prepared emotionally to make rational decisions consistent with his or her family and vocational tendencies and needs. Schools can provide vocational skills and knowledge, and, as importantly, can condition youth to evaluate openly biases about their own gender and the opposite sex and encourage them to examine the implications of different family and career orientations for likely personal, family, and career success. As youth approach adulthood, their ideas about family and career and the balance between the two frequently undergo radical transformations, so it is profitable for them to keep life-style options open for as long as they can and to follow an educational path that leaves maximum flexibility.

In chapter 2 we matched records of brothers and sisters to show how family background can work for or against educational or early career success. Traditionally young men in American society have had a major advantage in progressing through the educational system in terms of the variety of programs to which they had access as well as the level of education that they usually could complete. This sex difference in education has narrowed in recent years, but a gap still remains. We examined the extent to which this sex bias reflects certain differences emanating from the family. First, our data imply that the major educational handicap girls face is getting into college; once in college they compete effectively against their peers of the opposite sex. We also found that parental encouragement, independent of family size, parental education, and a number of other explanatory factors, is an important predictor of educational success. Undoubtedly reflecting societal influences, youth tend to gain special advantage when they are encouraged by a parent of the same sex to continue their education.

This socialization influence is also manifested in the substantial differences between boys and girls in how much education they want to complete. Regardless of parental education or encouragement, young men are more likely to want to attend and complete college than are their sisters. Although young women in some family situations have greater goals than others, in no situation does a young woman have an absolute advantage over her male counterpart. In fact in families where the girl perceives more educational encouragement than her brother, she is still less likely to attend or complete college than her brother. The apparent advantage that a daughter can receive from a parent is not sufficient to overcome all the other institutional forces that favor the young man.

Aside from the extent to which these family influences directly impinge on educational progress, we also have evidence that this parental encouragement perhaps has broader vocational implications. Young women who receive considerable parental encouragement from their mothers not only receive some educational advantage but, independent of this educational edge, are more likely (as of age 24) to expect to be working as of age 35 and are more likely than their female counterparts to expect to be employed in less-traditional occupations. Thus parental encouragement can have a more generalized payoff in terms of a woman's adult life intentions.

Chapter 3 more directly tests the link between a woman's family and work intentions and behaviors and how this linkage reflects her earlier experience. This chapter examines young women's fertility intentions in 1973 and changes in fertility intentions between 1973 and 1978 it finds that intentions are sensitive to both economic and noneconomic considerations when viewed in the aggregate. That is, white married women are more likely to expect fewer children and more likely to reduce their fertility intentions between 1973 and 1978 if they have more extensive prior employment. However, an important caveat accompanying this finding is that when the models are disaggregated by the number of children present in 1973, changes in fertility intentions are sensitive to prior work experience only for those women who already have two or more children. This is additional strong presumptive evidence that the work-fertility interaction becomes significant only at the life-cycle point where normative fertility behavior has already been accomplished. Societal pressures still encourage most women to meet the two-child norm, and it appears that true freedom of choice for many women in work versus family options occurs only after this normative constraint has been met.

Chapter 3 also provides evidence that white women who had more liberalized views about appropriate roles for women prior to 1973 were more likely to revise their fertility intentions downward. Thus in addition to the direct effect on family values implied by a prior work orientation, women who had earlier evidenced ideas consistent with the notion that their life-style should incorporate more than just the home were later more likely to verbalize reduced fertility desires.

There is also some evidence that only after two children have been born is a respondent's earnings potential, as measured by her education, associated with downward revisions in fertility intentions. Apparently the increasing realism about the need for more income and the desire for a diversified life-style clashes with desires for a large family only at that point. This finding is consistent with evidence from other research that shows how a woman's future work intentions increase substantially after she has had children, in comparison with less desire for life-long work before children have been born.

The need for including both economic and noneconomic orientations in evaluating women's work motivations is clarified more directly in chapter 4, which combines data from mother-daughter pairs. This chapter examines the determinants of young women's labor supply in 1977, including as explanatory factors both the usual neoclassical labor supply explanatory variables as well as additional information about how the young women's mothers themselves viewed work activity. We assume that standard economic motivations are important, but they are conditioned by other internalized socio-psychological constraints. This, of course, is the overriding theme of this book. We hypothesize that labor supply theory will be most effective in explaining female work behavior when women are psychologically able to make economically rational decisions—that is, when their personal work needs or desires are not severely constrained by emotional baggage from their family of orientation. We find strong support for this thesis as anticipated income and substitution effects appear only in the economic modeling limited to those women who are known to have mothers with less traditional views about women's roles. More specifically income and substitution effects are most apparent in a model limited to young women whose mothers not only had nontraditional attitudes but in addition worked themselves. These are the young women who were in a position to implement their internalized feelings and translate them into actual work. In addition these same women were least likely to be impeded in their work activity by the presence of small children. The fewer psychological constraints, the greater the possibility for economically rational behavior. If future generations of young women reaching adulthood come from backgrounds that support a work orientation, we can anticipate both higher levels of future work activity among women and more theoretically satisfactory results when we use neoclassical labor supply theory to predict their work activity.

Chapter 5 continues earlier research that documented how relatively large proportions of women now retain close labor force ties at those life-cycle points when traditionally women left employment, sometimes temporarily but more often permanently. We had hypothesized that women who showed strong work attachment in the period surrounding a first birth in all likelihood were part of a new wave of women who planned continuous work careers and a lifetime of work outside the home regardless of their family orientation. Our findings strongly support these ideas. First, women with strong early work ties are not substantially different from other women in their subsequent fertility behavior, a finding consistent with the earlier one that fertility intentions are essentially invariant for many women until they have achieved the two-child norm.

Most important we found that the determinants of work activity in 1977 had both strong economic and noneconomic components, which to a considerable degree could be identified. Women's work activity was sensitive to standard income and substitution considerations, but independent of these effects and independent of intervening fertility events, the earlier work activity surrounding the first birth powerfully predicted subsequent work activity. In other words many young women have strong continuing long-term ties to the job market regardless of their fertility behavior and independent of standard economic considerations. This finding suggests a strong psychological component to work activity conditioned by earlier work attitudes and largely independent of standard economic interpretations.

Chapter 6 documents the effect changing attitudes have had on the recent escalation in female work activity. Using neoclassical labor supply theory, this research compares the determinants of female work activity for 30 to 34 year olds in 1967 and 1978 and uses a decomposition technique to consider changes in that activity over the decade. The increasing education of young women and the declines in fertility have directly contributed to their increasing labor supply, while demand factors such as the increasing unemployment rate and the increasing real earnings of men have had only negligible effects in retarding the growth in female employment. Most important the study documented how the largest part of the increase in female work activity was due directly to changing attitudes. As it has become more acceptable for women to work, they have increased their participation. This phenomenon is documented partly by the fact that a woman's education has a greater positive effect on her probability of being employed in 1978 than it did in 1967. As in several of the preceding analyses, this one documents the importance of both economic and noneconomic factors, which in this instance interact.

The final chapter focuses on several different issues but emphasizes the invariance of many women's work activity in the face of other events, in this instance divorce and remarriage. In a society where perhaps half of all young women can be expected to end their first marriage through divorce and where the large majority of these divorcees will remarry, the issues of temporary and permanent income support and work attachment are of major interest. Contrary to some popular mythologies, we do not find any major differences in role attitudes and home-work activity patterns between women who are in their first marriage, in their second marriage, or between marriages. This finding is consistent with the notion that while changing social mores make it easier for couples to dissolve a marriage, the reasons behind most dissolutions (and remarriages) are essentially idiosyncratic and apparently do not relate to disagreements over women's roles, at least as they are verbalized in this survey. From an employment perspective we found that most remarrying women have well-established behavior patterns; they either work fairly continuously across life-cycle stages, or they do not. The large majority of women working between marriages also were working in their first and second marriages. Conversely nonworkers between marriages were also unlikely to be working before or after. While some women obtain employment only when they divorce, this is not the modal behavior pattern. Thus in a somewhat different way, our results support the idea that the motivation to work is a fairly permanent condition for many women and not sensitive only to economic stimuli.

In addition to documenting the recent trends and patterns of work activity for young adult women, we have emphasized the need to diversify the theoretical and empirical orientations in research in this area. Economic theory is an important component of any female labor supply analysis, and we suggest that its importance will increase in the years ahead as the motivations behind women's work more closely approximate male motivations and the normative constraints against not working become more similar between the sexes. We feel that to consider the motivations for female employment appropriately, however, careful consideration of noneconomic factors is required. As we have shown in many different ways, the propensity of American women to work or not work is sensitive not only to economic factors but also to the current milieu in which the woman lives, as well as her childhood and adolescent environment. Perhaps most important, to the extent that these sociopsychologically based considerations interact with the economic motivations, standard economic modeling and interpretations can be subject to considerable error.

Appendix to
Chapter 1

Sampling,
Interviewing,
and Estimating
Procedures

The Survey of Work Experience of Young Women is one of
the four longitudinal surveys sponsored by the Employment
and Training Administration of the U.S. Department of Labor.
Taken together these four surveys constitute the National Longitudinal Surveys (NLS). Each of the four NLS samples was
designed by the Bureau of the Census to represent the civilian
noninstitutional population of the United States at approximately the time of the initial survey. Samples were reweighted
in each year in order to compensate for attrition.

Sample Design

The cohort is represented by a multistage probability sample
located in 235 sample areas comprising 485 counties and independent cities representing every state and the District of Co-
lumbia. The 235 sample areas were selected by grouping all of
the nation's counties and independent cities into about 1,900
primary sampling units (PSUs), and further forming 235 strata
of one or more PSUs that are relatively homogeneous according to socioeconomic characteristics. Within each of the strata
a single PSU was selected to represent the stratum. Within
each PSU a probability sample of housing units was selected
to represent the civilian noninstitutional population.

Since one of the survey requirements was to provide separate reliable statistics for blacks, households in predominantly
black enumeration districts (EDs) were selected at a rate approximately three times that for households in predominantly
white EDs. The sample was designed to provide approximately
5,000 respondents—about 1,500 blacks and 3,500 whites.

An initial sample of about 42,000 housing units was selected, and a screening interview took place in March and April
1966. Of this number about 7,500 units were found to be va-
cant, occupied by persons whose usual residence was elsewhere, changed from residential use, or demolished. On the
other hand, about 900 additional units were found that had
been created within existing living space or had been changed
from what was previously nonresidential space. Thus 35,360
housing units were available for interview, of which usable information was collected for 34,622 households, a completion
rate of 98.0 percent.

Following the initial interview and screening operation, the
sample was rescreened in the fall of 1966, immediately prior

to the first Survey of Work Experience of Males 14 to 24. For the rescreening operation the sample was stratified by the presence or absence of a 14- to 24-year-old woman in the household. The rescreened sample was used to designate 5,533 young women aged 14 to 24 as of January 1, 1968, to be interviewed for the Survey of Work Experience. These were sampled differentially within four stata: whites in white EDs (EDs that contained predominantly white households); nonwhites in white EDs; whites in nonwhite EDs; and nonwhites in nonwhite EDs.

The Fieldwork

Over 300 interviewers were assigned to each of the surveys. Preference in the selection of interviewers was given to those who had had experience on one of the other longitudinal surveys. Since many of the procedures and the labor force and socioeconomic concepts used in this survey were similar to those used in the Current Population Survey (CPS), whenever possible the Bureau of the Census used interviewers with CPS experience.

Training for the interviewers consisted of a home study package that included a reference manual explaining the purpose, procedures, and concepts used in the survey and the home study exercises and a set of questions based on points explained in the manual. In addition to the home study package, in the early survey years there were one-day classroom training sessions that all interviewers were required to attend. All training materials were prepared by the Census Bureau staff and reviewed by the Employment and Training Administration and the Center for Human Resource Research of The Ohio State University. Professional members of the participating organizations observed both the training sessions and the actual interviewing.

In addition to training, a field edit was instituted to ensure adequate quality. This consisted of a full edit of the completed questionnaires by Data Collection Center staffs. The edit consisted of reviewing each questionnaire from beginning to end to determine whether the entries were complete and consistent and whether instructions which skipped respondents around various questions in the interview schedule were being followed. If there were minor problems, the interviewer was contacted by telephone, told of the error, and asked to contact the respondent for clarification. For more serious problems, the interviewer was retrained, either totally or in part, and the questionnaire was returned to her for completion.

Estimating Methods

The estimating procedure used in the NLS involved multistage ratio estimates.

Basic Weight

The first step was the assignment to each sample case of a basic weight consisting of the reciprocal of the final probability of selection. The probability reflects the differential sampling that was employed by race within each stratum.

Noninterview Adjustment

In the initial survey the weights for all those interviewed were adjusted to the extent needed to account for persons for whom no information was obtained because of absence, refusal, or unavailability for other reasons. This adjustment was made separately for the following groups: Census region, place of residence, and race.

Ratio Estimates

The distribution of the population selected for the sample may differ somewhat, by chance, from that of the nation as a whole with respect to residence, age, race, and sex. Since these population characteristics are closely correlated with the principal measurements made from the sample, the measurements can be substantially improved when weighted appropriately to conform to the known distribution of these population characteristics.[1] This was accomplished in the initial survey through two stages of ratio estimation.

The first stage takes into account differences at the time of the 1960 Census in the distribution by race and residence of the population as estimated from the sample PSUs and that of the total population in each of the four major regions of the country. Using 1960 Census data, estimated population totals by race and residence for each region were computed by appropriately weighting the Census counts for PSUs in the sample. Ratios were then computed between these estimates (based on sample PSUs) and the actual population totals for the region as shown by the 1960 Census.

In the second stage, the sample proportions were adjusted to independent current estimates of the civilian noninstitutionalized population by age and race. These estimates were prepared by carrying forward the most recent Census data (1960) to take account of subsequent aging of the population, mortality, and migration between the United States and other countries.[2] The adjustment was made by race within four age groupings.

Weights for Subsequent Years

In each survey year after the initial interview, the sample was reduced for reasons of noninterview. In order to compensate for these losses, the sampling weights of the individuals who were interviewed had to be revised. This revision was done in two stages. First, the out-of-scope noninterviews in each of the years were identified by the Bureau of the Census and eliminated from the sample of noninterviews. This group consisted of people who were institutionalized, had died, were members of the armed forces, or who had moved outside the United States—that is, they were no longer members of the noninstitutional, civilian population of the United States.

The second stage in the adjustment acknowledged the nonrandom characteristics of the in-scope interviews. For each of the survey years the eligible noninterviews and those interviewed were distributed into strata (cells) according to their race, years of school completed, education of their father, and years in 1968 place of residence. Within each of the cells the 1968 sampling weights of those interviewed were increased by a factor equal to the reciprocal of the reinterview rate in that year. The revised weight for each respondent in each survey year is on the 1968–1978 data tapes.

Coding and Editing

Most of the data on the interview schedules required no coding since a majority of the answers were numerical entries or in the form of precoded categories; however, clerical coding was necessary for the occupational and industrial classification of the several jobs referred to in the interview. The Census

Bureau's standard occupation and industry codes used for the CPS were employed for this purpose. Codes for other open-ended questions were assigned by the Census Bureau, in some cases on the basis of guidelines developed by the Center for Human Resource Research from tallies of subsamples of the returns.

The consistency edits for the interview schedules were completed on the computer by the Census Bureau. For the parts of the questionnaire that were similar to the CPS, a modified CPS edit was used. For all other sections separate consistency checks were performed. None of the edits included an allocation routine that was dependent on averages or random information from outside sources since such allocated data could not be expected to be consistent with data from previous or subsequent surveys. However, where the answer to a question was obvious from others in the questionnaire, the missing answer was entered on the tape. To take an example from the 1970 survey, if item 62a ("Is it necessary for you to make any regular arrangements for the care of your child[ren] while you are working?") was blank but legitimate entries appeared in item 62b and 62c ("What arrangements have you made?" and "What is the cost of these child care arrangements?"), a "Yes" was inserted in 62a since 62b and 62c could have been filled only if the answer to 62a was "Yes." Therefore the assumption was made that either the keypunch operator had failed to punch the item or the interviewer had failed to record it.

Attrition

As shown in appendix table 1A.1, sample attrition is somewhat nonrandom. In general respondents with lower socioeconomic status were more likely to leave the sample than respondents with higher status. A higher proportion of blacks than whites were noninterviews by 1978 and for both races blue collar/service occupations, city dwellers, marital disruptees, and those with lower education were most likely to leave the sample. For blacks, persons not living in the South, or with few years at their 1968 residence also have a high attrition rate. Thus even though only about one-quarter of the sample were dropped by 1978, there are slight sample selection biases for those respondents who remain.

Table 1A.1

Noninterview rate, by noninterview reason, selected characteristics of respondents in 1968, and race

Characteristic in 1968	Number interviewed, 1968	Number interviewed, 1978	Number leaving sample, 1968–1978
All respondents[b]	5,159	3,902	1,257
Whites	3,638	2,794	844
Blacks	1,459	1,064	395
Whites			
Enrolled			
Age 14–19	1,532	1,211	321
Age 20–24	253	202	51
Not enrolled			
Age 14–19	504	367	137
Age 20–24	1,329	994	335
Occupation of head of household when respondent was age 14			
White collar	1,229	982	247
Blue collar	1,609	1,197	412
Service	169	125	44
Farm	370	304	66
Area of residence			
Central city	900	668	232
Not central city	1,251	918	333
Not SMSA	1,483	1,204	279
Region of residence			
South	1,112	868	244
Non-South	2,526	1,926	600
Marital status			
Married, spouse present	1,154	904	250
Never married	2,345	1,792	553
Other	139	98	41
Dependents			
Child	802	619	183
No child	2,836	2,175	661
Lives with parents			
Yes	2,250	1,715	535
No	1,378	1,079	299

Total attrition rate	Reason for noninterview (percentage distribution)					
	Unable to locate	Institutionalized	Refused	Dead	Dropped[a]	Other
24.5	6.8	0.5	65.5	2.6	21.1	3.5
23.2	4.3	0.4	71.9	2.3	17.2	4.0
27.1	12.7	0.8	52.2	3.5	28.4	2.5
21.0	6.9	0.6	68.5	0.9	15.3	7.8
20.2	0.0	0.0	68.6	3.9	23.5	3.9
27.2	5.8	0.0	73.0	1.5	19.7	0.0
25.2	1.8	0.3	75.2	3.6	17.0	2.1
20.1	3.2	0.4	70.4	2.8	18.2	4.9
25.6	4.6	0.0	74.5	2.7	14.6	3.6
26.0	4.5	0.0	65.9	0.0	27.3	2.3
17.8	1.5	0.0	74.2	1.5	19.7	3.0
25.8	3.9	0.0	71.1	3.0	18.5	3.4
26.6	4.2	0.6	72.4	2.4	15.9	4.5
18.8	4.7	0.4	72.0	1.4	17.6	3.9
21.9	6.1	0.4	70.9	1.2	18.0	3.3
23.8	3.5	0.3	72.3	2.7	16.8	4.3
21.7	2.4	0.0	74.8	3.2	17.6	2.0
23.6	5.1	0.5	71.6	1.4	16.5	4.9
29.5	4.9	0.0	58.5	7.3	24.4	4.9
22.8	2.7	0.0	75.4	4.4	14.8	2.7
21.5	4.7	0.5	71.0	1.7	17.9	4.4
23.8	5.3	0.4	71.3	1.5	16.5	5.1
21.7	2.6	0.3	73.0	3.5	18.3	2.3

Table 1A.1 (continued)

Characteristic in 1968	Number interviewed, 1968	Number interviewed, 1978	Number leaving sample, 1968–1978
Number of years in 1968 residence			
Less than 1 year	381	292	89
1–4 years	590	452	138
5–9 years	370	273	97
10 or more years	568	431	137
All life	1,699	1,326	373
Years of schooling completed			
Enrolled			
12 years or less	1,492	1,179	313
More than 12 years	293	234	59
Not enrolled			
Less than 12 years	497	354	143
12 years	1,030	763	267
13 or more years	326	264	62
Blacks			
Enrolled			
Age 14–19	665	493	172
Age 20–24	51	38	13
Not enrolled			
Age 14–19	255	175	80
Age 20–24	488	358	130
Occupation of head of household when respondent was age 14			
White collar	103	74	29
Blue collar	658	471	187
Service	236	158	78
Farm	229	193	36
Area of residence			
Central city	689	457	232
Not central city	176	133	43
Not SMSA	593	473	120
Region of residence			
South	972	750	222
Non-South	486	313	173

Total attrition rate	Reason for noninterview (percentage distribution)					
	Unable to locate	Institutionalized	Refused	Dead	Dropped[a]	Other
23.3	3.4	0.0	67.4	5.6	27.5	1.1
23.4	5.8	0.7	69.6	0.7	18.8	4.3
26.2	1.0	0.0	59.8	3.1	26.8	9.3
24.1	8.0	0.0	67.9	1.5	17.5	5.1
22.0	3.5	0.5	78.8	1.9	12.6	2.7
21.0	6.7	0.6	68.4	1.3	15.0	8.0
20.1	1.7	0.0	69.5	1.7	23.7	3.4
28.8	4.2	0.7	63.6	1.4	28.0	2.1
19.0	2.6	0.0	82.0	3.7	10.9	0.7
19.0	1.6	0.0	67.7	3.2	24.2	3.2
25.9	13.4	1.2	54.7	2.9	24.4	3.5
25.5	c	c	c	c	c	c
31.4	15.0	0.0	45.0	0.0	37.5	2.5
26.6	10.0	0.8	53.8	6.2	27.7	1.5
28.2	3.4	0.0	65.5	3.4	27.6	0.0
28.4	11.2	1.1	53.5	3.2	26.7	4.3
33.1	16.7	0.0	51.3	2.6	26.9	2.6
15.7	13.9	2.8	44.4	2.8	36.1	0.0
33.7	12.9	0.4	55.2	3.4	25.4	2.6
24.4	16.3	0.0	44.2	2.3	34.9	2.3
20.2	10.8	1.7	49.2	4.2	31.7	2.5
22.8	13.1	0.5	49.1	5.4	29.7	2.3
35.6	12.1	1.2	56.1	1.2	26.6	2.9

Table 1A.1 (continued)

Characteristic in 1968	Number interviewed, 1968	Number interviewed, 1978	Number leaving sample, 1968–1978
Marital status			
Married, spouse present	310	234	76
Never married	1,060	766	294
Other	89	64	25
Dependents			
Child	451	348	103
No child	1,008	716	292
Lives with parents			
Yes	944	680	264
No	508	384	124
Number of years in 1968 residence			
Less than 1 year	115	79	36
1–4 years	151	99	52
5–9 years	113	81	32
10 or more years	211	159	52
All life	861	638	223
Years of schooling completed			
Enrolled			
12 years or less	667	497	170
More than 12 years	49	34	15
Not enrolled			
Less than 12 years	366	278	88
12 years	304	207	97
13 or more years	73	48	25

a. Any respondent who was not interviewed for two consecutive surveys was dropped from the sample.
b. Includes a small number of nonwhites other than blacks.
c. Percentage distribution not shown where base represents fewer than 20 respondents.

Total attrition rate	Reason for noninterview (percentage distribution)					
	Unable to locate	Institutionalized	Refused	Dead	Dropped[a]	Other
24.5	9.2	1.3	57.9	3.9	26.3	1.3
27.7	13.9	0.7	52.0	2.7	27.6	3.1
28.1	8.0	0.0	36.0	12.0	44.0	0.0
22.8	10.7	1.0	51.5	5.8	28.2	2.9
29.0	13.4	0.7	52.4	2.7	28.4	2.4
28.0	14.5	0.8	51.9	3.4	26.3	3.1
24.4	9.0	0.8	52.6	3.8	32.3	1.5
31.3	13.9	0.0	44.4	2.8	36.1	2.8
34.4	1.9	1.9	57.7	5.8	30.8	1.9
28.3	12.5	0.0	53.1	0.0	25.0	9.4
24.6	19.2	0.0	32.7	1.9	46.2	0.0
25.9	13.5	0.9	56.5	4.0	22.9	2.2
25.5	12.9	1.2	55.3	2.9	24.7	2.9
30.6	c	c	c	c	c	c
24.0	13.6	0.0	40.9	5.7	38.6	1.1
31.9	12.4	1.0	53.6	2.1	27.8	3.1
34.2	4.0	0.0	72.0	4.0	20.0	0.0

Notes

1. See U.S. Bureau of the Census (1963) for a more detailed explanation of the preparation of these estimates.

2. See U.S. Bureau of the Census (1966) for a description of the methods used in preparing these independent estimates.

References

U.S. Bureau of the Census. 1963. *The Current Population Survey—A Report on Methodology.* Technical Paper No. 7. Washington, D.C.: U.S. Government Printing Office.

————. 1966. Estimates of the population of the United States, by age, color, and sex: July 1, 1966. *Current Population Reports.* Series P-25, No. 352.

In 1966 the original sample of NLS young men aged 14 to 24
was interviewed by the U.S. Bureau of the Census. When the
NLS young women's cohort (age 14 to 24) was selected in
1968, the sample was drawn from the same households as
the young men in 1966; thus it is possible to match brothers
and sisters from the two different cohorts. This matching produces 1,913 brother-sister pairs for which data are merged
onto a single data tape. We cannot distinguish with complete
accuracy whether the boy and girl are stepbrother/stepsister,
adopted, or biological brother and sister, but we do know that
at some point in time, they had to have been living together in
the same household (usually 1966), and each respondent must
have listed the other as his or her brother/sister.

Of these 1,913 pairs, 1,177 pairs come from multiple-pair
families (representing a total of 467 families) and 736 come
from single-pair households. Since we limited our sample to
one pair per household and imposed the additional restriction
that the boy be interviewed in 1976 and the girl in 1978, we re-
tained a total of 749 pairs (522 white, 214 black, and 13 other
race pairs).

There were several criteria involved in selecting a single pair
from each multiple pair household. First, to offset the bias of
the boy's usually being older than the girl due to the original
cohort selection process (boys were age 14 to 24 in 1966 and
girls were age 14 to 24 in 1968), we generally chose the youngest boy in the household and matched him to the girl closest
in age. If there were two girls, one older and one younger but
equidistant in age from the boy, we chose the older girl. If
there was a significantly large gap (for example, five years)
between the youngest boy's age and the girl nearest him in
age, a different brother-sister pair was chosen who were
closer in age. When the choice between pairs was difficult, we
tended to favor pairs of high school age when first interviewed
so as to maximize the data available for analysis.

Table 2A.1 presents a comparison between the sibling sample and the overall cohorts for selected characteristics. The
only notable differences between the samples lies in the fact
that the boys are slightly older than the girls, and both boys
and girls in the sibling sample are on average younger than the
more general cohorts due to our bias toward selecting sibling
pairs of high school age. In addition sibling pairs more often

come from rural environments than the overall cohorts, a re-
flection of the generally larger family sizes in rural areas.

Attainment

For the separate male and female models (MCAs) a variable is
created for each sex. For example, in the case of the probability of completing high school, a dummy variable is created and
coded 1 for boys if the highest grade of schooling completed
by 1976 is 12 or more years, and 0 otherwise. For girls the reference point for years of schooling completed is 1978. In the
difference models (multiple logit), a difference is taken between the dummy probability for boys and the probability for
girls. This results in a trichotomous dependent variable with
the following categories: (− 1) girl completed high school and
boy did not, (0) both boy and girl completed or both did not
complete, and (1) boy completed but girl did not.

Similar procedures are used in defining the probability of attending and completing college. To have attended college, the
youth must have been enrolled at some time prior to and including the tenth survey date (1976 for young men and 1978
for young women). Completion of college requires that they received at least a bachelor's degree by the tenth survey.

In the model for actual educational attainment, the dependent variable is a continuous measure of the highest grade of
schooling completed by 1976 (boys) or 1978 (girls) and ranges
in value from 0 to 18 years.

Goals

Educational goals are based upon responses to the question,
"How much more education would you like to get?" As a continuous measure, aspirations range in value from 0 to 18 years
of schooling. If the respondent desired no additional schooling,
his or her highest grade completed was used instead. The reference point for obtaining information on goals was the survey
following the respondent's eighteenth birthday.

In the two models featuring the probability that the goal is to
attend or complete college, the continuous goal measure is
put into dummy variable form. For the separate sex models,
the variable created for the boys' probability of attending college is coded 1 if the respondent's educational goal is greater

than or equal to 13 years of schooling, and 0 otherwise. A similar variable is created for the girls. If a respondent has a goal greater than or equal to 16 years of school, he or she is coded 1 on the probability that the goal is to complete college and 0 otherwise.

The respondent's occupational goal is derived from her response to the question, "What would you like to be doing when you are 35 years old?" This question was asked in every survey year, and we reference the survey following the respondent's twenty-fourth birthday. Two dependent measures are created from this question. One is a dummy variable coded 1 if the respondent desired to be working at age 35 and 0 if she wished to be keeping house.

The continuous atypicality measure is linked to the particular occupation the respondent listed if she wished to be working at age 35. An atypicality score is the difference between the percentage of women found in the occupational category desired by the respondent (measured as of the 1970 Census) and the percentage of women represented in the experienced civilian labor force in 1970. For example, in 1970 women were 38.1 percent of the experienced civilian labor force. Women were also 4.6 percent of all architects. Hence the atypicality score for a woman who desires to be an architect is 4.6 − 38.1 = −33.5. The larger the positive value of the atypicality score, the more typical is the occupation for women. Conversely the larger the negative value of the atypicality score, the more atypical the occupation is for women. Women who desired to be keeping house at age 35 were assigned a value of 61.9 on the atypicality measure. This value results from the assumption that 100 percent of the incumbents in the occupation called "housewife" are women.

<table>
<tr><td>Independent
Variables</td><td>Siblings Outside of Pair</td></tr>
</table>

Variables included in this set are of several types. The number of siblings outside of the pair is simply a continuous measure of family size. It is used in continuous form in the multiple logit equations and categorized into three groups for use in the MCAs: (1) 0 to 1, (2) 2, and (3) 3 or more.

The sex and relative age of siblings outside of the pair are categorized as follows in the MCAs: (1) older siblings are all girls, (2) older siblings are all boys, (3) older siblings include both boys and girls, and (4) there are no older siblings outside of the pair (that is, the sibling pair are the only children in the family or they are the oldest such that remaining siblings are all younger). In the multiple logit models each of the above categories represents a dummy variable with category 4 omitted as the reference group.

Boy Oldest in Pair

This variable is a dummy variable coded 1 if the boy in the sibling pair is older than the girl and 0 otherwise.

Parents' Education

This variable combines separate information obtained on the highest grade of schooling completed by the respondents' mother and father. Data were taken from the 1966 boys' interview. If data were missing from that interview, information was then taken from the girls' 1968 interview. In order to maximize sample cases, an estimated value for father's education was derived for missing data cases by regressing father's SES and Duncan Index scores on education. The missing data rate for mother's education was minimal.

Categories of parental education used in the MCAs were defined as follows: (1) both parents completed 0 to 11 years of schooling, (2) father completed 0 to 11 years and mother completed 12 or more years, (3) father completed 12 or more years and mother completed 0 to 11 years, and (4) both parents completed 12 or more years of schooling. In the multiple logit models, each of the above categories represents a dummy variable with category (4) omitted as the reference group.

Encouragement

Parental encouragement is measured by the response to the question, "How much encouragement has your father [mother] given you to continue your education beyond high school?" Respondents were allowed the choices of "much," "some," or "none." This question was asked separately with reference to each parent and was asked in 1970 and 1971 for the boys and 1971 and 1972 for the girls. Data were taken from the second year only in cases where they were missing from the first year.

A particular problem exists for boys' information in 1970 because respondents who were not currently living with the parent in question were not asked about that parent's degree of encouragement. These missing data were not captured in the 1971 interview. On average respondents in this group come from larger families than boys in the more general sibling sample and are twice as likely to have served in the military (an additional reason for incorporating a military variable in our models). Otherwise these young men show no well-defined differences from the overall sample.

Since the questions on parental encouragement were asked independently of boys and girls and separately in reference to each parent, we created a single variable to determine the importance of the relative perceptions between brother and sister. Hence two variables for the MCAs (one for mother's encouragement and one for father's) contain comparisons categorized as follows: (1) no difference in perception of encouragement between boy and girl (that is, they perceived the same amount (much/much, some/some) or they perceived the same lack of encouragement (none/none)), (2) girl perceives more than boy (much/some, much/none, or some/none), (3) boy perceives more than girl (much/some, much/none, or some/none), and (4) either the boy or the girl has missing data on the encouragement question. In the multiple logit models, each category represents a dummy variable with categories 1 and 4 combined and omitted as the reference group.

Pair Lived with Both Parents at Age 14

This variable is a dummy variable coded 1 if both the boy and girl said they lived with their mother and father when they were age 14 and 0 otherwise.

Oldest in Pair Lived in Urban Area at Age 14

This variable is a dummy variable coded 1 if the oldest respondent in the pair said he or she lived in an urban area (as opposed to a rural-farm or rural nonfarm environment) when age 14 and 0 otherwise.

Pair Lived in South at Time of Initial Survey

Since for many of the respondents, no measure of geographic area was available that referenced age 14, we created a dummy variable coded 1 if the boy resided in a southern area in 1966 and the girl also resided in the South as of the 1968 survey.

IQ

This variable is a standardized measure of mental ability constructed by pooling scores from different achievement, aptitude, and intelligence tests. The construct has a mean of 100 and a standard deviation of 16. Data for the IQ measure were collected from the last secondary school attended by the respondent as of 1968. For further details regarding the separate tests involved and pooling technique, see Kohen (1973), appendix A.

Due to a reasonably high missing data rate on the IQ measure biased toward low-ability respondents and blacks, we estimated an IQ score for respondents who were missing data. This involved regressing a "Knowledge of the World of Work" score and the respondent's highest grade of schooling completed on IQ. IQ has been found to be a significant predictor of "Knowledge of the World of Work" scores. See Parnes and Kohen (1975) for further details.

In the MCAs separate IQ variables for boys and girls are combined into a single measure with four categories: (1) both boy and girl have IQs equal to or greater than 100, (2) boy's IQ is equal to or greater than 100 and girl's IQ is less than 100, (3) boy's IQ is less than 100 and girl's IQ is equal to or above 100, and (4) both respondents have IQs below 100. For the multiple logit models, each of the above categories represents a dummy variable with category 1 omitted as the reference group.

Boy Served in the Military

This variable is a dummy variable coded 1 if the boy served in the armed forces at any time prior to the 1976 survey and 0 otherwise.

Mother's Work Status When Girl Age 14

This variable is derived from the response to the question, "Did your mother work for pay when you were 14 years old?" asked in 1968. If the respondent said "yes," our variable was coded 1; if she said "no," a code of 2 was assigned; and if information was not available, our variable was coded 3.

Girl's Educational Attainment

This variable is taken from the highest grade completed (ranging from 0 to 18 years) as of the 1978 survey. A category of 1 was assigned if the girl completed between 0 and 11 years of education (inclusive); a code of 2 was assigned if she completed exactly 12 years; and a code of 3 was assigned if she completed 13 or more years of schooling.

References

Kohen, A. I. 1973. Determinants of early labor market success among young men: race, ability, quantity and quality of schooling. Unpublished manuscript. Columbus: Center for Human Resource Research, The Ohio State University, 1973.

Parnes, H. S., and Kohen, A. I. 1975. "Occupational information and labor market status: the case of young men." *Journal of Human Resources* 10:44–55.

Table 2A.1
Comparison of selected characteristics for sibling sample and total
NLS cohorts

Selected characteristics	Young men		Young women	
	Sibling sample	Total cohort	Sibling sample	Total cohort
Percent living with both parents at age 14	90.1	85.4	86.4	84.6
Percent residing in urban area at age 14	59.1	66.5	62.9	69.6
Mean age (1966 for boys and 1968 for girls)	16.9	18.4	17.8	18.9
Mean ratio of family income in base year to poverty level[a]	2.90	3.06	2.94	2.81
Mean years of education completed by father	11.1	10.6	11.1	10.9

Note: Means and percentages are based on weighted data.
a. Base survey year is 1966 for the young men and 1968 for the young women. Income information is for the year preceding the survey.

Table 2A.2
Models of educational progress for brothers in sibling sample: multiple classification analysis (adjusted percentages)

Independent variables	Number of respondents
Siblings outside of pair	
Number	
0–1	183
2	101
3 or more	214
Age and sex	
Older girls only	68
Older boys only	98
Older of both sexes	83
All younger or none	249
Boy oldest in pair	
Yes	310
No	188
Parents' education	
Both 0–11	138
Father 0–11/mother 12 or more	97
Father 12 or more/mother 0–11	41
Both 12 or more	222
Encouragement from mother	
No difference	217
Girl perceives more than boy	81
Boy perceives more than girl	109
Not ascertainable	91
Encouragement from father	
No difference	197
Girl perceives more than boy	64
Boy perceives more than girl	117
Not ascertainable	120
Pair lived with both parents at age 14	
Yes	428
No	70
Oldest in pair lived in urban area at age 14	
Yes	299
No	199

Dependent variables			
Probability of high school completion	Probability of college attendance	Probability of college completion	Actual educational attainment
(0.370)	(0.434)	(1.033)	(0.080)
0.888	0.688	0.369	13.90
0.909	0.669	0.299	13.82
0.908	0.652	0.328	13.91
(0.180)	(0.551)	(0.879)	(0.928)
0.881	0.619	0.264	13.57
0.896	0.659	0.337	13.97
0.904	0.669	0.355	13.76
0.906	0.686	0.352	13.98
(0.561)	(0.741)	(0.723)	(1.148)
0.907	0.657	0.350	13.96
0.889	0.688	0.317	13.76
(7.510)***	(22.867)***	(5.564)***	(19.736)***
0.812	0.486	0.257	13.05
0.920	0.640	0.327	13.72
0.944	0.544	0.216	13.16
0.939	0.818	0.415	14.60
(5.208)***	(2.309)*	(1.531)	(2.496)*
0.893	0.706	0.364	13.93
0.877	0.577	0.257	13.43
0.856	0.651	0.362	13.83
0.994	0.682	0.317	14.25
(15.691)***	(1.949)	(1.868)	(6.028)***
0.918	0.685	0.389	14.17
0.903	0.668	0.302	13.77
1.000	0.713	0.325	14.11
0.771	0.599	0.284	13.25
(0.026)	(1.877)	(0.531)	(0.757)
0.901	0.678	0.343	13.92
0.896	0.610	0.304	13.69
(1.595)	(0.714)	(0.553)	(1.217)
0.889	0.681	0.326	13.97
0.919	0.651	0.354	13.77

Table 2A.2 (continued)

Independent variables	Number of respondents
Pair lived in South at time of initial survey[a]	
Yes	137
No	361
IQ	
Both $\geq$ 100	249
Boy $\geq$ 100/girl < 100	67
Boy < 100/girl $\geq$ 100	90
Both < 100	92
Boy served in military	
Yes	
No	
Grand mean	498
_F_ ratio	
Adusted R^2	

Note: Numbers in parentheses are _F_ ratios. One, two, and three asterisks indicate that the _F_ is significant at the 0.10, 0.05, and 0.01 levels respectively. All variables are described in detail in appendix to chapter 2.
a. The initial survey year is 1966 for the young men and 1968 for the young women.
b. Variable is not included in this model.

Dependent variables			
Probability of high school completion	Probability of college attendance	Probability of college completion	Actual educational attainment
(0.720)	(0.473)	(0.314)	(0.333)
0.884	0.649	0.354	13.80
0.907	0.676	0.331	13.92
(34.756)***	(30.488)***	(22.507)***	(52.926)***
0.979	0.778	0.468	14.74
0.983	0.824	0.377	14.54
0.856	0.547	0.185	12.95
0.668	0.379	0.104	11.97
	(0.043)	(19.920)***	(1.270)
b	0.674	0.225	13.75
	0.666	0.398	13.96
0.901	0.669	0.337	13.89
8.765***	11.970***	8.169***	15.475***
0.249	0.327	0.241	0.393

Table 2A.3
Models of educational progress for sisters in sibling sample: multiple classification analysis (adjusted percentages)

Independent variables	Number of respondents
Siblings outside of pair	
Number	
0–1	183
2	101
3 or more	214
Age and sex	
Older girls only	68
Older boys only	98
Older of both sexes	83
All younger or none	249
Boy oldest in pair	
Yes	310
No	188
Parents' education	
Both 0–11	138
Father 0–11/mother 12 or more	97
Father 12 or more/mother 0–11	41
Both 12 or more	222
Encouragement from mother	
No difference	217
Girl perceives more than boy	81
Boy perceives more than girl	109
Not ascertainable	91
Encouragement from father	
No difference	197
Girl perceives more than boy	64
Boy perceives more than girl	117
Not ascertainable	120
Pair lived with both parents at age 14	
Yes	428
No	70
Oldest in pair lived in urban area at age 14	
Yes	299
No	199

Dependent variables			
Probability of high school completion	Probability of college attendance	Probability of college completion	Actual educational attainment
(1.211)	(2.947)*	(5.601)***	(3.789)**
0.903	0.560	0.363	13.67
0.898	0.438	0.213	13.17
0.860	0.497	0.262	13.15
(0.923)	(0.689)	(0.008)	(0.634)
0.908	0.519	0.295	13.50
0.918	0.535	0.286	13.54
0.864	0.451	0.291	13.27
0.870	0.513	0.288	13.26
(0.001)	(5.515)**	(0.577)	(0.097)
0.883	0.474	0.279	13.33
0.884	0.564	0.306	13.38
(6.515)***	(20.441)***	(9.233)***	(15.971)***
0.804	0.360	0.213	12.62
0.871	0.411	0.253	13.17
0.864	0.366	0.110	12.62
0.942	0.669	0.386	14.01
(4.733)***	(1.832)	(3.228)**	(3.943)***
0.912	0.531	0.345	13.62
0.951	0.566	0.259	13.50
0.831	0.477	0.207	12.85
0.820	0.438	0.280	13.15
(3.854)***	(4.920)***	(2.515)*	(2.262)*
0.866	0.572	0.324	13.60
0.791	0.544	0.307	13.31
0.920	0.390	0.203	13.00
0.926	0.499	0.306	13.28
(1.975)	(1.209)	(0.436)	(0.007)
0.891	0.500	0.294	13.35
0.838	0.559	0.260	13.33
(3.608)*	(0.005)	(0.379)	(0.000)
0.863	0.509	0.280	13.35
0.914	0.507	0.302	13.35

Table 2A.3 (continued)

Independent variables	Number of respondents
Pair lived in South at time of initial survey[a]	
Yes	137
No	361
IQ	
Both $\geq$ 100	249
Boy $\geq$ 100/girl $<$ 100	67
Boy $<$ 100/girl $\geq$ 100	90
Both $<$ 100	92
Boy served in military	
Yes	
No	
Grand mean	498
F ratio	
Adjusted *R*^{2}	

Note: Numbers in parentheses are *F* ratios. One, two, and three aster-isks indicate that the *F* is significant at the 0.10, 0.05, and 0.01 levels respectively. All variables are described in detail in appendix to chapter 2.
a. The initial survey year is 1966 for the young men and 1968 for the young women.
b. Variable is not included in this model.

Dependent variables			
Probability of high school completion	Probability of college attendance	Probability of college completion	Actual educational attainment
(0.067)	(0.090)	(1.559)	(0.002)
0.889	0.517	0.325	13.35
0.881	0.505	0.276	13.34
(20.367)***	(16.539)***	(13.656)***	(30.363)***
0.933	0.612	0.390	14.00
0.947	0.357	0.150	12.91
0.917	0.550	0.283	13.53
0.670	0.296	0.123	11.71
	(1.396)	(8.148)***	(3.382)*
b	0.478	0.221	13.12
	0.524	0.326	13.47
0.884	0.508	0.289	13.35
6.107***	11.296***	8.290***	13.561***
0.177	0.313	0.244	0.357

Table 2A.4
Models of educational goals for brothers in sibling sample: multiple classification analysis (adjusted percentages)

Independent variables	Number of respondents
Siblings outside of pair	
Number	
0–1	176
2	92
3 or more	201
Age and sex	
Older girls only	66
Older boys only	90
Older of both sexes	78
All younger or none	235
Boy oldest in pair	
Yes	297
No	172
Parents' education	
Both 0–11	131
Father 0–11/mother 12 or more	91
Father 12 or more/mother 0–11	34
Both 12 or more	213
Encouragement from mother	
No difference	212
Girl perceives more than boy	75
Boy perceives more than girl	104
Not ascertainable	78
Encouragement from father	
No difference	192
Girl perceives more than boy	60
Boy perceives more than girl	111
Not ascertainable	106
Pair lived with both parents at age 14	
Yes	404
No	65
Oldest in pair lived in urban area at age 14	
Yes	282
No	187

Dependent variables		
Educational goal as of age 18	Probability goal is to attend college	Probability goal is to complete college
(0.342)	(0.158)	(0.171)
14.73	0.695	0.594
14.72	0.722	0.595
14.88	0.703	0.616
(0.872)	(0.840)	(1.211)
14.55	0.674	0.548
14.65	0.670	0.572
14.73	0.684	0.588
14.94	0.731	0.636
(3.065)*	(0.106)	(0.373)
14.92	0.708	0.612
14.58	0.696	0.589
(17.450)***	(16.089)***	(19.322)***
13.88	0.538	0.449
14.69	0.669	0.555
14.30	0.654	0.428
15.48	0.829	0.747
(2.503)*	(1.940)	(0.615)
14.94	0.703	0.627
14.20	0.616	0.580
14.85	0.728	0.601
14.88	0.757	0.565
(3.477)**	(4.031)***	(3.206)**
15.01	0.733	0.646
14.68	0.727	0.517
14.99	0.749	0.641
14.26	0.590	0.535
(0.025)	(0.027)	(0.585)
14.80	0.702	0.609
14.76	0.711	0.569
(16.965)***	(8.025)***	(10.905)***
15.11	0.745	0.652
14.31	0.642	0.531

Table 2A.4 (continued)

Independent variables	Number of respondents
Pair lived in South at time of initial survey[a]	
Yes	131
No	338
IQ	
Both ⩾ 100	240
Boy ⩾ 100/girl < 100	58
Boy < 100/girl ⩾ 100	84
Both < 100	87
Grand mean	469
F ratio	
Adjusted R^2	

Note: Numbers in parentheses are *F* ratios. One, two, and three asterisks indicate that the *F* is significant at the 0.10, 0.05, and 0.01 levels respectively. All variables are described in detail in appendix to chapter 2.
a. The initial survey year is 1966 for the young men and 1968 for the young women.

Dependent variables		
Educational goal as of age 18	Probability goal is to attend college	Probability goal is to complete college
(2.639)	(3.671)*	(9.655)***
15.04	0.758	0.693
14.70	0.682	0.569
(52.319)***	(27.447)***	(39.713)***
15.65	0.813	0.749
15.50	0.846	0.742
14.14	0.587	0.432
12.59	0.421	0.276
14.79	0.704	0.603
16.369***	10.274***	14.095***
0.408	0.294	0.370

Table 2A.5
Models of educational goals for sisters in sibling sample: multiple classification analysis (adjusted percentages)

Independent variables	Number of respondents
Siblings outside of pair	
Number	
0–1	181
2	100
3 or more	204
Age and sex	
Older girls only	67
Older boys only	95
Older of both sexes	79
All younger or none	244
Boy oldest in pair	
Yes	301
No	184
Parents' education	
Both 0–11	132
Father 0–11/mother 12 or more	93
Father 12 or more/mother 0–11	40
Both 12 or more	220
Encouragement from mother	
No difference	213
Girl perceives more than boy	79
Boy perceives more than girl	106
Not ascertainable	87
Encouragement from father	
No difference	193
Girl perceives more than boy	61
Boy perceives more than girl	115
Not ascertainable	116
Pair lived with both parents at age 14	
Yes	416
No	69
Oldest in pair lived in urban area at age 14	
Yes	291
No	194

Dependent variables		
Educational goal as of age 18	Probability goal is to attend college	Probability goal is to complete college
(3.094)**	(1.811)	(2.385)*
14.38	0.621	0.498
13.86	0.525	0.391
14.02	0.569	0.430
(0.741)	(0.429)	(0.691)
14.20	0.596	0.469
14.29	0.569	0.496
13.89	0.536	0.427
14.11	0.593	0.429
(2.527)	(3.660)*	(1.681)
14.02	0.551	0.428
14.29	0.626	0.479
(19.881)***	(20.483)***	(16.450)***
13.51	0.468	0.341
13.62	0.420	0.323
13.47	0.427	0.284
14.82	0.741	0.594
(9.306)***	(6.272)***	(10.953)***
14.53	0.668	0.550
14.27	0.553	0.482
13.74	0.506	0.359
13.45	0.474	0.273
(2.413)*	(0.857)	(3.551)**
14.17	0.605	0.443
14.24	0.605	0.473
13.74	0.531	0.355
14.35	0.570	0.533
(0.231)	(0.023)	(3.071)*
14.14	0.578	0.461
14.02	0.586	0.365
(0.872)	(1.100)	(0.689)
14.18	0.596	0.460
14.03	0.555	0.428

Table 2A.5 (continued)

Independent variables	Number of respondents
Pair lived in South at time of initial survey[a]	
Yes	131
No	354
IQ	
Both ≥ 100	247
Boy ≥ 100/girl < 100	64
Boy < 100/girl ≥ 100	87
Both < 100	87
Grand mean	485
F ratio	
Adjusted R^2	

Note: Numbers in parentheses are *F* ratios. One, two, and three asterisks indicate that the *F* is significant at the 0.10, 0.05, and 0.01 levels, respectively. All variables are described in detail in appendix to chapter 2.
a. The initial survey year is 1966 for the young men and 1968 for the young women.

Dependent variables		
Educational goal as of age 18	Probability goal is to attend college	Probability goal is to complete college
(1.152)	(0.431)	(1.746)
14.27	0.600	0.489
14.07	0.572	0.432
(24.220)***	(13.713)***	(15.327)***
14.68	0.667	0.563
13.87	0.573	0.326
14.06	0.580	0.418
12.77	0.334	0.238
14.12	0.579	0.447
13.560***	10.294***	10.216***
0.353	0.287	0.286

Table 2A.6
Difference between brothers and sisters in the probability of completing high school: multiple choice logit estimation

Independent variables	Probability of completing high school		
	Boy(yes)-girl(no)/ girl(yes)-boy(no)	No difference/ girl(yes)-boy(no)	Boy(yes)-girl(no)/ no difference
Siblings outside of pair			
Number (continuous)	−0.038 (−0.26)	−0.028 (−0.25)	−0.010 (−0.09)
Older girls only	−1.134 (−0.94)	−0.371 (−0.40)	−0.764 (−0.92)
Older boys only	−0.899 (−1.01)	−0.570 (−0.86)	−0.329 (−0.51)
Older of both sexes	0.331 (0.33)	−0.336 (−0.39)	0.667 (1.12)
Boy oldest in pair	1.085 (1.53)*	1.019 (1.79)**	0.065 (0.14)
Parents' education			
Both 0–11	0.552 (0.52)	−0.649 (−0.78)	1.201 (1.73)**
Father 0–11/mother 12 or more	0.230 (0.22)	−1.523 (−1.89)**	1.752 (2.62)
Father 12 or more/ mother 0–11	1.227 (0.83)	−0.186 (−0.15)	1.413 (1.68)**
Encouragement from mother			
Girl perceives more than boy	−1.552 (−1.30)*	−0.271 (−0.35)	−1.280 (−1.35)*
Boy perceives more than girl	0.252 (0.25)	−0.270 (−0.31)	0.523 (0.89)
Encouragement from father			
Girl perceives more than boy	1.928 (1.58)	0.511 (0.51)	1.417 (1.83)
Boy perceives more than girl	2.508 (1.92)**	2.329 (1.94)**	0.180 (0.30)
Pair lived with both parents at age 14	−0.027 (−0.03)	0.867 (1.19)	−0.894 (−1.67)
Oldest in pair lived in urban area at age 14	0.122 (0.17)	−0.218 (−0.39)	0.340 (0.72)
Pair lived in South at time of initial survey[a]	−0.910 (−1.20)	−0.317 (−0.55)	−0.592 (−1.13)
IQ			
Boy ≥ 100/girl < 100	9.048 (0.05)	8.940 (0.05)	0.108 (0.16)
Boy < 100/girl ≥ 100	−3.378 (−2.60)***	−3.046 (−2.78)***	−0.332 (−0.45)
Both < 100	−2.350 (−1.87)*	−3.423 (−2.97)***	1.073 (1.94)*
Constant	1.420 (0.83)	5.142 (3.49)***	−3.722 (−4.00)***

Note: All variables are described in detail in appendix to chapter 2. All independent variables are dichotomous unless specified otherwise. Numbers in parentheses represent asymptotic t statistics. One, two, and three asterisks indicate that the t is significant at the 0.10, 0.05, and 0.01 levels respectively. Sample size is 493 pairs. Mean probabilities for each category of the dependent variable are as follows: boy(yes)-girl(no) = 0.055; girl(yes)-boy(no) = 0.039; and no difference = 0.907.
a. The initial survey year is 1966 for the young men and 1968 for the young women.

Table 2A.7
Difference between brothers and sisters in the probability of attending college: multiple choice logit estimation

Independent variables	Probability of attending college		
	Boy(yes)-girl(no)/ girl(yes)-boy(no)	No difference/ girl(yes)-boy(no)	Boy(yes)-girl(no)/ no difference
Siblings outside of pair			
Number (continuous)	0.038 (0.37)	−0.006 (−0.06)	0.044 (0.76)
Older girls only	−0.371 (−0.52)	0.251 (0.40)	−0.622 (−1.55)*
Older boys only	−0.405 (−0.71)	−0.262 (−0.53)	−0.142 (−0.43)
Older of both sexes	0.262 (0.37)	0.062 (0.10)	0.200 (0.55)
Boy oldest in pair	0.408 (0.90)	0.111 (0.27)	0.297 (1.17)
Parents' education			
Both 0–11	−0.182 (−0.32)	−0.053 (−0.11)	−0.129 (−0.39)
Father 0–11/ mother 12 or more	0.876 (1.36)	0.487 (0.82)	0.389 (1.21)
Father 12 or more/ mother 0–11	0.708 (0.77)	0.577 (0.68)	0.131 (0.29)
Encouragement from mother			
Girl perceives more than boy	−1.759 (−2.55)***	−0.967 (−1.77)**	−0.791 (−1.64)*
Boy perceives more than girl	−0.078 (−0.11)	0.018 (0.03)	−0.096 (−0.26)
Encouragement from father			
Girl perceives more than boy	0.126 (0.16)	0.024 (0.04)	0.102 (0.20)
Boy perceives more than girl	1.246 (1.72)**	0.261 (0.38)	0.985 (2.87)***
Pair lived with both parents at age 14	1.205 (1.98)**	0.547 (1.08)	0.658 (1.67)**
Oldest in pair lived in urban area at age 14	0.563 (1.24)	0.676 (1.67)	−0.113 (−0.44)
Pair lived in South at time of initial survey[a]	0.025 (0.05)	0.550 (1.21)	−0.525 (−1.79)
IQ			
Boy ⩾ 100/girl < 100	11.679 (0.11)	10.609 (0.10)	1.070 (3.28)***
Boy < 100/girl ⩾ 100	−1.717 (−3.05)***	−1.080 (−2.36)***	−0.637 (−1.63)*
Both < 100	−1.011 (−1.59)	−0.637 (−1.13)	−0.373 (−1.00)
Boy served in military	−0.122 (−0.28)	−0.849 (−2.17)**	0.727 (2.95)
Constant	−0.197 (−0.22)	2.079 (2.74)***	−2.276 (−4.33)***

Note: All variables are described in detail in appendix to chapter 2. All independent variables are dichotomous unless specified otherwise. Numbers in parentheses represent asymptotic t statistics. One, two, and three asterisks indicate that the t is significant at the 0.10, 0.05, and 0.01 levels respectively. Sample size is 493 pairs. Mean probabilities for each category of the dependent variable are as follows: boy(yes)-girl(no) = 0.233; girl(yes)-boy(no) = 0.069; and no difference = 0.698.
a. The initial survey year is 1966 for the young men and 1968 for the young women.

Table 2A.8
Difference between brothers and sisters in the probability of completing college: multiple choice logit estimation

Independent variables	Probability of completing college		
	Boy(yes)-girl(no)/ girl(yes)-boy(no)	No difference/ girl(yes)-boy(no)	Boy(yes)-girl(no)/ no difference
Siblings outside of pair			
Number (continuous)	0.077 (0.72)	0.144 (1.60)*	−0.067 (−0.94)
Older girls only	−0.788 (−1.26)	−0.155 (−0.33)	−0.632 (−1.34)*
Older boys only	−0.024 (−0.05)	−0.129 (−0.31)	0.104 (0.29)
Older of both sexes	0.194 (0.30)	0.071 (0.13)	0.124 (0.30)
Boy oldest in pair	0.373 (0.96)	−0.160 (−0.51)	0.533 (1.86)**
Parents' education			
Both 0–11	−0.012 (−0.02)	0.155 (0.36)	−0.168 (−0.45)
Father 0–11/mother 12 or more	0.244 (0.49)	0.043 (0.10)	0.200 (0.57)
Father 12 or more/ mother 0–11	0.960 (1.03)	1.199 (1.51)*	−0.239 (−0.43)
Encouragement from mother			
Girl perceives more than boy	−0.032 (−0.05)	0.237 (0.48)	−0.269 (−0.54)
Boy perceives more than girl	0.924 (1.45)*	0.187 (0.33)	0.737 (1.89)**
Encouragement from father			
Girl perceives more than boy	−0.482 (−0.69)	−0.387 (−0.75)	−0.095 (−0.17)
Boy perceives more than girl	0.856 (1.36)*	0.635 (1.13)	0.221 (0.58)
Pair lived with both parents at age 14	0.076 (0.13)	−0.167 (−0.37)	0.242 (0.60)
Oldest in pair lived in urban area at age 14	−0.136 (−0.34)	−0.121 (−0.37)	−0.015 (−0.05)
Pair lived in South at time of initial survey[a]	−0.278 (−0.66)	−0.291 (−0.86)	0.013 (0.04)
IQ			
Boy ≥ 100/girl < 100	1.515 (1.88)**	1.216 (1.59)*	0.299 (0.83)
Boy < 100/girl ≥ 100	−1.255 (−2.50)***	−0.626 (−1.78)**	−0.629 (−1.49)*
Both < 100	−0.538 (−0.63)	1.427 (2.16)**	−1.965 (−3.39)***
Boy served in military	−0.627 (−1.51)*	0.105 (0.32)	−0.732 (−2.41)***
Constant	0.014 (0.02)	1.524 (2.46)**	−1.510 (−2.74)***

Note: All variables are described in detail in appendix to chapter 2. All independent variables are dichotomous unless specified otherwise. Numbers in parentheses represent asymptotic *t* statistics. One, two, and three asterisks indicate that the *t* is significant at the 0.10, 0.05, and 0.01 levels respectively. Sample size is 493 pairs. Mean probabilities for each category of the dependent variable are as follows: boy(yes)-girl(no) = 0.166; girl(yes)-boy(no) = 0.118; and no difference = 0.716.
a. The initial survey year is 1966 for the young men and 1968 for the young women.

Table 2A.9
Occupational goals for age 35 for sisters in sibling sample: multiple classification analysis (adjusted percentages)

Independent variables	Number of respondents	Dependent variables	
		Proportion expecting to work at age 35	Atypicality of goal for age 35[a]
Siblings outside of pair			
Number		(2.273)	(2.996)*
0–1	142	0.485	43.28
2	84	0.626	37.60
3 or more	158	0.528	35.84
Age and sex		(1.761)	(1.792)
Older girls only	54	0.582	46.22
Older boys only	72	0.418	40.53
Older of both sexes	63	0.568	37.78
All younger or none	195	0.552	36.75
Boy oldest in pair		(4.855)**	(0.562)
Yes	218	0.581	38.12
No	166	0.472	40.24
Parents' education		(0.515)	(1.164)
Both 0–11	101	0.580	36.77
Father 0–11/mother 12 or more	76	0.521	38.05
Father 12 or more/mother 0–11	32	0.475	46.75
Both 12 or more	175	0.523	39.15
Encouragement from mother			
Girl's perception		(3.803)**	(1.072)
Much	209	0.550	39.43
Some	99	0.599	35.84
None	76	0.404	41.75
Not ascertainable			
Girl's compared to boy's perception		(5.588)***	(3.552)**
No difference	172	0.591	37.56
Girl perceives more	60	0.673	31.25
Boy perceives more	82	0.426	45.32
Not ascertainable	70	0.402	41.62
Encouragement from father			
Girl's perception		(1.359)	(0.848)
Much	165	0.496	37.96
Some	105	0.514	41.93
None	111	0.610	37.26
Not ascertainable	3	0.449	49.53
Girl's compared to boy's perception		(1.626)	(1.699)
No difference	155	0.527	37.59
Girl perceives more	42	0.393	42.49
Boy perceives more	95	0.560	35.29
Not ascertainable	92	0.583	43.20

Table 2A.9 (continued)

Independent variables	Number of respondents	Dependent variables	
		Proportion expecting to work at age 35	Atypicality of goal for age 35[a]
Pair lived with both parents at age 14		(0.022)	(0.402)
Yes	331	0.532	39.29
No	53	0.543	36.72
Oldest in pair lived in urban area at age 14		(5.243)**	(2.506)
Yes	241	0.577	37.19
No	143	0.461	41.66
Pair lived in South at time of initial survey[b]		(0.046)	(0.157)
Yes	92	0.524	39.87
No	292	0.537	38.62
IQ		(0.103)	(3.469)**
Both ≥ 100	202	0.532	36.44
Boy ≥ 100/girl < 100	54	0.566	38.27
Boy < 100/girl ≥ 100	67	0.520	37.84
Both < 100	61	0.527	49.13
Mother's work status when girl age 14		(2.083)	(1.551)
Working	121	0.601	40.95
Not working	233	0.494	35.95
Not ascertainable	30	0.576	36.17
Girl's educational attainment		(10.074)***	(7.743)***
0–11	44	0.564	37.08
12	160	0.406	45.35
13 or more	180	0.640	33.92
Grand mean	384	0.534	38.95
F ratio		1.973***	2.148***
Adjusted R^2		0.071	0.074

Note: Numbers in parentheses are F ratios. One, two, and three asterisks indicate that the F is significant at the 0.10, 0.05, and 0.01 levels respectively. All variables are described in detail in appendix to chapter 2.

a. Occupational goals for age 35 were measured as of age 24 for the respondents. Each number represents the mean atypicality score for each category of each independent variable. An atypicality score is the difference between the percentage of women found in the occupational category desired by the respondent (measured as of the 1970 Census) and the percentage of women represented in the experienced civilian labor force in 1970. For example, in 1970, women were 38.1 percent of the experienced civilian labor force. Women were also 4.6 percent of all architects. Therefore the atypicality score for a woman who desires to be an architect is 4.6 − 38.1 = −33.5. The larger the positive value of the atypicality score, the more typical is the occupation for women. The larger the negative value of the atypicality score, the more atypical the occupation is for women.

b. The initial survey year is 1966 for the young men and 1968 for the young women.

Appendix to Chapter 3

Table 3A.1

Determinants of downward and upward revisions in birth expectations for women married in 1973 and 1978, by race: logit results

Explanatory variables	Whites		Blacks	
	Down	Up	Down	Up
Duncan index	0.002	0.006	−0.005	−0.013
	(0.56)	(1.78)*	(−0.36)	(−1.07)
Number of siblings	0.000	0.029	−0.005	0.057
	(0.01)	(0.84)	(−0.07)	(1.12)
Husband's education	−0.021	0.006	0.067	−0.020
	(−0.58)	(0.20)	(0.80)	(−0.34)
Years worked before 1973	0.133	−0.000	0.236	0.017
	(3.99)***	(−0.01)	(2.57)**	(0.24)
Respondent's education	0.063	−0.023	0.159	0.012
	(1.34)	(−0.53)	(1.35)	(0.14)
Respondent's age	−1.26	−0.091	−0.270	−0.129
	(−3.77)***	(−2.99)***	(−2.88)***	(−1.97)**
Whether any children in 1973	−1.224	0.308	−1.251	0.355
	(−6.32)***	(1.64)	(−2.55)**	(0.77)
1973 expectations	1.119	−0.292	0.660	−0.127
	(11.95)***	(−3.24)***	(3.96)***	(−0.89)
Propriety	0.049	−0.046	−0.117	−0.114
	(1.86)*	(−1.96)**	(−1.52)	(−1.97)**
Economic necessity	0.018	−0.035	−0.178	0.012
	(0.44)	(−0.97)	(−1.82)*	(0.15)
Work plans at age 35	−0.204	−0.041	0.510	0.442
	(−1.26)	(−0.28)	(1.18)	(1.39)
Constant	−1.38	3.31	6.69	5.32
Log likelihood	−1,160.85		−223.99	
Number of respondents	1130		251	

Note: Asymptotic *t* values in parentheses.
* Significant at the 0.10 level.
** Significant at the 0.05 level.
*** Significant at the 0.01 level.

Table 3A.2
Determinants of downward and upward revisions in birth expectations, by marital status in 1973 and 1978 and number of children in 1973: logit results

Explanatory variables	Single to married	
	Down	Up
Duncan index	0.011	0.014
	(1.71)*	(1.59)
Number of siblings	−0.120	0.171*
	(−1.42)	(1.74)*
Husband's education	−0.148	−0.094
	(−2.08)**	(−1.06)
Respondent's education	−0.040	0.247
	(−0.34)	(1.49)
Years worked before 1973	0.091	0.335
	(0.68)	(1.68)*
Respondent's age	0.115	−0.473
	(0.86)	(−2.44)**
Birth expectations in 1973	1.468	−1.020
	(6.26)***	(−3.98)***
Economic necessity	−0.025	−0.043
	(−0.31)	(−0.40)
Propriety	0.020	−0.122
	(0.32)	(−1.72)*
Plans for work at age 35	0.599	0.437
	(1.67)*	(0.91)
Constant	−5.111	11.655
Log likelihood	−204.05	
Number of respondents	265	

Note: Asymptotic *t* values in parentheses.
* Significant at the 0.10 level.
** Significant at the 0.05 level.
*** Significant at the 0.01 level.

Married both years, no children in 1973		One child in 1973		Two or more children in 1973	
Down	Up	Down	Up	Down	Up
−0.001	0.016	0.010	−0.001	−0.002	0.004
(−0.26)	(2.57)**	(1.40)	(−0.15)	(−0.27)	(0.069)
−0.017	0.029	−0.135	0.012	0.070	0.023
(−0.25)	(0.36)	(−1.70)*	(0.21)	(0.93)	(0.43)
−0.095	0.018	−0.007	0.005	−0.036	0.026
(−1.67)*	(0.26)	(−0.10)	(0.09)	(−0.47)	(0.52)
−0.130	−0.059	−0.293	−0.033	0.371	0.033
(−1.71)*	(−0.62)	(−2.81)***	(−0.39)	(3.28)***	(0.47)
0.017	0.031	−0.128	−0.066	0.166	0.045
(0.25)	(0.38)	(−1.86)*	(−1.12)	(2.49)**	(1.03)
0.131	−0.034	0.192	−0.108	−0.309	−0.184
(2.03)**	(−0.42)	(2.51)**	(−1.66)*	(−4.08)***	(−3.70)***
1.080	−0.536	2.105	−0.583	1.672	0.214
(6.37)***	(−3.09)***	(7.98)***	(−2.63)***	(8.38)***	(1.46)
−0.019	0.078	0.164	−0.019	0.024	−0.080
(−0.29)	(1.02)	(1.92)*	(−0.28)	(0.27)	(−1.47)
0.075	−0.001	0.060	−0.090	0.035	−0.038
(1.83)*	(−0.00)	(1.12)	(−2.04)**	(0.62)	(−1.03)
0.320	0.041	0.015	0.049	−0.772	−0.318
(1.21)	(0.13)	(0.00)	(0.20)	(−2.15)**	(−1.35)
−4.677	−0.116	−10.044	5.907	−2.594	4.684
−385.84		−316.83		−371.73	
427		390		513	

Appendix to Chapter 4	Nontraditional	A mother who scored less than 17 on the sex-role scale of social acceptability (see Mother's traditionality).
Variable Construction	Traditional	A mother who scored 17 or greater on the sex-role scale of social acceptability (see Mother's traditionality).
	Workers	A mother who worked 33.3 percent or more of the six-month period between the birth of her first child and her 1967 interview (see Mother's work history).
	Nonworkers	A mother who worked less than 33.3 percent of the six-month period between the birth of her first child and her 1967 interview (see Mother's work history).
	Weeks worked	A continuous variable denoting the number of weeks worked between the 1977 and 1978 surveys.
	Husband's earnings	A continuous variable of the husband's income from wages and salary in the year preceding the 1978 interview.
	South	A 0, 1 variable, with 1 denoting residence in the South in 1978.
	Labor force size	A variable ranging from 25,000 to 4 million, indicating the 1970 Census size of the labor force in which the respondent resides in 1978.
	Youngest child under 6	A 0, 1 variable with 1 indicating that the respondent has a child under the age of six. Zero indicates no children or no children under 6 are present in the household.

Mother's work history

A continuous variable from 0 to 1 denoting the percentage of six-month intervals that the mother was employed between the birth of her first child and 1967. For example, a 0 denotes no employment during that period, 0.50 denotes employment half of the time, and 1 denotes employment during the entire period.

Mother's traditionality

A continuous variable ranging from 6 to 30 showing the traditionality of the mother, with the higher scores indicating traditionality. Scores were based on agreement or disagreement with the following statements (which were scored from 1 to 5):

Modern conveniences permit a wife to work without neglecting her family.

A woman's place is in the home, not in the office or shop.

A job provides a wife with interesting outside contacts.

A wife who carries out her full family responsibilities doesn't have time for outside employment.

The employment of wives leads to more juvenile delinquency.

Working wives lose interest in their homes and families.

Table 4A.1
Comparison of mother-daughter sample to NLS mature and young women's cohorts

Characteristic	Mature women's cohort	Young women's cohort	Mother/daughter sample
Mother's education in 1967 (mean years)	11.4		11.1
Mother's age in 1967 (mean years)	37.3		39.4
Mother's traditionality (mean score)	15.8		16.5
Mother's work history (proportion)[a]	0.262		0.257
Daughter's education as of 1978 (mean years)		12.8	13.0
Daughter's age in 1966 (mean)		19.0	16.9
Husband's earnings (mean 1977 dollars)		13,098	12,608
Percent in South in 1978		34.5	31.6
Labor force size of 1978 area of residence (mean)		460,857	395,095
Age of youngest child in 1978 (mean)		3.1	1.6
Weeks worked between 1977 and 1978 (mean)		27.4	27.2
Number of respondents	3,606	2,112	633

Note: Statistics for the mature women's cohort are for white women only. Statistics for the young women's cohort are for young white women married and interviewed in 1978. Statistics for the mother/daughter group are for our sample: young white women who were married and interviewed in 1978 and who lived with their mother at age 14.
a. Proportion working at least one-third of years between birth of first child and 1967. See appendix to chapter 4 for further details.

Table 4A.2
Mean weeks worked between 1977 and 1978 for white women: multiple classification analysis (adjusted means)

Explanatory variables	Mean weeks worked
Daughter's education	(11.61)*
0–11 years	17.6
12 years	26.4
13 years or more	31.0
Husband's earnings[a]	(4.51)*
Less than $5000	27.00
$5,000–$9,999	32.33
$10,000–$12,999	29.61

Table 4A.2 (continued)

Explanatory variables	Mean weeks worked
Husband's earnings (continued)	
$13,000–$17,999	28.85
$18,000–$22,999	22.14
$23,000 and over	16.08
Not ascertainable	27.22
South	(2.67)
No	26.28
Yes	29.32
Labor force size	(0.88)
Less than 125,000	27.96
125,000–299,999	25.59
300,000–449,999	24.26
450,000–649,999	30.00
650,000–899,999	29.04
900,000–1,499,999	28.26
1,500,000–3,999,999	31.24
4,000,000 or more	32.77
Age of youngest child	(89.66)*
Under 6	20.96
6 and over	37.87
Nontraditional worker	(2.35)
No	26.62
Yes	30.11
Traditional nonworker	(0.86)
No	26.68
Yes	28.39
Nontraditional nonworker	(6.26)*
No	25.77
Yes	30.43
Traditional worker	(0.07)
No	27.14
Yes	27.86
Grand mean	27.22
Adjusted R^2	0.201
F ratio	8.141
Number of respondents	597

Note: F ratios in parentheses.
a. In 1977 dollars.
* Significant at the 0.01 level.

Table 4A.3

Estimated mean weeks worked between 1977 and 1978 for white women, by mothers' work orientation and attitude: regression results

Explanatory variables	All women	All women	Nontraditional worker	Traditional nonworker
Daughter's education	2.086 (4.70)	2.019 (4.52)	3.928 (4.18)	1.837 (2.27)
Husband's earnings[a]	−0.0003 (2.52)	−0.0003 (2.63)	−0.0005 (2.02)	−0.0003 (1.16)
South	2.650 (1.30)	2.851 (1.40)	3.392 (0.74)	0.330 (0.09)
Labor force size/1,000	0.001 (0.80)	0.001 (0.88)	0.001 (0.39)	0.003 (1.13)
Youngest child under 6	−16.752 (8.50)	−16.551 (8.35)	−11.244 (2.62)	−16.682 (4.79)
Mother nontraditional worker		2.02 (0.76)		
Mother nontraditional nonworker		3.14 (1.38)		
Mother traditional worker		−0.546 (0.17)		
Mother's traditionality				
Mother's work history				
Constant	13.874	13.316	−10.665	15.191
Adjusted R^2	0.185	0.184	0.229	0.131
F ratio	25.05	15.95	7.01	6.45
Number of respondents	532	532	102	182

Note: Absolute t values in parentheses.
a. In 1977 dollars.

Nontraditional nonworker	Traditional worker	Nontraditional	Traditional	Worked	Did not work
1.232	1.674	2.253	1.784	3.023	1.604
(1.62)	(1.18)	(3.83)	(2.57)	(3.89)	(2.91)
− 0.0003	− 0.004	− 0.0003	− 0.0003	− 0.0005	− 0.0003
(1.31)	(0.91)	(2.05)	(1.54)	(2.32)	(1.78)
7.145	−1.009	5.660	−0.155	0.598	3.345
(2.03)	(0.16)	(2.06)	(0.05)	(0.17)	(1.33)
−0.002	− 0.0004	0.00001	0.002	0.0004	0.002
(0.38	(0.08)	(0.002)	(1.02)	(0.17)	(0.92)
18.548	−21.57	−15.486	−17.748	−15.237	−17.141
(5.46)	(3.27)	(2.67)	(5.87)	(4.30)	(7.13)
				−0.403	−0.128
				(1.08)	(0.52)
		−3.006	−0.109		
		(0.70)	(0.02)		
27.309	23.132	12.938	17.335	10.006	21.821
0.203	0.126	0.208	0.143	0.208	0.169
10.39	2.78	16.01	7.76	8.17	13.42
185	63	287	245	165	367

Table 4A.4
Means (standard deviations) for regression models

Variables	All women	All women	Nontraditional worker	Nontraditional nonworker
Weeks worked	27.73 (23.76)	27.73 (23.76)	29.78 (23.25)	25.86 (24.04)
Daughter's education	13.05 (2.14)	13.05 (2.14)	13.39 (2.24)	12.85 (2.08)
Husband's earnings	12,920 (7,472)	12,920 (7,472)	13,390 (7,994)	12,946 (7,322)
South	0.32 (0.47)	0.32 (0.47)	0.36 (0.48)	0.33 (0.47)
Labor force size/1,000	368.84 (622.83)	368.84 (622.83)	428.18 (673.90)	406.32 (768.40)
Youngest child under 6	0.63 (0.48)	0.63 (0.48)	0.59 (0.49)	0.64 (0.48)
Mother nontraditional worker		0.19 (0.39)		
Mother nontraditional nonworker		0.35 (0.48)		
Mother traditional worker		0.12 (0.32)		
Mother's traditionality				
Mother's work history				

Note: Labor force estimates in the model were divided by 1,000. Numbers in parentheses are the standard deviations associated with the mean characteristic for the selected universe.

Traditional nonworker	Traditional worker	Nontraditional	Traditional	Worked	Did not work
29.83 (23.56)	23.65 (23.96)	29.82 (23.41)	25.29 (23.99)	27.44 (23.64)	27.86 (23.85)
13.23 (2.15)	12.52 (2.04)	13.29 (2.18)	12.77 (2.07)	13.06 (2.20)	13.04 (2.12)
13,435 (7,235)	10,572 (7,452)	13,419 (7,499)	12,336 (7,414)	12,314 (7,889)	13,193 (7,272)
0.27 (0.45)	0.38 (0.49)	0.30 (0.46)	0.34 (0.48)	0.37 (0.48)	0.30 (0.46)
326.35 (402.74)	289.29 (596.44)	362.54 (516.84)	376.22 (728.71)	375.15 (647.12)	366.00 (612.49)
0.61 (0.49)	0.75 (0.44)	0.60 (0.49)	0.67 (0.47)	0.65 (0.48)	0.62 (0.49)
				15.39 (4.55)	16.89 (4.69)
		0.28 (0.29)	0.22 (0.29)		

It was first determined between which two surveys (1968 to 1973) a woman's first child was born. Taking the first survey date in that interval, five months was added to get a midpoint date. If the birth of the child came before the midpoint date, the last survey in her birth interval was selected in order to obtain data on the first year of work after her baby was born since data on weeks worked are in reference to work experience during the previous year. If the baby's birthday was equal to or greater than the midpoint date, the next survey following the last survey in the birth interval was selected. Having then determined a survey to represent the first year for each woman, each subsequent survey represented a second to tenth year depending on the starting survey point. (See appendix table 5A.1 for clarification.)

As represented in figures 5.2 and 5.3, data on weeks worked in the past year were obtained for whatever survey represented her first year, and a separate variable was created for each of the first through tenth years, which is coded 1 if the weeks worked for the woman were greater than or equal to 25.99 and 0 otherwise (provided data on weeks worked were available). Data for 1974 and 1976 were unobtainable and are therefore NA for all women regardless of which year (relative to the birth) they represent. For tables 5.2 and 5.3 a cumulative technique was used. The base figure represents the total number of years she had available to her after the birth minus the number in which she was missing data on weeks worked. Of those years in which she had data a percentage was taken of the number in which she worked six months or more.

Table 5A.1
Survey year assignment for obtaining data on postbirth work behavior

Baby born between survey dates Year[a]	Baby's birthday less than midpoint date									
	1	2	3	4	5	6	7	8	9	10
1968–1969	1968	1969	1970	1971	1972	NA	1974	NA	1976	1977
1969–1970	1969	1970	1971	1972	NA	1974	NA	1976	1977	
1970–1971	1970	1971	1972	NA	1974	NA	1976	1977		
1971–1972	1971	1972	NA	1974	NA	1976	1977			
1972–1973	1972	NA	1974	NA	1976	1977				

a. Except for the 1978 backfill question used in construction of tables 5.2 and 5.3, data for any one year represented here were taken from the succeeding survey point (for example, for year 1968 data were taken from the 1969 interview) because data on weeks worked are for the preceding year.

Baby's birthday greater than or equal to midpoint date

1	2	3	4	5	6	7	8	9	10
1969	1970	1971	1972	NA	1974	NA	1976	1977	
1970	1971	1972	NA	1974	NA	1976	1977		
1971	1972	NA	1974	NA	1976	1977			
1972	NA	1974	NA	1976	1977				
NA	1974	NA	1976	1977					

Table 5A.2
Determinants of 1968 work attachment

Independent variables[a]	Dependent variables	
	Weeks employed during preceding year	
	Coefficient (t value)	
Whites		
EDUC	1.526	(3.93)
INCHUS	−0.647	(−6.70)
LFSIZE	−2.078	(−1.93)
SOUTH	−0.239	(−0.14)
SPAN	0.137	(3.98)
KIDS	−4.540	(−3.42)
BEFORE	5.364	(3.10)
AFTER	9.175	(5.39)
CONSTANT	6.520	(1.12)
$\bar{R}^2/X^2$	0.250	
Number of respondents	706	
Blacks		
EDUC	1.876	(3.22)
INCHUS	0.0625	(0.35)
LFSIZE	−4.112	(−3.09)
SOUTH	−0.486	(−0.17)
SPAN	0.150	(3.06)
KIDS	−4.169	(−2.48)
BEFORE	7.983	(3.24)
AFTER	5.783	(2.32)
CONSTANT	0.621	(0.07)
$\bar{R}^2/X^2$	0.270	
Number of respondents	317	

a. See note 8 in chapter 5 for definitions of all variables.

Coefficient (t value)		Employment status as of 1978 survey			
		Partial derivative (t value)		Partial derivative (t value)	
1.687	(4.35)	0.036	(3.55)	0.039	(3.91)
−0.672	(−6.92)	−0.015	(−5.67)	−0.015	(−5.83)
−2.291	(−2.11)	−0.074	(−2.61)	−0.079	(−2.84)
0.272	(0.15)	0.015	(0.35)	0.034	(0.78)
0.211	(7.90)	0.0023	(2.57)	0.0045	(6.49)
		−0.135	(−3.86)		
5.628	(3.23)	0.098	(2.25)	0.108	(2.49)
9.413	(5.49)	0.269	(6.14)	0.267	(6.15)
−4.097	(−0.83)	−0.374	(−2.47)	−0.675	(−5.21)
0.238		192.37		177.04	
706		744		744	
2.249	(3.96)	0.078	(4.43)	0.084	(4.93)
0.0728	(0.41)	0.00078	(0.17)	0.00062	(0.13)
−3.890	(−2.91)	−0.095	(−2.63)	−0.090	(−2.49)
−0.314	(−0.11)	0.031	(0.40)	0.038	(0.49)
0.227	(6.02)	0.0028	(2.23)	0.0041	(4.11)
		−0.072	(−1.62)		
8.391	(3.39)	0.118	(1.81)	0.125	(1.95)
6.265	(2.50)	0.177	(2.76)	0.182	(2.85)
−13.389	(−1.88)	−0.992	(−3.82)	−1.232	(−5.69)
0.258		90.50		87.82	
317		325		325	

Table 6A.1
Variable means and standard deviations for whites

Variable	1967 Mean	Standard deviation	1978 Mean	Standard deviation
Highest grade completed	11.7	2.4	12.8	2.4
Age of youngest child				
Under age 3	0.317	0.466	0.261	0.440
Ages 3–5	0.293	0.455	0.265	0.442
Ages 12 and over	0.036	0.185	0.037	0.189
No children	0.070	0.255	0.085	0.279
Number of children	2.8	1.6	2.1	1.2
Husband's earned income[a]	15.0	8.1	17.0	10.2
Health dummy	0.124	0.330	0.109	0.311
Unemployment rate	4.3	1.7	6.3	2.3
South dummy	0.293	0.455	0.350	0.477
Attitudes toward women working	10.1	2.4	12.0	2.2
Multiple marriage dummy	0.115	0.319	0.147	0.354
Log_{10} labor market size	5.4	0.7	5.2	0.7
Labor force participation rate	0.401	0.490	0.544	0.248
Weeks worked in preceding year	15.9	21.0	24.4	23.3

a. In thousands of 1977 dollars.

Table 6A.2
Variable means and standard deviations for blacks

Variable	1967 Mean	Standard deviation	1978 Mean	Standard deviation
Highest grade completed	10.4	2.8	11.8	2.5
Age of youngest child				
Under age 3	0.380	0.487	0.182	0.387
Ages 3–5	0.259	0.439	0.200	0.401
Ages 12 and over	0.083	0.276	0.077	0.267
No children	0.078	0.269	0.094	0.293
Number of children	4.0	2.8	2.6	1.7
Husband's earned income[a]	8.7	4.9	10.7	6.3
Health dummy	0.141	0.349	0.135	0.343
Unemployment rate	4.7	1.6	6.6	2.6
South dummy	0.561	0.497	0.776	0.418
Attitudes toward women working	11.0	2.5	11.9	2.0
Multiple marriage dummy	0.166	0.373	0.141	0.349
Log_{10} labor market size	5.5	0.8	5.3	0.7
Labor force participation rate	0.649	0.479	0.694	0.462
Weeks worked in preceding year	28.3	22.5	31.5	23.4

a. In thousands of 1977 dollars.

Table 6A.3
Labor supply equations for white married women age 30 to 34: estimated coefficients

Independent variables	Labor force participation rate 1967		1978		Weeks worked in preceding year 1967		1978	
Highest grade completed	0.024	(3.3)	0.041	(5.2)	1.1	(3.4)	1.9	(5.4)
Age of youngest child								
Under age 3	−0.327	(−7.7)	−0.277	(−6.3)	−13.4	(−7.5)	−12.4	(−6.2)
Ages 3–5	−0.172	(−4.0)	−0.136	(−3.2)	−8.1	(−4.4)	−5.4	(−2.8)
Ages 12 and over	−0.006	(−0.1)	0.050	(0.6)	−2.5	(−0.7)	6.0	(1.5)
No children	0.193	(2.6)	0.023	(0.3)	8.7	(2.7)	6.0	(1.8)
Number of children	−0.001	(−0.1)	−0.037	(−2.1)	−0.7	(−1.2)	−2.2	(−2.8)
Husband's earned income[a]	−0.011	(−5.2)	−0.011	(−6.6)	−0.4	(−4.7)	−0.5	(−6.1)
Health dummy	−0.118	(−2.4)	−0.136	(−2.6)	−1.7	(−0.8)	−5.4	(−2.2)
Unemployment rate	−0.013	(−1.4)	−0.016	(−2.3)	−0.2	(−0.6)	−0.8	(−2.5)
South dummy	0.040	(1.1)	−0.022	(−0.6)	2.3	(1.5)	0.2	(0.1)

Table 6A.3 (continued)

Independent variables	Labor force participation rate				Weeks worked in preceding year			
	1967		1978		1967		1978	
Multiple marriage dummy	0.094	(1.8)	0.128	(2.8)	2.2	(1.0)	7.6	(3.6)
Log_{10} labor market size	0.003	(0.1)	−0.075	(−3.0)	−0.7	(−0.7)	−3.7	(−3.3)
Constant	0.464	(2.8)	0.893	(4.8)	21.8	(3.1)	40.2	(4.7)
Adjusted R^2	0.147		0.155		0.153		0.186	
Number of respondents	816		811		816		811	

Note: t values are in parentheses.
a. In thousands of 1977 dollars.

Table 6A.4
Labor supply equations for black married women age 30 to 34: estimated coefficients

Independent variables	Labor force participation rate				Weeks worked in preceding year			
	1967		1978		1967		1978	
Highest grade completed	−0.019	(−1.3)	0.044	(2.9)	−0.2	(−0.3)	2.2	(2.9)
Age of youngest child								
Under age 3	−0.354	(−3.8)	−0.191	(−1.9)	−18.7	(−4.6)	−10.7	(−2.1)
Ages 3–5	−0.181	(−1.9)	−0.047	(−0.5)	−7.5	(−1.8)	−3.4	(−0.7)
Ages 12 and over	−0.035	(−0.3)	0.102	(0.7)	−0.2	(−0.0)	3.3	(0.5)
No children	−0.085	(−0.6)	−0.093	(−0.7)	0.8	(0.1)	−2.5	(−0.4)
Number of children	−0.025	(−1.5)	−0.014	(−0.5)	−1.0	(−1.4)	−1.4	(−1.1)
Husband's earned income[a]	−0.004	(−0.5)	0.002	(0.3)	−0.4	(−1.2)	−0.1	(−0.5)
Health dummy	−0.308	(−3.3)	−0.077	(−0.8)	−15.4	(−3.8)	−8.1	(−1.6)
Unemployment rate	−0.001	(−0.1)	0.005	(0.4)	0.1	(0.1)	−1.0	(−1.3)
South dummy	0.046	(0.5)	0.364	(3.6)	8.3	(2.1)	6.9	(1.4)
Multiple marriage dummy	0.005	(0.1)	−0.083	(−0.8)	5.1	(1.3)	−0.7	(−0.0)
Log_{10} labor market size	0.074	(1.2)	0.055	(0.9)	7.5	(2.8)	−1.0	(−0.3)
Constant	0.786	(1.8)	0.343	(−0.7)	1.3	(0.1)	20.1	(0.8)
Adjusted R^2	0.144		0.115		0.251		0.107	
Number of respondents	205		170		205		170	

Note: t values are in parentheses.
a. In thousands of 1977 dollars.

Table 6A.5
Labor supply equations controlling for attitudes toward women working for white married women age 30 to 34: estimated coefficients

Independent variables	Labor force participation rate				Weeks worked in preceding year			
	1967		1978		1967		1978	
Highest grade completed	0.017	(2.4)	0.035	(4.5)	0.8	(2.7)	1.7	(4.7)
Age of youngest child								
Under age 3	−0.320	(−7.8)	−0.269	(−6.2)	−13.2	(−7.4)	−12.1	(−6.1)
Ages 3–5	−0.174	(−4.2)	−0.138	(−3.3)	−8.1	(−4.6)	−5.5	(−2.9)
Ages 12 and over	0.011	(0.1)	0.056	(0.6)	−1.9	(−0.5)	6.2	(1.5)
No children	0.228	(3.1)	0.040	(0.6)	9.9	(3.2)	6.7	(2.1)
Number of children	0.002	(0.1)	−0.027	(−1.6)	−0.6	(−1.1)	−1.8	(−2.2)
Husband's earned income[a]	−0.010	(−5.1)	−0.011	(−6.6)	−0.4	(−4.6)	−0.5	(−6.1)
Health dummy	−0.103	(−2.1)	−0.138	(−2.7)	−1.1	(−0.5)	−5.5	(−2.3)
Unemployment rate	−0.015	(−1.6)	−0.016	(−2.3)	−0.3	(−0.7)	−0.8	(−2.5)
South dummy	0.037	(1.0)	−0.033	(−0.9)	2.2	(1.4)	−0.2	(−0.1)
Attitudes toward women working	0.043	(6.5)	0.039	(5.1)	1.5	(5.4)	1.6	(4.7)
Multiple marriage dummy	0.078	(1.6)	0.114	(2.5)	1.6	(0.8)	7.0	(3.4)
Log$_{10}$ labor market size	0.002	(0.1)	−0.089	(−3.6)	−0.7	(−0.8)	−4.3	(−3.8)
Constant	0.094	(0.5)	0.550	(2.8)	8.7	(1.2)	25.7	(2.9)
Adjusted R^2	0.189		0.180		0.181		0.207	
Number of respondents	816		811		816		811	

Note: t values are in parentheses.
a. In thousands of 1977 dollars.

Table 6A.6
Labor supply equations controlling for attitudes toward women working for black married women age 30 to 34: estimated coefficients

Independent variables	Labor force participation rate				Weeks worked in preceding year			
	1967		1978		1967		1978	
Highest grade completed	−0.016	(−1.2)	0.043	(2.8)	−0.1	(−0.2)	2.1	(2.8)
Age of youngest child								
Under age 3	−0.353	(−3.9)	−0.191	(−1.9)	−18.7	(−4.6)	−10.7	(−2.1)
Ages 3–5	−0.169	(−1.8)	−0.035	(−0.4)	−7.3	(−1.7)	−2.0	(−0.4)
Ages 12 and over	0.017	(0.1)	0.010	(0.7)	0.7	(0.1)	3.1	(0.5)
No children	−0.013	(−0.1)	−0.096	(−0.7)	2.1	(0.3)	−2.8	(−0.4)
Number of children	−0.017	(−1.0)	−0.012	(−0.5)	−0.9	(−1.2)	−1.2	(−0.9)
Husband's earned income[a]	−0.005	(−0.6)	0.002	(0.3)	−0.4	(−1.2)	−0.1	(−0.4)
Health dummy	−0.302	(−3.3)	−0.073	(−0.7)	−15.3	(−3.7)	−7.7	(−1.5)
Unemployment rate	0.002	(0.1)	0.007	(0.5)	0.2	(0.2)	−0.9	(−1.2)
South dummy	0.028	(0.3)	0.368	(3.7)	8.0	(2.1)	7.4	(1.5)
Attitudes toward women working	0.035	(2.7)	0.013	(0.7)	0.6	(1.1)	1.5	(1.6)
Multiple marriage dummy	−0.019	(−0.2)	−0.076	(−0.8)	4.6	(1.2)	0.7	(0.1)
Log_{10} labor market size	0.094	(1.5)	0.053	(0.8)	7.9	(2.9)	−1.2	(−0.4)
Constant	0.230	(0.5)	−0.504	(−1.0)	−8.5	(−0.4)	2.7	(0.1)
Adjusted R^2	0.170		0.113		0.251		0.116	
Number of respondents	205		170		205		170	

Note: t values are in parentheses.
a. In thousands of 1977 dollars.

Appendix to
Chapter 7

Construction of
the Remarriage
Sample and
Reference
Group of
Nonremarriers

In order to study a woman's activities and attitudes surrounding her divorce and remarriage, data were drawn from four periods: two surveys prior to divorce, one survey prior to divorce, the survey after divorce, and the survey after remarriage. For the most part all women divorced for the first time between 1968 and 1973 are included in each of the four samples.

The primary analytical reference point for predicting remarriage for those once-divorced respondents was the first survey after the divorce. Thus the characteristics used to predict remarriage were ones reported at that survey date. If the woman was not interviewed in that survey, data were drawn from the next year in which she was interviewed. This presents a problem only when the woman has divorced and remarried without being interviewed in between, which happened in less than 20 percent of the cases. In such cases data were taken from the survey preceding the divorce. If the woman was not interviewed in that year, she was excluded from the sample.

Another set of data was drawn from the survey after remarriage or a comparable point for those not remarrying. For those who remarried, the first survey interview in which the respondent reported herself married was used. For those women who did not remarry, a comparable year was needed to compare remarriers with nonremarriers while controlling for temporal changes. To do this we broke the sample into groups depending, first, on when the woman divorced and, second, whether she remarried (see appendix table 7A.1). Women who remarried were then classified by year of remarriage. (To be defined as remarried the remarriage must have occurred within five years after divorce.) The nonremarriers were then randomly assigned a "remarried" year based on the proportion of women remarrying in that year. For example, between 1969 and 1970, 44 women divorced. Twenty-six remarried within five years of divorce and 18 did not. Of the 26 who remarried, 42.3 percent had remarried by 1970. Therefore 42.3 percent of the nonremarriers (7 women) were randomly assigned 1970 as their year of remarriage. By randomly assigning nonremarriers years of remarriage equivalent to the remarriage year of women who were divorced in the same year as the nonremarriers, we can compare characteristics of remarriers and nonremarriers at comparable points.

In order to portray changes surrounding these events, another set of data was taken from periods preceding divorce

Table 7A.1
Assigning nonremarriers a reference year for remarriage

Year	Total	1969	1970
Divorced 1968–1969			
Remarriers	26	5 (19.2)	13 (50.1)
Nonremarriers	12	2	6
Divorced 1969–1970			
Remarriers	26		11 (42.3)
Nonremarriers	18		7
Divorced 1970–1971			
Remarriers	49		
Nonremarriers	31		
Divorced 1971–1972			
Remarriers	35		
Nonremarriers	36		
Divorced 1972–1973			
Remarriers	63		
Nonremarriers	55		
Total	352	7	37
Remarriers	200	5	24
Nonremarriers	152	2	13

Note: Numbers in parentheses represent a percentage distribution.

whenever possible. In general data were drawn from the first survey preceding the divorce and from the second survey preceding the divorce. For women divorcing between 1968 and 1969, data are not available two years preceding divorce since the surveys started in 1968. Women who remarried before being interviewed must be treated differently. If a woman divorces and remarries before being interviewed, data for the period following divorce are drawn from the year preceding divorce; hence when looking at her predivorce behavior we must go back a year further. For example, if a woman divorced and remarried between 1970 and 1971, 1970 would be used as the year data were taken for the first survey before divorce, and 1968 would be the year data were drawn for the second survey before divorce. If the woman was not interviewed in one of those surveys, we go back one preceding year to draw data.

1971	1972	1973	1975	1977
4 (15.4)	2 (7.7)	2 (7.7)		
2	1	1		
10 (38.5)	4 (15.4)	2 (7.7)		
7	3	1		
15 (30.6)	17 (34.7)	6 (12.2)	11 (22.4)	
9	11	4	7	
	12 (34.3)	13 (37.1)	10 (28.6)	0
	12	14	10	0
		21 (33.3)	24 (38.1)	18 (28.6)
		19	21	15
47	62	83	83	33
29	35	44	45	18
18	27	39	38	15

Variable Specification

Kids

No = had own child in home survey after divorce.

Yes = other.

Education

0–11 = completed 0 to 11 years of school.

12 = completed 12 years of school.

13 or more = completed 13 or more years of schooling.

Log of marriage duration

The exponential logarithm (years) of first-marriage duration.

low = less than 5 years of marriage.

high = 5 or more years of marriage.

SMSA

Yes = lived in Standard Metropolitan Statistical Area at survey following divorce.

No = other.

Finances T-1 to T

Whether a respondent perceived that her personal finances were better, the same, or worse over the year preceding the divorce.

Hours worked and satisfaction

Not working at first survey after divorce.

Dissatisfied = dissatisfied with current job at first survey after divorce.

Satisfied—part time = satisfied with part-time job (less than 35 hours) held at first survey after divorce.

Satisfied—full time = self-explanatory.

Health problems

No = no health problem at first survey after divorce.

Yes = had health problem.

Lived with parents at 14

Yes = lived with both parents when 14 years of age.

No = other.

Welfare receipt

Yes = respondent or respondent's family received AFDC or other public transfer payment in the year preceding the divorce.

No = other.

Worked 2 surveys before divorce

Yes = was employed second survey before divorce.

No = was not employed.

Work experience

One year or less = had one year or less of lifetime work experience.

1½–3 = had 1½–3 years of lifetime work experience.

3½ years and over = had 3½ or more years of lifetime work experience.

Table 7A.2
Adjusted remarriage probabilities for selected time periods following a first divorce: whites

Explanatory variables	Number of respondents
Kids	
No	87
Yes	151
Education	
0–11	85
12	116
13 or more	37
Log of marriage duration	
Low	156
High	82
Age at divorce	
Under 20	23
20–23	112
24–26	64
27 and over	39
SMSA residence	
No	84
Yes	154
Finances T-1 to	
Better	109
Same	64
Worse	65
Hours worked and satisfaction	
Not working	102
Dissatisfied/working	11
Satisfied—part time	31
Satisfied—full time	94
Health problem	
No	206
Yes	26
Lived with parents at age 14	
No	61
Yes	177
Welfare receipt	
No	184
Yes	54

Probability of remarriage within years

1	2	3	4	5
(2.39)	(2.96)*	(1.58)	(0.83)	(1.18)
0.222	0.431	0.549	0.580	0.683
0.144	0.324	0.467	0.522	0.614
(3.51)**	(1.42)	(3.13)**	(5.50)***	(2.34)**
0.258	0.409	0.592	0.662	0.713
0.118	0.367	0.474	0.518	0.628
0.156	0.256	0.364	0.360	0.515
(1.09)	(0.02)	(0.64)	(1.25)	(0.05)
0.191	0.368	0.480	0.518	0.635
0.138	0.358	0.533	0.591	0.650
(1.18)	(2.48)*	(1.44)	(1.61)	(0.39)
0.286	0.578	0.637	0.620	0.670
0.158	0.377	0.528	0.599	0.669
0.133	0.322	0.450	0.483	0.597
0.209	0.270	0.411	0.447	0.612
(0.47)	(0.06)	(1.21)	(3.23)*	(4.90)**
0.150	0.375	0.546	0.621	0.735
0.185	0.359	0.473	0.504	0.591
(0.10)	(1.18)	(0.28)	(0.61)	(0.58)
0.179	0.400	0.514	0.579	0.675
0.181	0.375	0.510	0.503	0.617
0.156	0.290	0.459	0.521	0.602
(3.34)**	(1.93)	(1.83)	(0.68)	(0.32)
0.251	0.416	0.554	0.565	0.640
0.050	0.143	0.474	0.438	0.778
0.206	0.442	0.589	0.619	0.645
0.094	0.308	0.412	0.507	0.624
(0.83)	(1.81)	(3.82)**	(3.95)**	(4.07)**
0.173	0.372	0.524	0.567	0.670
0.216	0.385	0.386	0.456	0.485
(0.00)	(2.59)	(1.50)	(0.05)	(0.27)
0.175	0.277	0.428	0.531	0.669
0.173	0.391	0.519	0.547	0.631
(0.53)	(2.13)	(3.49)*	(4.46)**	(0.19)
0.182	0.387	0.529	0.578	0.647
0.140	0.281	0.386	0.419	0.615

Table 7A.2 (continued)

Explanatory variables	Number of respondents
Employed 2 surveys before divorce	
No	94
Yes	109
Not ascertainable	35
Work experience	
1 year or less	126
1½–3 years	82
3½ years and over	20
Not ascertainable	10
Grand mean	238
Adjusted R^2	
F ratio	

Note: Numbers in parentheses are F ratios.
* Significant at the 0.10 level.
** Significant at the 0.05 level.
*** Significant at the 0.01 level.

Table 7A.3
Adjusted remarriage probabilities for selected time periods following a first divorce: blacks

Explanatory variables	Number of respondents
Kids	
No	11
Yes	81
Education	
0–11	42
12	41
13 or more	9
Log of marriage duration	
Low	58
High	34
Age at divorce	
Under 20	13
20–23	29
24–26	31
27 and over	19
SMSA residence	
No	20
Yes	72

Probability of remarriage within years				
1	2	3	4	5
(0.37)	(1.09)	(0.26)	(1.54)	(0.41)
0.153	0.400	0.501	0.547	0.650
0.178	0.316	0.479	0.502	0.614
0.215	0.417	0.547	0.665	0.694
(0.45)	(1.74)	(0.65)	(0.90)	(0.64)
0.156	0.346	0.497	0.524	0.649
0.175	0.339	0.487	0.585	0.631
0.256	0.431	0.451	0.428	0.544
0.208	0.672	0.700	0.670	0.793
0.173	0.364	0.498	0.544	0.640
0.035	0.074	0.058	0.085	0.024
1.39	1.86**	1.66**	2.00***	1.26

Probability of remarriage within years				
1	2	3	4	5
(0.82)	(0.16)	(0.03)	(0.17)	(0.01)
0.263	0.286	0.251	0.250	0.362
0.169	0.238	0.270	0.303	0.348
(9.82)***	(10.30)***	(11.89)***	(9.01)***	(6.92)***
0.122	0.135	0.160	0.187	0.280
0.123	0.220	0.234	0.275	0.291
0.578	0.692	0.754	0.748	0.794
(0.79)	(0.78)	(4.82)**	(6.82)**	(4.96)**
0.205	0.271	0.337	0.385	0.432
0.143	0.202	0.164	0.164	0.226
(1.47)	(0.55)	(0.44)	(0.79)	(0.39)
0.300	0.222	0.245	0.209	0.295
0.198	0.302	0.271	0.246	0.293
0.181	0.260	0.319	0.376	0.402
0.071	0.165	0.203	0.299	0.375
(1.94)	(2.33)	(2.18)	(0.90)	(2.57)
0.287	0.376	0.396	0.385	0.514
0.159	0.217	0.242	0.279	0.317

Table 7A.3 (continued)

Explanatory variables	Number of respondents
Finances T-1 to	
Better	37
Same	43
Worse	12
Hours worked and satisfaction	
Not working	44
Dissatisfied/working	5
Satisfied—part time	8
Satisfied—full time	35
Health problem	
No	81
Yes	9
Lived with parents at age 14	
No	42
Yes	50
Welfare receipt	
No	57
Yes	35
Employed 2 surveys before divorce	
No	37
Yes	44
Not ascertainable	11
Work experience	
1 year or less	44
1½–3 years	35
3½ years and over	8
Not ascertainable	5
Grand mean	92
Adjusted R^2	
F ratio	

Note: Numbers in parentheses are F ratios.
* Significant at the 0.10 level.
** Significant at the 0.05 level.
*** Significant at the 0.01 level.

Probability of remarriage within years				
1	2	3	4	5
(7.19)***	(4.00)**	(4.38)**	(2.60)*	(1.43)
0.335	0.368	0.402	0.409	0.431
0.055	0.133	0.155	0.204	0.269
0.171	0.273	0.277	0.299	0.395
(1.93)	(1.75)	(1.17)	(1.90)	(1.08)
0.263	0.322	0.310	0.377	0.388
0.107	0.308	0.291	0.274	0.533
0.116	0.255	0.425	0.424	0.472
0.096	0.136	0.186	0.178	0.258
(1.16)	(1.38)	(1.13)	(1.51)	(0.31)
0.201	0.274	0.290	0.329	0.366
0.121	0.115	0.206	0.181	0.288
(8.69)***	(6.50)**	(6.09)**	(4.64)**	(6.16)**
0.060	0.126	0.154	0.190	0.215
0.264	0.326	0.347	0.372	0.444
(1.45)	(2.49)	(3.15)	(3.58)*	(0.39)
0.211	0.290	0.320	0.357	0.371
0.126	0.164	0.179	0.194	0.313
(2.39)	(5.90)***	(5.30)***	(5.32)***	(7.07)***
0.199	0.304	0.303	0.367	0.408
0.125	0.134	0.174	0.181	0.216
0.362	0.536	0.570	0.584	0.750
(1.97)	(1.59)	(2.54)	(1.55)	(1.98)
0.193	0.268	0.312	0.333	0.353
0.109	0.162	0.146	0.202	0.282
0.438	0.486	0.510	0.531	0.722
0.191	0.248	0.354	0.303	0.287
0.180	0.243	0.268	0.297	0.349
0.285	0.266	0.313	0.248	0.174
2.65***	2.50***	2.88***	2.37***	1.87**

Index